# SCHILLER

## THE DRAMATIC WRITER

# SCHILLER

## THE DRAMATIC WRITER

### A STUDY OF STYLE IN
### THE PLAYS

---

H. B. GARLAND

OXFORD
AT THE CLARENDON PRESS
1969

*Oxford University Press, Ely House, London W.1*

GLASGOW NEW YORK TORONTO MELBOURNE WELLINGTON
CAPE TOWN SALISBURY IBADAN NAIROBI LUSAKA ADDIS ABABA
BOMBAY CALCUTTA MADRAS KARACHI LAHORE DACCA
KUALA LUMPUR SINGAPORE HONG KONG TOKYO

PRINTED IN GREAT BRITAIN

TO MARY

Und mein geflügelt Werkzeug ist das Wort

SCHILLER: *Die Huldigung der Künste*

# PREFACE

THIS study had its beginning in the pleasure which reading
Schiller's plays has given me for many years. I have come
to realize more and more clearly that the fascination of Schiller
derives, not from ideas or messages, not from political attitudes
or philosophical postures of sublimity, but from his singular
power to manipulate words, making the commonplace unique
and the dingy luminous. I have tried in the following pages to
demonstrate the working of this striking linguistic gift and in so
doing to encourage others to share the experience of listening to
Schiller, which I have found so rewarding.

I express my gratitude to my friend and colleague, Professor
W. H. Bruford, who kindly read and commented on the draft
of the chapter on *Die Räuber*, and to my wife for her patient
encouragement and constructive criticism. I acknowledge also
with thanks the permission given by Messrs. Faber & Faber Ltd.,
London, and Messrs. Harcourt, Brace & World, Inc., New York,
to quote in the Introduction certain lines from *Burnt Norton* in
*Four Quartets* by T. S. Eliot; and I express a like obligation to
Limes Verlag, Wiesbaden, for allowing me to quote the stanza
from Gottfried Benn's poem *Ein Wort*.

Schiller's plays are quoted in the text of *Friedrich Schiller,
Sämtliche Werke*, 1958–9, edited by G. Fricke and H. G. Göpfert.
References to the Nationalausgabe are indicated by the abbrevia-
tion *NA*, and 'Jonas' denotes *Schillers Briefe*, edited by F. Jonas.
The numeration of lines in *Don Carlos* follows the Säkular-
Ausgabe.                                                    H. B. G.

*Exeter 1968*

# CONTENTS

# INTRODUCTION

THIS book intends a discussion of a matter which is obvious, yet neglected—which may, indeed, have been neglected because it is obvious. Whatever thoughts he may conceive, whatever passions or emotions he may experience, whatever visions he may see, the writer communicates through language and through language alone. This may seem so clearly self-evident as to be hardly worth saying, yet the history of Schiller criticism shows plainly how easy it is to take language for granted and to go on to discuss the poet's thought or passion or imagining without paying the slightest heed to the means by which we apprehend these things. And we may go further and discover how easy it is to ignore what the poet is saying with subtlety and precision and to assume meanings which an alert examination of what he says will not support.

Difficulties encumber the path of any attempt to discuss Schiller's style or that of any other writer; for words are the means by which we must discuss words and, just as words may be misconceived, so they may themselves deceive. But notwithstanding the difficulties, and even dangers, the effort, it seems to me, ought to be made. An examination of Schiller's style, if it is pursued honestly and with good will, may well yield points of understanding which have hitherto been appreciated only dimly or have even passed unperceived.

The words which make up a literary work, and which so often pass without remark, are not identical bricks to be individually ignored in the structure of a wall. Neither are they algebraic symbols with constant values. They have their 'meaning', but they have, too, their undertones, which we can describe as colour, temperature, shape, and consistency; they have diverse and shifting associations, and a sensuous aural quality, which is compounded not only of vowel and consonant, but of syllabic length and stress as well. And all these elements are variable according to the way in which they are combined. Small wonder that their treacherous instability has led a poet to write:

> Words strain,
> Crack and sometimes break, under the burden,
> Under the tension, slip, slide, perish,
> Decay with imprecision, will not stay in place,
> Will not stay still.[1]

Yet poets know, too, their fleeting potency:

> Ein Wort — ein Glanz, ein Flug, ein Feuer,
> ein Flammenwurf, ein Sternenstrich —
> und wieder Dunkel, ungeheuer,
> im leeren Raum um Welt und Ich.[2]

The accumulation of these subtle, sensitive, volatile units in shifting groups, in repeated patterns constantly renewed, imparts to a literary work its particular climate. And no account of its 'meaning' which ignores this can be valid. This is not to say that the normal categories of traditional interpretation should be disregarded. Philosophical and moral attitudes are a part of literature and a proper object of criticism, but they are all too easily condensed to abstract formulas, which give the reader the impression that the poet might well have put his point in a fraction of the words he has actually used. Accounts of a work in terms of metaphysics, ideology, generalized psychology, social factors, or historical development can deprive it of its unique individuality, reducing it to anatomical simplicity or to abstract concepts of function.

For generations the word has suffered almost complete neglect in writings on Schiller. Careful, solid, well-informed books such as the studies by Berger, Kühnemann, and Buchwald[3] have

---

[1] T. S. Eliot in *Burnt Norton*.
[2] Gottfried Benn in *Ein Wort*.
[3] K. Berger, *Schiller*, 1905; E. Kühnemann, *Schiller*, 1905; R. Buchwald, *Schiller*, 1937.

analysed dramatic structure, assessed characters, and established underlying ideas, but when it comes to style, they have spared at most a page out of thirty or forty for a few perfunctory remarks. Even Benno von Wiese's recent large-scale work has remarkably little to say about the language of the plays.[1] Slowly, over the last twenty years, signs of change have appeared, beginning with a stimulating essay by Kurt May on *Wallenstein*.[2] Notwithstanding its patronizing tone, Thomas Mann's *Versuch über Schiller* (1955) abounds in perceptive observations on Schiller's use of words. Gerhard Storz[3] has given more space and more thought to some aspects of Schiller's style than any of his predecessors. Articles by Ilse Appelbaum-Graham[4] have examined the language in its revelatory significance. More recently Marga Parzeller has devoted an essay to 'Die Sprache bei Schiller', treating the language of poems and plays in a boldly generalizing philosophical spirit.[5] And the completion of the present book coincides with the publication of a monograph by Emil Staiger,[6] in which a chapter headed 'Sprache' is given up to a discussion of style.

The study which follows examines the language of the plays. It takes no note of the lyric poetry and ballads, nor of the theoretical works, which form so important a part of Schiller's *œuvre*. These matters lie outside my purview, for I am not concerned with Schiller's style in general, but with the way in which it functions in the drama and illuminates it. Plays involve a special problem, since they are intended to make their impact through other factors than the word alone—physical presence of actors, movement, gesture, and setting. Yet all these factors are determined by a reading of the text, which is therefore no less important than in works for reading, though some of its effect reaches the audience at second hand. Of course, actors, director, and designer

---

[1] *Schiller*, 1959.

[2] *Friedrich Schiller. Idee und Wirklichkeit im Drama*, 1948.

[3] *Der Dichter Friedrich Schiller*, 1959.

[4] 'Passions and Possessions in Schiller's *Kabale und Liebe*', in *German Life and Letters*, vi, 1952–3, p. 12; 'The Structure of the Personality in Schiller's Tragedies', in *Schiller Bicentenary Lectures*, 1960.

[5] *Neue Folge des Jahrbuchs der Goethe-Gesellschaft*, 25. Band, 1963.

[6] *Friedrich Schiller*, 1967.

bring something personal and individual to the play and not infrequently impose something extraneous upon it. But productions pass and the text remains. And plays should not be approached solely with an eye upon stage representation. The author who has seen fit to publish his play in book form does not imagine that he is merely furnishing actors with a text to memorize. He is well aware that in the long run the readers will outnumber the spectators, and that the majority of performances will take place, not on the stage, but in the mind. Schiller was clearly as much interested in publication as in stage production, and not primarily for financial reasons, important though these may have been. His lavish provision of stage directions was much more valuable as a help to mental performance than as an instruction to actors. No one knew better than he how little attention actors pay to the printed direction; and he did not hesitate to provide indications which (as with blushing or turning pale) the actor cannot use. For Schiller, whether on the stage or in the study, the word remained paramount.

Though my study is extensive it is not exhaustive. I have excluded the Swabian peculiarities in Schiller's dramatic speech, believing that, interesting historically and dialectally though they are, they do little to help the understanding of the plays (the Swiss dialect in *Wilhelm Tell* is another matter). And I have not attempted to infer peculiarities of temperament, construing the personality from linguistic evidence. Such a retrospective, Freudian approach is legitimate and may yield conclusions on personal conduct or even on structural perversion; but it lies outside the scope of my intention. I have sought through the study of the style to detect the differing climate of each of the plays, and so to complement in an important respect the many excellent and authoritative accounts in which other aspects of Schiller are in the foreground. The climate, I am well aware, is not the whole work, and what I offer is not complete interpretation, but a contribution to interpretation, from a standpoint which I believe to be of more consequence than has often been supposed.

# I · *DIE RÄUBER*

## I. REALISM

'ABER ist Euch auch wohl, Vater? Ihr seht so blaß.'

These opening words of *Die Räuber* are pregnant with deceit, part of a calculated, far-reaching, wicked plan. Yet in themselves they appear harmless, colourless, spontaneous, and natural. Both Franz and his father speak in a tone and tempo which resemble easy, real speech, with cliché-like images ('wie dem Fisch im Wasser'), with halts, gropings, and restarts ('Hm! Hm! — So ist es. Aber ich fürchte — ich weiß nicht — ob ich — Eurer Gesundheit'). This muted opening, however, is deceptive. When Franz makes his fifth short speech a transition begins; the style is heightened, expressions such as 'Träne des Mitleids' and 'auf ewig' make their appearance and (especially important) an indication of movement associated with emotion is given ('Laßt mich vorerst auf die Seite gehen und eine Träne des Mitleids vergießen'). The 'auf ewig' is repeated in a balanced parallelism:

ich sollte schweigen auf ewig — denn er ist Euer Sohn; ich sollte seine Schande verhüllen auf ewig — denn er ist mein Bruder.

The drabness of the beginning is no doubt intentional. It implies a state of humdrum normality extending backwards into the past, and so gives the situation a pre-existence, which is the more necessary since Schiller only sporadically alludes to the past of his characters in *Die Räuber*.[1] This introductory passage, however, is brief, and quickly yields to the intensity which is an obvious primary characteristic of the play. Only at one other point does similarly relaxed dialogue appear, in the second scene of Act Four, when Amalia introduces the supposed stranger into

[1] Cf. G. Storz, op. cit., pp. 52 ff.

the picture gallery; and this passage is even shorter—seven brief
sentences. Schiller knew how to write realistic dialogue of this
kind, but he contents himself with the minimum for his purpose
and escapes into tension, and so into that dynamic use of language which, more than any feature of character, plot, or situation,
gives this play its unmistakable identity.

There are, indeed, other passages of realistic dialogue. When
the Leipzig students talk of their situation and their prospects,
the language is strikingly appropriate, because it reproduces the
energetic, bounding vitality of young men conscious of their
intellectual power and their physical vigour, translating them
into thrust and parry with devil-may-care insouciance and
youthful delight in the shocking and provocative. In a brief
dialogue in Act I. Sc. ii each participant seeks ostentatiously to
cap his companion's point:

SPIEGELBERG. So gefällt mirs! Wenn ihr Mut habt, tret einer auf und
  sag: Er habe noch etwas zu verlieren, und nicht alles zu gewinnen! —
SCHWARZ. Wahrhaftig, da gäbs manches zu verlieren, wenn ich das
  verlieren wollte, was ich noch zu gewinnen habe!
RAZMANN. Ja, zum Teufel! und manches zu gewinnen, wenn ich das
  gewinnen wollte, was ich nicht verlieren kann.
SCHUFTERLE. Wenn ich das verlieren müßte, was ich auf Borgs auf
  dem Leibe trage, so hätt ich allenfalls morgen nichts mehr zu
  verlieren.

This is recognizably the forced competitive language of
students, wringing the last drop out of a given phrase. It arises
from a state of semi-intoxication which derives as much from
irrepressible energy as from grosser stimulants. And it is precisely the element of intoxication which leads Schiller to prefer
this dynamic realism to the flat and expressionless lifelikeness of
the opening words of the play. A tiny fragment of just such
student speech survives from real life in a note left by Schiller
for his friends one evening at the end of 1781:

Seid mir schöne Kerls. Bin da gewesen und kein Petersen, kein
Reichenbach. Tausensakerlot! Wo bleibt die Manille heut? Hol euch

alle der Teufel! Bin zu Hauß, wenn ihr mich haben wollt. Adieu. Schiller.[1]

Intoxication of another kind underlies the passage of realistic speech in which Schweizer and Roller give an account of the rescue of the latter. Here the mingled sense of oppressive danger and relief at its removal unties their tongues, imparting to them an eloquence which is the symptom of crisis surmounted, be it only by a hair's breadth. Schweizer's words tumble over each other:

Wir paßten die Zeit ab, bis die Passagen leer waren. Die ganze Stadt zog dem Spektakel nach, Reuter und Fußgänger durch einander und Wagen, der Lärm und der Galgenpsalm johlten weit. Itzt, sagt der Hauptmann, brennt an, brennt an! Die Kerl flogen wie Pfeile, steckten die Stadt an dreiunddreißig Ecken zumal in Brand ... Wir indes Gasse auf, Gasse nieder, wie Furien — Feuerjo! Feuerjo! durch die ganze Stadt — Geheul, — Geschrei — Gepolter ...          (ii. iii)

From the moment when Schweizer repeats 'brennt an' it is clear that he is reliving the experience, carried away in a form of intoxication, which expresses itself in acceleration and finally in the abandonment of syntax.

Roller, in this episode, safeguards himself against loss of self-control by a staccato insistence on brutal detail:

Es war Hülfe in der Not, ihr könnts nicht schätzen. Ihr hättet sollen — den Strick um den Hals — mit lebendigem Leib zu Grabe marschieren wie ich, und die sackermentalischen Anstalten und Schinderszeremonien ...

At the end Roller, emphasizing in throwing down his glass that this cup has been taken from him, utters words of complete realism which yet echo the subdued intoxication of relief:

Nein, bei allen Schätzen des Mammons! ich möchte das nicht zum zweiten Mal erleben. Sterben ist etwas mehr als Harlekinssprung, und Todesangst ist ärger als Sterben.

At one other point Schiller employs realistic dialogue. In the evocative scene on the banks of the Danube (iii. ii) the robbers

[1] *NA* 23. 29. Jonas, i. 53.

Schwarz and Grimm punctuate the utterances of Karl Moor with short matter-of-fact sentences, which could be fragments of any real conversation—'Es gibt ein fruchtbares Jahr' and 'Das ist leicht möglich. Es kann alles zugrund gehen, wenig Stunden vorm Schneiden' and 'Alle Teufel! was hat er? wird ihm übel?' Here the realism performs a different function. These interpolations of normality reveal the gulf between the insensitive, unimaginative robbers and their suffering and conscience-rent captain. Karl has passed through a great crisis, comparable with that experienced by Roller and Schweizer in Act Two; his soul is still remote from actuality, though the passing of the paroxysm and the expenditure of nervous energy have left upon him a great lassitude. True to his mobile and sensitive nature, he expresses himself, in this phase of gentle, post-climactic intoxication, in words which breathe a melancholy, elegiac poetry. Schwarz and Grimm answer tersely and plainly, yet without abruptness or aggressiveness, so that they provide a norm for Karl's emotions and at the same time leave the delicate mood unimpaired.

## 2. THE LANGUAGE OF FRENZY

These were the gentler uses of intoxication, occurring within the framework of realism. Most of the language of *Die Räuber*, however, is understandable only as the expression of a state of poetic elevation, rapture, fury, or despair. The words *Rausch*, *Taumel*, *Wirbel* constantly recur, drawing attention to an overriding condition of mind. In this intoxication the inhibitions are lifted, concealed violence is revealed, brutality and libidinousness make their appearance side by side with noble emotions and sublime conceptions, and the whole pours forth in the torrential eloquence which has made this play notorious for the extravagant dynamism of its language.[1]

Karl Moor seems indeed 'a part to tear a cat in', and so wild

[1] Cf. R. Buchwald, *Schiller. Leben und Werk*, 4th edn., 1959, pp. 267 f.

and ferocious is the tone that it is not surprising that this style has mostly been explained away in terms of youth, inexperience, or repression, or else rejected outright.[1] It is obvious, however, even to a casual glance, that the language of *Die Räuber* is something essential to and inseparable from the play, and not a mere tactless indiscretion.

The techniques of expression which enable this language to function are few and simple. Fundamental to Schiller's poetic imagination is antithesis. It underlies the character structure of the play, reproducing the striking dualistic pattern which is already fixed in the two opposed and opposing brothers. It shapes the contrast of scene with scene. Most of all it pervades and inspires the dialogue.

Frequently these antitheses are of the most direct and simple kind: Heaven and Hell, creation and destruction, rats and lions. 'Seine Küsse sind Pest', insinuates Franz (I. iii) and he acclaims lamentation and remorse as 'ewige Zerstörerinnen und ewige Schöpferinnen eures Giftes' (II. i); or he eggs Hermann on to action with the contrast 'Was kann so eine Ratze gegen einen Löwen?' (II. i). '*Ich* bin mein Himmel und meine Hölle", exclaims Karl (IV. v). The examples can be multiplied—body and soul, rags and purple, spirit and matter, ugly and beautiful, day and night, whore and nun, prolong and cut short, win and lose, north and south ('Mitternacht . . . Mittag'), all these occur, several of them repeatedly.

Commoner than the simple antithesis are the refinements of opposition. Contrasting things are made to associate—'Da krabbeln sie nun wie die Ratten auf der Keule des Herkules' (I. ii), or 'Bettler sind Könige' (I. iii) or 'den Gifttrank dieser Seligkeit' (IV. iii). This leaning to oxymoron culminates in such expressions as 'ein so blutdürstiges Mitleid' (V. ii) or 'verwilde zum Tiger, sanftmütiges Lamm' (I. ii). Their impetuous rhythm, their unrestrained violence, together with their ubiquity, make it apparent that their source is not a mode of thought, but a spontaneous act of feeling. They betoken the fundamental

[1] K. Berger, *Schiller*, i. 1905, p. 158.

principle of division in Schiller, which is simultaneously the principle of drama. It is doubtful if any dramatist has felt and shaped more dramatically. And antithesis is one of the most conspicuous patterns for expressing this dualism with its ever-present tension of pro and contra.

Tension, in its turn, engenders intensity. No doubt the stresses of Schiller's life at the Academy accentuated a natural tendency. It is equally likely that his first major work was an outlet for accumulated pressures, a formidable geyser breaking the surface with a violence and a heat which are never sub-sequently repeated, simply because such rigid and prolonged restraint without opportunity for escape does not recur in Schiller's life. These explanations account in some degree for the *excessive* intensity present in *Die Räuber*. Its real and deeply-rooted first cause, however, is the dualistic structure of Schiller's mind.

The intensity of the play manifests itself primarily in poetico-rhetorical form. The hyperbolical mode pervades the speech of the play. It occurs repeatedly in numerical form—'tausend blutige Tränen' (I. i) or 'wie von tausend Donnern getroffen' (III. ii) or 'der mit zehntausendfachem Zentnergewicht auf deine stolze Seele fallen wird' (V. i), or even 'Ich höre mit tausend Ohren' (II. i). It appears even more frequently in the extreme of temporality—'auf ewig', 'nie und nimmer', or 'die große Schand-tat soll er mit sich in die Ewigkeit hinüber schleppen' (V. ii). Even where nothing more than 'constant' is meant, 'eternal' is used—'dessen ewiges Studium' (I. i), 'mein ewiger Wunsch' (II. i); or two words of perpetuity are tautologically yoked together—'laß mich immer ewig davon rennen' (V. ii).

This intensification applies to the whole range of Schiller's vocabulary in *Die Räuber*. *Totenbleich* and *totenblaß* reinforce the idea of pallor. Images of fire proliferate. They are used to indicate intense energy, enthusiasm, or indignation. In the first scene twice we read of 'der feurige Geist'. 'Das wird Feuer in deine Adern blasen', says Spiegelberg (I. ii),[1] and Karl in his

---

[1] *NA* 3. 357, Lesarten. The sentence occurs only in the first edition.

rage cries 'so fange Feuer, männliche Gelassenheit' (i. ii) and reinforces with fire one of his sternest maledictions—'diese Flamme brenne in deinem Busen, bis die Ewigkeit grau wird' (ii. iii). Franz describes his brother's eyes as 'schwarzen, feuer-werfenden Augen' (iv. ii). Apart, however, from this direct use of the image to denote an intense activity of the mind, numerous images make the speech vivid in terms of fire. Franz alludes to the lamp of life burning out—'das Öl seines Lebens in sechs Jährchen so rein weggebrannt hat' (i. i), an image which is repeated in the next act: 'Ein Licht ausgeblasen, das ohnehin nur mit dem letzten Öltropfen wuchert' (ii. i). The true dynamism and the false are contrasted as 'Der lohe Lichtfunke Prometheus' and 'die Flamme von Bärlappenmehl — Theaterfeuer, das keine Pfeife Tabak anzündet' (i. ii). And the depth of the decline of humanity from its original vitality is further crystallized in the exclamation 'Ah! daß der Geist Hermanns noch in der Asche glimmte!' (i. ii). As Robber Moor nears his end he uses a cognate image when he asks to be allocated 'irgendeinen eingeäscherten Weltkreis' (iv. v). Truly, we might feel that *Die Räuber* is on fire from end to end.[1]

The high blood-pressure of the play is also maintained by a means which is particularly apt in a play dealing with brigands—the use of oaths. Many of these are in themselves commonplace, the familiar stormy terms of conventional German profanity; they do, however, seek to heighten and intensify by the multipli-cation of their elements, as in the quadruple oath—'Blitz, Donner, Hagel und Wetter!' (ii. ii). More significant are the invocations of murder, death, and Hell ('Mord und Tod!', 'Hölle, Tod und Teufel!', 'Tod und Verdammnis!', 'Holen mich zehn Teufel!', or 'Zum Henker!'), and still more closely adapted to the gloomy intensity of the last scene is Karl's oath—'bei meiner grimmigen Seele!' These explosions of profanity, with their underlining by imprecation, serve a purpose in the process of intensification, but more important are the three solemn oaths sworn deliberately, yet fervently, by Karl Moor. The exclamation 'so wahr meine

[1] In all there are some forty instances of words or images of fire in *Die Räuber*.

Seele lebt, ich bin euer Hauptmann' is only a prelude to the solemn oath:

bei dieser männlichen Rechte! schwör ich euch hier, treu und standhaft euer Hauptmann zu bleiben bis in den Tod! Den soll dieser Arm gleich zur Leiche machen, der jemals zagt oder zweifelt oder zurücktritt! Ein Gleiches widerfahre mir von jedem unter euch, wenn ich meinen Schwur verletze! (I. ii)

Here the gesture of swearing a solemn oath with upraised arm, the use of 'treu und standhaft' (the formula of virtue applied in the context of vice), and the triple alliterative association in the second phrase combine to evoke a mood of awe. That the seriousness is weakened by the use of a substitute ('Ein Gleiches') in the last limb of this threefold asseveration is no doubt a miscalculation on Schiller's part.

The second of Karl's three oaths is the shortest; its simple formula of affirmation ('so wahr meine Seele lebt') is this time intensified by the gesture of raising the dagger which has been the instrument of murder (III. ii).

It is when the crisis of the fourth act reveals the full wickedness and horror of his brother's actions that Karl swears the oath which, in rhetorical majesty and soul-chilling splendour, elevates the language of the play to a new pitch of solemn intensity. A triple invocation supported by anaphora provides a prelude:

Höre mich Mond und Gestirne! Höre mich mitternächtlicher Himmel! der du auf die Schandtat herunter blicktest! Höre mich dreimal schröcklicher Gott, der da oben über dem Monde waltet, und rächt und verdammt über den Sternen, und feuerflammt über der Nacht;

and the oath itself is underlined by the ritual of gesture and posture:

Hier knie ich — hier streck ich empor die drei Finger in die Schauer der Nacht.

It is only after these awe-inspiring preliminaries that the oath itself is sworn:

Hier schwör ich, und so speie die Natur mich aus ihren Grenzen wie eine bösartige Bestie aus, wenn ich diesen Schwur verletze, schwör ich,

das Licht des Tages nicht mehr zu grüßen, bis des Vatermörders Blut,
vor diesem Steine verschüttet, gegen die Sonne dampft. (IV. v)

All three sections of this passage of anathema are noticeably
repetitive. Saying a thing again and again is the simplest form of
emphasis, and it can also serve as a means of intensification. *Die
Räuber* abounds in repetition, often in its most elementary form.
'Menschen — Menschen!' exclaims Karl Moor in his paroxysm
of wounded rage, and 'Er, Er', and each time the duplication
conveys a choking in the throat, an inability to voice and articulate the torrent of emotion within him (I. ii).

The scene (II. ii) in which the tormented father is shattered and
apparently killed by the false report of Karl's death achieves its
effect by an intense language of despair, horror, and impotent
anger, which is largely conveyed by repetition. The stereotyped
'Wehe, wehe' which the afflicted father twice utters invokes
biblical images and so heightens and intensifies the situation.[1]
And, in the extremity of his grief, Graf Moor reveals the excess of
emotion, inhibiting its own expression, in a series of repetitions,
in which the inadequate word is repeated with effect similar to
Karl's utterances quoted above. The old man stammers 'Fluch,
Fluch, Verderben, Fluch . . .', 'Scheusal, Scheusal!', and—more
clearly than at any other point—'du hast mir den Fluch aus dem
Herzen geschwätzt, du — du —' (II. ii), in which the attempt at
expression is abandoned in the overfullness of his heart.

It may sometimes seem as if *Die Räuber* were a play written
for the deaf, so insistent are the emphases, so hammer-like
the repetitions. Yet one perceives, on closer examination, that
even the most innocent-looking reduplications have a purpose.
Thus Karl in II. iii, addressing his robbers and underlining the
apparent hopelessness of their plight, calls out 'Schaut doch um
euch, schaut doch um euch!', so that it becomes clear that they
are listening to him spellbound, and only on the second exhor-
tation does the order to look and see for themselves translate
itself in their minds into an action.

---

[1] Cf. also, below, the similar ritualistic recurrence of the same phrase in *Die
Braut von Messina*.

A more sophisticated, augmentative use of repetition occurs in Karl's apostrophe of his native soil—'Sei mir gegrüßt, Vaterlandserde! Vaterlandshimmel! Vaterlandssonne!' (IV. i)—in which the swelling tide of emotion, powerful though it is, falls short of the pitch where it inhibits expression. And a related use appears in the scene by the Danube (III. ii), where the pensive mood is indicated by a threefold repetition, of which the second element is simply a matter-of-fact assent by another speaker:

MOOR. ... Aber es kann ja über Nacht ein Hagel fallen und alles zugrund schlagen.
SCHWARZ. Das ist leicht möglich. Es kann alles zugrund gehen, wenig Stunden vorm Schneiden.
MOOR. Das sag ich ja. Es wird alles zugrund gehn.

Here the symbolical character of Moor's language is unobtrusively yet unmistakably pointed, not only by the repetition, but also by the simple shift from 'kann' to 'wird'.

Most frequent of all repetitions, however, is the agonized expression of despair, the response to the knowledge that what is gone is gone beyond recall; paradoxically it underlines in the form of recurrence the fact of non-recurrence. So Graf Moor cries out 'Nimmer, nimmer, nimmer aus dem Grabe zurückholen!' (II. ii) and 'Kein Sohn mehr — kein Sohn mehr' (v. ii); and Karl expresses by utterances of 'Nimmer, nimmer' and 'Dahin! dahin!' (IV. ii) the realization that, though he return in the flesh, yet there is no return in the spirit.

Repetition, too, can simultaneously communicate both passion and solemnity, as in the triple vow of revenge which follows Karl Moor's discovery of the treatment which Franz has inflicted upon their father: 'Rache, Rache, Rache dir!' (IV. v). Here, in the sacred trinitarian formula, are the magic and the force of an incantation.

Intensification is also achieved in *Die Räuber* by accumulation; brand is added to brand until the fire burns more and more fiercely. It is by this simple means that the frenzied outbursts of Karl Moor rise to a sublime and frightening climax. Already in

the 'Schenke' scene of Act One he piles vehement demand upon
vehement demand:

wer mir itzt ein Schwert in die Hand gäb, dieser Otterbrut eine
brennende Wunde zu versetzen! wer mir sagte, wo ich das Herz ihres
Lebens erzielen, zermalmen, zernichten —

So compulsive is this mode of expression for Schiller that we see
him here doubly accumulating, adding verb to verb as well as
clause to clause. And no sooner has he reached this point than a
further series begins, this time in swift augmentation: 'er sei
mein Freund, mein Engel, mein Gott.'

In the first crisis of remorse, by the bank of the Danube, the
same crescendo of ejaculation expresses Moor's lament: 'Ich
allein der Verstoßene, ich allein ausgemustert aus den Reihen der
Reinen' (III. ii). In this complex form of repetition synonymy,
anaphora, accumulation, assonance, and alliteration all play a
part. A similar yet simpler parallelism occurs in 'Und ich so
häßlich auf dieser schönen Welt und ich ein Ungeheuer auf
dieser herrlichen Erde' (III. ii). The augmentation is here not
obvious, yet the slight lengthening of the second limb imparts a
feeling of intensification, which the words, viewed as statements,
would not have conveyed.

The language of accumulation reaches its culmination in the
explosive fury with which Karl Moor reacts to his father's
heart-rending disclosures: 'Die Gesetze der Welt sind Würfelspiel worden, das Band der Natur ist entzwei, die alte Zwietracht
ist los'; and this triple asseveration gives to the final conclusion
('der Sohn hat seinen Vater erschlagen') a force and weight
which alone it would never have possessed. No sooner is this
point reached than, after a mere drawing of breath, the torrent
of augmentation resumes with renewed fury: 'Nein, nicht erschlagen! das Wort ist Beschönigung! — der Sohn hat den Vater
tausendmal gerädert, gespießt, gefoltert, geschunden!' And, as if
the succession of single words were too weak, an accumulation of
clauses follows: 'worüber die Sünde rot wird, worüber der
Kannibale schaudert, worauf seit Äonen kein Teufel gekommen
ist —' (IV. v).

Again and again this cumulative mode of speech serves to express emotion, real or feigned. Moor's father uses it in his crazed misery:

drei volle Monde schmacht ich schon in diesem finstern unterirdischen Gewölbe, von keinem Strahle beschienen, von keinem warmen Lüftchen angeweht, von keinem Freunde besucht, wo wilde Raben krächzen und mitternächtliche Uhus heulen.          (IV. v)

Amalia conserves the pattern, using it anaphorically and hence in obvious parallel, to reveal the depth and power of her love:

hier hielt er mit himmlischer Musik die Hörer der Lüfte gefangen — hier an diesem Busch pflückte er Rosen . . . für mich — hier, hier lag er an meinem Halse, brannte seinen Mund auf den meinen.          (IV. iv)

The augmentation is accentuated by the final repetition of *hier* and the original transitive use of *brennen*.

Even Franz Moor speaks in accumulation when he feigns emotion, as in the parallel clauses already quoted[1] or the sentences which begin 'Ahndete mirs nicht . . .' (I. i). Here the long spacing of the anaphora is less compelling, differentiating the passage from those tracts where swift recurrence implies the power and conviction of genuine emotion.

The fundamental structure of Schiller's syntax in *Die Räuber* rests on antithesis, repetition, accumulation, and parallelism, powerfully reinforced by a vivid rhythmic sense. It is not difficult to see that a duplicating form of thought is at the root of all. One of the simplest and most obvious of mental processes expresses itself here in a range of variations. That process is a fundamental one to the dramatist, who must deploy and, so to speak, pluralize the oneness of himself into opposites and similarities.

### 3. THE VOCABULARY OF VIOLENCE

The arrangement of words in *Die Räuber* is significant enough. The words themselves are equally informative. They fall into a number of groups, which frequently prove to be related.

---

[1] See above, p. 5.

Mention has already been made of the words denoting or implying fire—*brennend*, *Flamme*, *Fünkchen*, *Asche*, and so on. They
constitute a substantial group conveying passionate intensity, or
the loss of it. Important though they are, they do not possess in
this play the weight of certain other groups. Foremost among
these are the words and expressions of violence, horror, and
cruelty.

Schiller's zoological collection in this play is limited, but
almost all the creatures represented are ravening beasts of prey,
and they are for the most part placed in a setting which emphasizes their ferocity, or alternatively stresses the even greater
ferocity of the human species. So Karl Moor, in his first passionate explosion, describes mankind as 'falsche, heuchlerische
Krokodilbrut' and compares human beings, to their great
disadvantage, to the mildness of lions, leopards, and ravens
(I. ii). Twice in this speech the tiger appears as the climax of
ferocity, and, as Karl's torrent of indignation and wounded
pride sweeps him on, men are seen as wolves and as broods of
hyenas and adders. Franz, as he plans his insidious lethal assault
upon his father, calls to his aid the image of the wolf and (three
times) of the serpent. And his wit is 'Skorpionstich' (I. i). The
lion and the eagle serve as symbols of ferocity allied to nobility.
But the savage mode predominates, Karl Moor 'schäumt wie ein
Eber', he reiterates 'wir müssen fechten wie angeschossene Eber',
and Schweizer continues the image with 'ich will ihnen mit
meinen Fangern den Bauch schlitzen' (II. iii). 'Die Klauen des
Tigers' (III. iii), 'grimmig wie die Tigerin dem siegbrüllenden
Räuber ihrer Jungen nach' (this from Amalia, III. i), 'Das
Erbarmen ist zu den Bären geflohen' (v. ii)[1]—all these amplify
the catalogue of ferocious zoological examples which illustrate or
heighten the ferocity of man.

This, however, is only a prelude to the language of horror in
*Die Räuber*. At the time of writing the play, Schiller was a
medical student, and many phrases testify to his anatomical,

---

[1] *NA* 3. 363, Lesarten. Text of the first edition only; subsequent editions read
'in die Bären gefahren'.

physiological, and pathological knowledge. The manner in which these medical accomplishments are exhibited is nevertheless far removed from the dispassionate observation, scientific objectivity, or human sympathy which, in some degree or other, may reasonably be expected in the physician. A streak of brutality and even of venom runs through this clinical language, which sometimes accidentally recalls the casual or ostentatious callousness of the medical student, but in general belongs to another deeper, more alarming, and more sinister world.

Expressions such as 'aus Mutterleib gekrochen' (i. ii) or 'dein Gehirnchen soll sich im Schädel undrehen' can perhaps be dismissed as a grim facetiousness remaining near the surface. But Karl's vivid visceral image of the tyrant's sycophants has a sour crudeness which seeks less to shock the listener than to vent suppressed indignation and *ressentiment*: 'Sie verpalisadieren sich ins Bauchfell eines Tyrannen, hofieren der Laune seines Magens und lassen sich klemmen von seinen Winden' (i. ii).[1] Such an image testifies to a powerful and original imagination which will stop at nothing. As savagely brutal is Schweizer's promise to slit the attackers' bellies 'daß ihnen die Kutteln schuhlang herausplatzen' or Razmann's account of Karl's murder of the Reichsgraf's attorney—'der Dolch stak in seinem Bauch wie ein Pfahl in dem Weinberg',[2] or Spiegelberg's story of the rape of the nuns (ii. iii).

The combination of physiological detail with savage bias reaches its fullest development in the circumstantial description of the man dying of syphilis, with which Franz Moor regales Amalia in the third scene of Act One:

da blickts schrecklich durch den gelben, bleifarbenen Augenring; — da verrät sichs im totenblassen, eingefallenen Gesicht und dreht die Knochen häßlich hervor — da stammelts in der halben, verstümmelten

---

[1] 'Bogen B', replaced by Schiller before publication, had this form: 'Warum sollen sich tausende und wieder tausend unter die Laune Eines Magens krümmen, und von seinen Blähungen abhängen' (*NA* 3. 248).

[2] Text of the first edition only, *NA* 3. 359, Lesarten. Subsequent reading, 'Wie ein Nagel in der Wand'.

Stimme — da predigts fürchterlich laut vom zitternden, hinschwan-
kenden Geripppe — da durchwühlt es der Knochen innerstes Mark
und bricht die mannhafte Stärke der Jugend — da, da spritzt es den
eitrigten, fressenden Schaum aus Stirn und Wangen und Mund und
der ganzen Fläche des Leibes zum scheußlichen Aussatz hervor und
nistet abscheulich in den Gruben der viehischen Schande.

And, as if this were not enough, he goes on to compare the
noxious exhalations with 'den Geruch eines berstenden Aases'.
And coprophagy joins in with the picture of remorse, 'grabende
Schlange, die ihren Fraß wiederkäut und ihren eigenen Kot
wiederfrißt'. That this is spoken by the wicked Franz does not
dispose of it. The riot of horrifying detail underlines the brutality
which at this time was a component of Schiller's poetic imagination, and runs through the fable as well as the language.

The most extended of these medical images, such as Spiegelberg's account of the raid on the nunnery and Franz Moor's
symptomatic description of syphilis, have discernible erotic
undertones. And others are concerned with procreation and
childbirth. The language of sex in this play falls into two
antithetical rubrics—ethereal and carnal—and the latter predominates. Franz and the mass of the robbers see love as corrupt,
venal, despicable—as an exercise of muscle, nerve, and epi-
dermis. Its characteristic words are *Wollust*, *gierig*, and *geil*, this
last once spoken by Amalia (III. i). Though she can hurl this
temperamental epithet at Franz, she, the only woman character
of the play, is clearly viewed as a figure of immaculate purity.
Numerous non-appearing women of easier virtue are referred to
as 'Koketten' or possessing 'die Reize einer Phryne'. Franz
proposes to make Amalia his 'Mätresse', and the robbers term
her 'eine Metze'. Elaborate images of rape are reinforced by
equally circumstantial descriptions of subsequent humiliation.
Spiegelberg's revolting account of the treatment of the nuns ends
with 'meine Kerls haben ihnen ein Andenken hinterlassen, sie
werden ihre neun Monate dran zu schleppen haben'; and Franz
follows up his threats to Amalia by gloating over her imagined
future social degradation: 'daß die ehrlichen Bauernweiber mit

Fingern auf dich deuten, wenn du es wagst und über die Gasse gehst.' He indulges in sadistic imaginings:

> mich ergötzt der Grimm eines Weibes, macht dich nur schöner, begehrenswerter. Komm — dieses Sträuben wird meinen Triumph zieren und mir die Wollust in erzwungenen Umarmungen würzen;
> (III. i)

—and even the chaste Amalia speaks of the absent Karl's burning kisses and weaves into her recollections an image of death gladly embraced: 'hier lag er auf meinem Halse, brannte seinen Mund auf den meinen, und die Blumen starben gern unter der Liebenden Fußtritt' (IV. iv). A similar association of violence and love infuses the death of Amalia at Karl's hands, and the link between murder and love is unmistakably, though grotesquely, underlined in the stage version (*Trauerspiel*), when, in her death-throes, she gives an obedient assent to Karl's leading question, whether such a death be sweet. And Kosinsky conjures up vividly the perpetual violence and shame to which *his* Amalia is subjected by her self-sacrificing love (III. ii).

An impulse to degrade and tread in the mire governs Franz Moor's variations on the theme of procreation. He terms it 'viehischer Prozeß zur Stillung viehischer Begierden' (I. i),[1] and later expatiates on this conception:

> Hängt nicht das Dasein der meisten Menschen mehrenteils an der Hitze eines Juliusmittags, oder am anziehenden Anblick eines Bettuchs, oder an der waagrechten Lage einer schlafenden Küchengrazie, oder an einem ausgelöschten Licht? die ... Geburt des Menschen das Werk einer viehischen Anwandlung. ... der Mensch entstehet aus Morast....
> (IV. ii)

Franz is here outlining a theory of casual causation and fortuitous creation, but the crude terms which he deliberately uses impart a tone of brutality and violence to his language; and this is underlined by his equating the father's impulsive act of pro-creation with his own coldly intended act of murder. Love—or

---

[1] *NA* 3. 357, Lesarten. The words are omitted in all editions after the first. The analogous phrase quoted immediately below from IV. ii is, however, retained in all editions by Schiller: 'das Werk einer viehischen Anwandlung.'

what passes for it—and death go hand in hand, as they do in the murder of Amalia or in the description of the syphilitic.

The brutal violence of action and language is not restricted to any one figure or group of figures. Karl Moor skirts the field of sexual brutality with his 'und studieren sich das Mark aus dem Schädel, was das für ein Ding sei, das er in seinen Hoden geführt hat' or 'Die Kraft seiner Lenden ist versiegen gegangen, und nun muß Bierhefe den Menschen fortpflanzen helfen',[1] or with his diatribe over 'das schlappe Kastratenjahrhundert' (I. ii).

Spiegelberg strews crudities through every speech, reaching his nadir in the sickening climax of the raid on the nunnery:

und endlich gar die alte Schnurre, die Äbtissin, angezogen wie Eva vor dem Fall — du weißt, Bruder, daß mir auf diesem weiten Erdenrund kein Geschöpf so zuwider ist als eine *Spinne* und ein *altes Weib*, und nun denk dir einmal die schwarzbraune, runzligte, zottige Vettel vor mir herumtanzen, und mich bei ihrer jungfräulichen Sittsamkeit beschwören — alle Teufel! ich hatte schon die Ellbogen angesetzt, ihr die übriggebliebenen *wenigen Edlen* [her teeth] vollends in den Mastdarm zu stoßen . . . . (II. iii)

Spiegelberg's momentary 'poetic' touch ('auf diesem weiten Erdenrund') and his parody of Klopstock ('wenigen Edlen')[2] make it clear that this passage is a form of comedy; its brutality is made all the more frightening by this mood of callous enjoyment.

Roller, in his turn, describes himself as 'schon mit Haut und Haar an die Anatomie verhandelt' (II. iii). Schufterle piles brutal atrocity on atrocity, to reach the culmination of the infant thrown alive into the blaze; and the point here is not the horror of the action but the cold callousness of his account—'Armes Tierchen, sagt ich, du verfrierst ja hier, und warfs in die Flamme' (II. iii). This sentence is in his eyes a splendid joke and the actor playing the part needs to accompany it with a loud guffaw.

Schweizer abstains from such sadistic humour, but what he says in seriousness and anger is scarcely less brutal—'bis wir

---

[1] *NA* 3. 357, Lesarten. The sentence occurs only in the first edition.
[2] *Messias*, IV. i. 20. Cf. note in *NA* 3. 412.

ihnen die Streu unterm Arsch angezündt haben' and 'daß du im Kloak ersticktest, Dreckseele du!', till it takes a more dangerous and cruel turn in 'man soll dich in eine Sauhaut nähen, und durch Hunde verhetzen lassen' (II. iii). His rage against the Pater-emissary precipitates an even more revolting excess of brutality— 'Soll ich hingehn, und diesem abgerichteten Schäferhund die Gurgel zusammenschnüren, daß ihm der rote Saft aus allen Schweißlöchern sprudelt?' (II. iii).

With Franz the brutality is usually controlled, in accord with his sharp and rationally schooled intellect; but anger draws him, too, into brutal threats when he encounters Amalia's resistance— 'an den Haaren will ich dich in die Kapelle schleifen, den Degen in der Hand' (II. i); and terror causes him to turn on Pastor Moser with 'Ich will dir die verfluchte Zunge aus dem Munde reißen'. Even Pastor Moser uses a drastic unclerical image when he refers to the churchyard—'wie des lebendig Begrabenen im Bauche des Kirchhofs' (v. i).

Karl Moor, too, sublime and noble though he is meant to be, twice adds brutality to his customary violence of expression. In the scene on the banks of the Danube he speaks thus to Kosinsky: 'hast du dein Fechten nur darum gelernt, arme Reisende um einen Reichstaler niederzustoßen, oder Weiber hinterrücks in den Bauch zu stechen?' (III. ii). These words are uttered in contempt, but the terms Karl Moor chooses are nevertheless significant in their crudity. Furthermore Karl in Act Five refers directly to his own deeds of rapine and murder in phrases of crass savagery: 'Euer banges Sterbegewinsel — euer schwarz-gewürgtes Gesicht — eure fürchterlich klaffenden Wunden . . .' (IV. v).

Oppressive though all this brutality and bestiality can be, it is lifted out of the merely disgusting by its dynamic violence. The figurative uses of language are less crude than these factual examples, but they are no less violent. Franz, wishing to suggest that the news about Karl would kill their father, says 'wir würden alle noch heute die Haare ausraufen über Eurem Sarge', and the pain the feigned letter will inflict is expressed by 'dein brüderliches Herz durchbohren'; similarly he hypocritically simulates his intention to spare his father with 'meine arme Lippen sollen nimmermehr einen Vater ermorden' (I. i). The choice of these phrases may in part be dictated by the imagined fulfilment of wishes which may not be disclosed. Such language, however, is not restricted to Franz. Mankind is for Karl 'dies mörderisch Geschlecht': in his frenzied rage he would poison the ocean to destroy the world—'den Ozean vergiften, daß sie den Tod aus allen Quellen saufen'; would summon up the elements against 'das Hyänengezücht'; and would wield a sword to annihilate this brood of creeping things—'dieser Otterbrut eine brennende Wunde zu versetzen'. He promises royal reward to him among his followers, 'der am wildesten sengt, an gräßlichsten mordet' (I. ii). *Grimm, grimmig, fürchterlich,* and *schröcklich* are words which are constantly on his lips. In his soliloquy he likens himself to the brazen bull of Perillus—'einen Ochsen aus mir gemacht, daß die Menschen in meinem glühenden Bauche bratet' (IV. v). His oath of vengeance on his brother is sworn by 'allen schröcklichen Seufzern derer, die meine Flamme fraß und mein fallender Turm zermalmte'; and the injunction to Schweizer's 'Würgengel' to deliver Franz alive is couched in terms of ferocious menace—'dessen Fleisch will ich in Stücken reißen, und hungrigen Geiern zur Speise geben, der ihm nur die Haut ritzt . . .' (IV. v).

The universal violence fixes the tone of the play; and its even distribution through action and persons disqualifies it as a means of characterization.

Born of the violence which dominates this play are also the frequent references to blood.[1] They include such horrifying examples as: 'wenn mein erboster Feind mir mein eigen Herzblut zutrinkt' (I. ii), 'Blut saufst du wie Wasser' (set in the mouth of the Pater of all people) (II. iii), 'schwarzes, rauchendes Blut' (IV. i), and 'bis des Vatermörders Blut, vor diesem Steine verschüttet, gegen die Sonne dampft' (IV. v).

It is tempting to relate such repeated outbursts of frightfulness,

---

[1] They number twenty.

horror, savagery, and violence to Schiller's circumstances, to the strains, stresses, constraints, and limitations which pressed upon him during the years in which *Die Räuber* was written. These environmental conditions supplied a favourable situation for explosive speech; they cannot alone explain its extreme virulence. The source of this frenzied vehemence was clearly deep down in Schiller himself.[1] Pressures at which we can only guess were exerting themselves far beneath the surface. Sexual stresses are discernible, touches of sadism and masochism, and a profound and anguished sense of guilt. This is the mixture which ignites in *Die Räuber*, flaming into incandescence. But the threatened degeneration into chaos is averted, and powerful factors, making for order, assert themselves.

The word *Gewissen* plays no great part in this tragedy. Yet conscience is one of its main nerves, operating half hidden and barely recognized. The acknowledgement of crime can be an act of conscience, and the constant insistence upon the word *Mord*, alone or in various compounds or derivatives, is itself a testimony to the power and prestige of conscience in *Die Räuber*. Even more significant are the references to sin. Franz encourages himself to attempt to murder his brother by the confession 'Bin ich doch ohnehin schon bis an die Ohren in Todsünden gewatet, daß es Unsinn wäre zurückzuschwimmen, wenn das Ufer schon so weit hinten liegt' (IV. ii). And in the hour of crisis he cries, 'so ruf doch den Beichtvater, daß er mir meine Sünden hinwegsegne' (V. i). Karl Moor, too, acknowledges the claims of conscience without ever mentioning the word. His exclamation in the Bohemian forests, 'Wie beugt mich diese Tat!', is an indirect affirmation of its power. Even clearer is his self-accusation on the banks of the Danube—'Und ich so häßlich auf dieser schönen Welt — und ich ein Ungeheuer auf dieser herrlichen Erde. . . . Meine Unschuld! Meine Unschuld!' (III. ii). When at last the tragedy is consummated he utters the cry, 'da steh ich am Rand

---

[1] The macabre vocabulary of horror occurs in several contemporary poems, especially the *Elegie auf den Tod eines Jünglings*, the *Leichenphantasie*, and the 'Laura' odes. Violence is also evident in the handling of the syntax of the poems.

eines entsetzlichen Lebens' (v. ii), by which the abyss of Hell is implied.

Behind the violence, then, lurks a consciousness of wrongdoing, which is reinforced by many of the expressions of violence and brutality themselves. Over and over again the dialogue turns around acts of savagery, cruelty, pain, and death which constitute punishments. The gallows is constantly on the robbers' lips; *Galgen* and *Henker* and 'das dreibeinige Tier' are always present in mind, and one of the central features of the play, the rescue of Roller, is reflected in a graphic account of execution seen from the standpoint of the escaped criminal. The gallows itself, the pillory, breaking on the wheel, pinching with glowing pincers, scourging, and loading with chains all provide repeated motifs belonging to the penal system of the eighteenth century.[1] Though these are the occupational risks of the robber, they are also images revealing a preoccupation of the author's mind with penal horror.

Thrice there appears in detail the picture of a prisoner incarcerated in the foulest and most savage conditions, twice as a threat and once as a fact. The terms in which this image is set have a remarkable similarity. The letter sent by Franz to Karl threatens dire imprisonment, should the prodigal return—'im untersten Gewölb seiner [his father's] Türme mit Wasser und Brot so lang traktiert werden, bis deine Haare wachsen wie Adlersfedern und deine Nägel wie Vogelsklauen werden' (I. ii). Franz holds over Daniel's head a similar fate when he seeks to induce him to poison Karl—'dein Leben im tiefsten meiner Türme, wo der Hunger dich zwingen wird, deine eigne Knochen abzunagen, und der brennende Durst, dein eignes Wasser wieder zu saufen' (IV. ii). And Graf Moor thus describes his treatment at Franz's hands:

drei volle Monde schmacht ich schon in diesem finstern unterirdischen Gewölbe, von keinem Strahle beschienen, von keinem warmen Lüftchen angeweht, von keinem Freunde besucht . . . drei Monden schon hab ichs tauben Wänden zugewinselt, aber ein hohler Widerhall

[1] There are more than sixty such expressions in *Die Räuber*.

äffte meine Klagen nur nach . . . dieser Mann brachte mir Brot und Wasser. . . . So ward ich kümmerlich erhalten diese lange Zeit, aber der unaufhörliche Frost — die faule Luft meines Unrats, — der grenzenlose Kummer — meine Kräfte wichen, mein Leib schwand, tausendmal bat ich Gott mit Tränen um den Tod.                    (IV. v)

We know the source of these images in the cruel imprisonment inflicted at Hohentwiel on Colonel Rieger and at Hohenasperg on C. D. Schubart, both of whom Schiller knew at a time when their sufferings were over or diminished.[1] The threefold repetition of the motif suggests that the horrors have stirred Schiller's imagination, exercising, as well as horrified repulsion, a ghoulish attraction. The fascination of the horrible, savage, and violent is evident, but the vital relationship is indicated by old Graf Moor when he refers to his affliction as a punishment from God. The horrible is harnessed to the idea of justice.

The full force of the motif of justice is embodied even more directly in the repeated references to courts, judges, and judgement. In the very first scene when Franz hypocritically refers to 'Gottes Richterstuhl', the aged Graf Moor exclaims 'Das ist ein Gericht über mich' (I. i) and 'Mit diesem Zeugnis belastet trete ich vor den Richterstuhl Gottes'(II. ii). Franz sees himself secure from the temporal courts, Spiegelberg cocks a snook at justice, while Razmann, rogue though he is, praises Karl for punishing the 'Schelm, der die Gerechtigkeit zur feilen Hure gemacht' (II. iii). In Schweizer's sardonic allusion to Roller's plight—'wenn der Himmel beizeit noch einfallen wollte' (II. iii)—there sounds an echo of *fiat justitia, ruat coelum*. Bitterly Karl Moor reproaches himself—'du bist der Mann nicht, das Rachschwert der obern Tribunale zu führen' (II. iii); Franz shudders at 'gräßliche Bilder von Strafgerichten' (II. ii), and hears from Pastor Moser the solemn admonition: 'Ihr fordert einen Höheren vor Euren Richterstuhl' (V. i). In this scene the images of judgment are multiplied—'ein innerer Tribunal . . . bestechen', 'Gericht über Euch halten', and 'sein Name heißt *Richter*' follow close upon each other.

---

[1] He met both in 1781, when Rieger, after his release, was Governor of Hohenasperg and Schubart a relatively privileged prisoner.

The judge who is cited in these abundant references is only rarely an earthly judge. The justice which Graf Moor and Pastor Moser revere, which Franz fears and Karl arrogates to himself, is divine; and this God is the Jehovah of the Old Testament, the God of retribution. References to *Rache* and *Wiedervergeltung* receive heavy emphasis. So Karl at his most arrogantly godlike exclaims, 'mein Handwerk ist Wiedervergeltung — Rache ist mein Gewerbe' (ii. iii), and with triple stress he vows to avenge his father—'Rache, Rache, Rache dir!' (iv. v). Franz Moor, in his paroxysm of terror at the height of his tragedy, utters a fourfold question—'Rächet denn droben über den Sternen einer?...Richtet droben einer über den Sternen! Entgegengehen dem Rächer über den Sternen diese Nacht noch! . . . Rechenschaft geben dem Rächer droben über den Sternen — und wenn er gerecht ist?' (v. i), proving by his reiteration that the answer is the 'Yes!' which he dreads. It is at a climax, too, that the tormented and frantic Karl exclaims, 'Das ist Vergeltung!' (v. ii); and in his final self-judgement he twice refers to revenge, condemning himself—'Ich nannte es Rache und Recht', and (inclining before God) '*Dein* eigen allein ist die Rache' (v. ii).

The New Testament has its part in this play primarily in the vision of judgement inspired by Revelation. The apocalyptic dream is dreamed by Franz:

siehe, da war mirs, als säh ich aufflammen den ganzen Horizont in feuriger Lohe, und Berge und Städte und Wälder, wie Wachs im Ofen zerschmolzen, und eine heulende Windsbraut fegte von hinnen Meer, Himmel und Erde — da erscholls wie aus ehernen Posaunen; Erde gib deine Toten, gib deine Toten, Meer! (v. i)

The tremendous vision presently displays 'auf drei rauchenden Stühlen drei Männer'. The first asserts faith, truth, and justice. The second tears the veil from the false and hypocritical. But the third, the figure of divine justice, thunders: 'ich wäge die Gedanken in der Schale meines Zorns! und die Werke mit dem Gewicht meines Grimms!' Even the images of divine justice are woven out of violence and horror.

To the group of words and images of judgment belongs also

*Gesetz*, which, though infrequent, is stressed at critical points. 'Ich soll', cries Karl, '... meinen Willen schnüren in Gesetze' (the image of the corset provides a note of constriction, related to the emphasis on chains, bonds, and imprisonment) (I. ii). And he reproaches 'das Gesetz' with its impotence to produce even *one* great man. It is not till the discovery of his father's wretched fate that Karl again invokes 'das Gesetz', which, in the meantime, has evolved from the arid restrictive code of men to the universal law governing hearts as well as hands—'Die Gesetze der Welt sind Würfelspiel worden' (IV. v). And finally the word occurs three times in the climax of self-knowledge at the end of the play—'ich wähnete . . . die Gesetze durch Gesetzlosigkeit aufrechtzuhalten' and 'noch blieb mir etwas übrig, womit ich die beleidigte Gesetze versöhnen ... kann'. With these pregnant uses of *Gesetz* are linked 'den ganzen Bau der sittlichen Welt' und 'die mißhandelte Ordnung' (v. ii).

God, the Devil, Heaven, and Hell are threads woven through the stuff of this play. God the judge, the avenger, dominates. Only once, through the mouth of the father, does He appear as a God of mercy—'die Gottheit ermüdet nicht im Erbarmen' (v. ii)—a belief which the action and the rest of the speech seem to contradict. Elsewhere God appears in stern contexts—'den Richterstuhl Gottes' (II. ii), 'die Schrecknisse Gottes' (IV. ii), 'Gott und mein Gewissen' (IV. ii), and 'ein Greuel vor Gott und den Menschen' (IV. ii). Once and once only does Karl Moor disclose the fundamental scope of his revolt, when he exclaims: 'schon wieder ein Kläger wider die Gottheit' (III. ii). But, if God is unyielding, Heaven sounds a more conciliatory note. Though it sometimes stands in simple antithesis to Hell, it more often functions independently as a symbol of hope and harmony. Though Franz derides the belief in an after-life, he speaks of 'die Freuden des Himmels' (I. i), recognizing the symbol, if not the substance. For Amalia and Graf Moor, the symbol of Heaven gives an assurance of the power of goodness and of happier days to come; Amalia speaks of 'die seraphische Harfe' and 'die himmlischen Hörer', and Graf Moor says to her, 'Himmlischer

Trost quillt von deinen Lippen' (II. ii). For Karl Moor 'dies himmlische Licht' (v. ii) remains, in spite of all the crimes he has committed, the sweet, beckoning symbol of goodness. Striking is the contrast with Franz, whose attempt at total disbelief has alienated him from the entire metaphysical structure of the universe, so that both Heaven and Hell are his enemies— 'diesen Sieg soll der Himmel nicht haben, diesen Spott mir nicht antun die Hölle' (IV. v).

References to the Devil and to Hell are not unnaturally abundant in a play concerned with robbers and murderers. Considering that Milton's Satan was in Schiller's mind not only when he wrote about the completed play, but also actually during its composition,[1] *Die Räuber* is remarkably free from satanism. Karl Moor seeks to substitute himself for God, but he does so in what he conceives to be a godlike spirit. He seeks to restore the divine order, not to overthrow it. And Franz, as we have just seen, fears and hates both parties in the cosmic struggle. The absence of a Lucifer-worshipping romanticism gives a hint that the violence, the brutality, and the cruelty are symptoms of emotional turbulence, not an expression of conviction, still less a confession of faith.

The sinister gloom of *Die Räuber* is lit repeatedly by vivid flashes of lightning, and here the figurative yields to the literal, for the lightning flash is one of the most important of the recurrent words and images, and from this terrifying and awful element there arises the sense of sublimity, which is one of the positive elements of the play. When Spiegelberg uses it in the scene *Schenke an der Grenze von Sachsen* it is merely the conventional image of speed. But in the mouth of Schweizer in the scene *Die böhmischen Wälder*, pluralized into a constant flickering, it acquires a more menacing tone—'Wir wollen über sie her wie die Sündflut und auf ihre Köpfe herabfeuren wie Wetterleuchten', a remarkable association of water, fire, and lightning. The note of menace here takes on a touch of the sublime. The images of lightning soon become less conventional and more vivid, spreading

---

[1] Cf. the 'Selbstbesprechung' in the *Wirtembergisches Repertorium der Literatur*, 1782.

across the play and refusing to be tied to one character. Amalia screams at Franz: 'Warum spaltet der Blitz die ruchlose Zunge nicht, die das Frevelwort ausspricht!' (III. i). 'Der Gefangene', laments Karl, 'hatte das Licht vergessen, aber der Traum der Freiheit fuhr über ihm wie ein Blitz in die Nacht, der sie finsterer zurückläßt' (IV. i), so achieving by the antithetical coupling of the profound darkness of the dungeon and the brilliance of the sudden flash of lightning a maximum of tension. Karl's electric halt before the portrait of his father evokes from Daniel the image 'wie vom Donner gerührt' (IV. ii). And his sudden recognition of the terrible deceit which has been practised upon him is given in similar sublime terms—'da fährt es über meine Seele wie der Blitz!' (IV. iii). And the lightning flickers and flashes through Franz's vision of judgement. Of course it is a symbol of divine justice, as well as of swiftness and of sudden irruption. But the most important aspect of the lightning for this play is its vertical dimension: from a sublime height it is launched downwards; it is the act of Jove, increasing the stature of the hero-god, diminishing the scale of the lesser creatures beneath him. It is the gesture of power, of poise leaping to sudden irresistible action, and in this, too, it is sublime.

If the lightning is the perfect combination of the sublime and the violent, other images and words of the sublime also abound. Among these are *ewig, nimmer, Himmel*, all of which have been mentioned already in other functions. Karl Moor quotes the heroes of Plutarch's Lives, specifically mentioning Scipio and Alexander and throwing in Hannibal for good measure. He refers to 'ein Tropfen deutschen Heldenbluts' and invokes Germanic heroism in the name of 'der Geist Hermanns' (I. ii). Twice in the scene in the Bohemian forests he speaks of 'dying like heroes'; and in the scene by the Danube he exclaims of the setting sun 'so stirbt ein Held!' On each occasion the heroic appears as the token of a height of sublimity no longer attainable by men. The sublime tone is further strengthened by the 'royal' vocabulary—'König seiner Triebe' (I. i), 'die Last der Kronen', 'königlich belohnet' (I. ii), 'ein königlicher Blick' (I. iii), 'der Arm höherer Majestäten' (IV. v), or 'ihre unverletzbare Majestät' (V. ii).

It is often asserted that *Die Räuber* is a *Freiheitsdrama*, and it would clearly be wrong to dispute that the tragedy of an attempt at freedom, at escape from the domination and constriction of law, is an important component of it; whilst in certain details it reflects political hostility to the tyrant in the shape of Franz Moor, the Reichsgraf, and the unnamed oppressor of Kosinsky and his bride. Nevertheless the verbal references to 'freedom' are less frequent than might be expected. Notwithstanding the title-page motto '*in Tirannos*', the word 'tyrant' occurs only five times, thrice with political significance, once in hypocrisy (I. iii.) and once in a reference to the tyrannical power of fate— 'Ich poche dem Tyrannen Verhängnis' (V. ii). *Frei* and *Freiheit* are not much more frequent,[1] and even then some of the occurrences are merely conventional or literal. The most significant uses come from Karl Moor in the opposition 'Freiheit : Gesetz'— 'Das Gesetz hat noch keinen großen Mann gebildet, aber die Freiheit brütet Kolosse und Extremitäten aus', and 'Mein Geist dürstet nach Taten, mein Atem nach Freiheit' (I. ii), in both of which a sense of some mysterious force in the word is perceptible, something which makes Karl's—and, we may fairly think, Schiller's—heart beat faster. The same spell is also felt, though in a more conventional way, in Karl's 'Tod oder Freiheit' at the end of Act Two. The much more frequent references to bondage, duress, and constriction, which are primarily connected with punishment and so with judgment, are linked antithetically with the idea of freedom, as is clearly demonstrated in Karl's speech in Act Four:

Wie dem Gefangenen, den der klirrende Eisenring aus Träumen der Freiheit aufjagt . . . der Gefangene hatte das Licht vergessen, aber der Traum der Freiheit fuhr über ihm wie ein Blitz in die Nacht. (IV. i)

When we know, as we do from other writings, how powerful was the emotive force of the word 'free' for Schiller, it is striking

---

[1] *Frei* and *Freiheit* occur eleven times in all.

that it occurs so rarely in this play in comparison with the words and images of bondage. This suggests that *Die Räuber* is a play in which the repressive and the constrictive dominate, in which Karl's revolt is foredoomed from the outset, the rule of law never for a moment endangered.

The language of the Lutheran Bible permeates the dialogue of *Die Räuber*. There are direct references to Jacob and Joseph (II. i), to Lot's wife and the destruction of Sodom and Gomorrha (II. iii), to the company of Korah (II. iii), and to Tobias (I. i). When Graf Moor listens to the reading of Scripture, the story of Joseph prophesies to him the course of events in his own family. And an allusion to the prodigal son (IV. v)[1] acquires irony by a reversal of roles. There are also references to Abraham's bosom, to Elijah's ravens (IV. v), and to the Apocalypse (V. i). Less obvious but nevertheless unmistakable footprints of Scripture occur over and over again. 'Mein Witz ist Skorpionstich' (I. i—I Kings 12 : 11), 'dankt dir . . ., daß er nicht ist wie dieser' (I. i—Luke 18 : 11), 'den Weg alles Fleisches' (II. iii—Genesis 6 : 13) are random examples. And in addition to these there are numerous turns of phrase which are not biblical quotations, but owe their shape to a thorough familiarity with Holy Writ. Such are 'saß liebreich lächelnd am Tor' (II. ii), 'unter euch treten und fürchterliche Musterung halten' (II. iii). Some expressions are hybrids, such as 'Dein Pfund vergraben' (I. ii), which is compounded of Matthew 25 : 18 and Luke 19 : 13. Whether Schiller devised this and other expressions or used a current phrase is immaterial; in using them he could not but be conscious of their biblical flavour; if, as sometimes occurs, their form owes something to Klopstock's *Messias*, their origin is still avowed, their use deliberate.

The scriptural tone in *Die Räuber* gives the dialogue solemnity and an exalted poetic tone. It reveals how deeply Schiller was involved in the play, how its issue is human destiny in the eye of God. It is particularly significant that this very expression occurs

---

[1] 'Ich hab gesündigt im Himmel und vor dir', Luke 25 : 18.

in the mouth of Franz—'ob das Vergangene nicht vergangen ist oder ein Auge findet über den Sternen' (v. i).

Sometimes quite small verbal components suffice to indicate an element of importance. A wave of anger against the perversion of religion emerges in the choice of 'bigott' (twice) and 'die Inquisition' (II. iii), but its subordinate import is made clear by the limitation of these occurrences to a single scene.

The bitterness of Karl's outburst, 'Betrogen, betrogen!' (IV. iii), sharply pointed by the preceding stage direction (*auffahrend nach schröcklichen Pausen*), focuses the tragedy upon the motif of deceit; and with an astonishing irony, Schiller achieves this at the moment when the *Larve*, which is the symbol of subterfuge, is attributed by Franz to Karl for the second time (I. i and IV. iii). Yet, for all his dishonesty, Franz's reference to the mask is true; for Karl has not only been deceived; he has deceived himself, as the reiterated subjunctives of non-return emphasize: 'Es hätte mich einen Fußfall gekostet, es hätte mich eine Träne gekostet ... Ich hätte glücklich sein können.' In this critical moment of self-recognition Schiller's beginning touches his end, for Karl Moor's flash of vision is a crude prestatement of the psychological subtlety intended in the central revelation scene of *Demetrius*.

This episode is quickly followed by a threat of total defeat for Karl, the near-collapse of the heroic figure; for, in the suicide monologue of Act IV. v, Karl for a moment adopts the phrasing of his brother to express a determinism which, if true, would be the negation of all he has lived for:

eure fürchterlich klaffenden Wunden ... hangen zuletzt an meinen Feierabenden, an den Launen meiner Ammen und Hofmeister, am Temperament meines Vaters, am Blut meiner Mutter.

Three words, occurring singly, acquire tremendous weight by their placing. Once and once only, and again it is at a moment of self-recognition, Karl substitutes for divine justice the classical Nemesis—'O unbegreiflicher Finger der rachekundigen Nemesis!' (IV. v)—and so establishes in anticipation a link with the plays to come.

In Karl's closing words the unmistakable vision of harmony is evoked ('die Harmonie der Welt') and his self-restoration driven home by the heavy emphasis on free will ('mit Willen für sie gestorben'). And finally the scope and circular motion of the play is brilliantly illuminated by a significant similarity of phrase. The Karl of Act I. ii says: 'Stelle mich vor ein Heer Kerls wie ich, und aus Deutschland soll eine Republik werden, gegen die Rom und Sparta Nonnenklöster sein sollen'—in which all the arrogance and dynamism of his youthful personality rings out. The defeated Karl of the last act echoes the phrasing and rhythm of his once confident self-assertion: 'daß zwei Menschen wie ich den ganzen sittlichen Bau der Welt zugrund richten würden.'

## 4. DYNAMIC RHETORIC

The language of *Die Räuber* is powerfully rhetorical, and its rhetoric employs two modes, one sardonic, the other exalted. Both are distributed without regard to character.

The sardonic mode belongs to Franz in his moments of monologue, to all the lesser robbers, and occasionally to Karl. The exalted mode is the normal vehicle for Karl Moor, and is used also by his father, by Amalia, and by Franz himself in moments of hypocrisy and likewise of panic. Both modes are closely related. Their mainspring is a fluent rhetoric which employs all the arts of persuasion and is at the same time animated by an irresistible impulsion. The linguistic elements composing it are often commonplace; simple words like *groß, heiß, heftig, schön* make up a large part of its vocabulary. Obvious images like *Feuer, Strom, eherne Bande, königlich, paradiesisch* abound. The structure is compounded of straightforward elements, of which antithesis, repetition, and accumulation are the most conspicuous. The result might easily have been schematic and monotonous. The actual texture is very different. A relentless dynamism animates the language of *Die Räuber* from beginning to end. The rhythm possesses an extraordinary flexibility, as in this passage from Franz Moor's first monologue:

Ich habe große Rechte über die Natur ungehalten zu sein, und bei
meiner Ehre! ich will sie geltend machen. — Warum bin ich nicht der
erste aus Mutterleib gekrochen? Warum nicht der einzige? Warum
mußte [sie] mir diese Bürde von Häßlichkeit aufladen? Gerade mir?
Nicht anders, als ob sie bei meiner Geburt einen Rest gesetzt hätte.

(I. i.)

The first statement is swept into aggressive thrustfulness. Four
rhetorical questions follow, skilfully varied in length and ellipsis,
culminating not in the longest, but in the shortest and tersest.
And the blunt reply draws an angry and contemptuous retort,
enforcing a momentary pause before the torrent of questions is
renewed.

The magnificent speech which concludes the second scene of
Act Four[1] offers a further example of Franz's compelling and
dynamic rhetoric. Its supple and flexible rhythm quickens and
checks its pace, its tone rises and falls. This is the sinuous course
of the serpent, the apex of the sardonic. Later Franz, rising to an
emotion which expresses itself in his characteristic paradoxical
form, a sincere cynicism, puts, with a touch of the sublime, his
philosophy of nihilism:

Es war etwas und wird nichts — Heißt es nicht ebenso viel als: es war
nichts und wird nichts und um nichts wird kein Wort mehr gewech-
selt — der Mensch entstehet aus Morast, und watet eine Weile im
Morast, und macht Morast, und gärt wieder zusammen im Morast,
bis er zuletzt an den Schuhsohlen seines Urenkels unflätig anklebt.
Das ist das Ende vom Lied — der morastige Zirkel der menschlichen
Bestimmung, und somit — glückliche Reise, Herr Bruder!

The rhetoric of *Die Räuber* is distributed among all the
principal characters, including the most unlikely. Spiegelberg
exclaims:

Wenn Scharen vorausgesprengter Kuriere unsere Niederfahrt melden,
daß sich die Satane festtäglich herausputzen, sich den tausendjährigen
Ruß aus den Wimpern stäuben und Myriaden gehörnter Köpfe
aus der rauchenden Mündung ihrer Schwefelkamine hervorwachsen,
unsern Einzug zu sehen?

---

[1] Part of this speech is quoted above on p. 20.

As with everything put in the mouth of Spiegelberg there is here a touch of parody; yet Spiegelberg's speech still makes its contribution to the dynamic rhetoric which is the dominant style of the play.

Amalia's speech is frequently Klopstockian in flavour,[1] as in the following specimen:

Ja süß, himmlisch süß ists, eingewiegt zu werden in den Schlaf des Todes von dem Gesang des Geliebten — vielleicht träumt man auch im Grabe noch fort — ein langer, ewiger, unendlicher Traum von Karln, bis man die Glocke der Auferstehung läutet — und von itzt an in seinen Armen auf ewig.                                                (II. ii)

Nevertheless she is equally at home in impetuous dynamic denunciation:

Ha des liebevollen, barmherzigen Vaters, der seinen Söhnen Wölfen und Ungeheuern preisgibt! daheim labt er sich mit süßem, köstlichem Wein und pflegt seiner morschen Glieder in Kissen von Eider, während sein großer, herrlicher Sohn darbt — schämt euch, ihr Unmenschen! schämt euch ihr Drachenseelen, ihr Schande der Menschheit! — seinen einzigen Sohn!                                               (I. iii)

Accumulation, augmentation, hyperbole, and an irony so obvious that it becomes sarcasm, all these features of rhetorical speech are here exhibited. And Amalia can go further, breaking into the savageness of tone so frequent in *Die Räuber*:

Ich bin ein Weib, aber ein rasendes Weib — wag es einmal, mit unzüchtigem Griff meinen Leib zu betasten — dieser Stahl soll deine geile Brust mitten durchrennen, und der *Geist* meines Oheims wird mir die Hand dazu führen . . . .                                         (III. i)

Graf Moor, too, notwithstanding his feebleness and flaccidity, achieves rhetorical speech after he receives the false news of Karl's death, and rises to powerful, though brief, denunciation; whilst Hermann in his account of Karl's alleged death (II. ii) and the Pater in his swingeing diatribe (II. iii) both exhibit rhetorical parodies.

---

[1] Cf. Schiller's remark in his so-called Selbstbesprechung (*NA* 22. 130), published in the *Wirtembergisches Repertorium*: 'Das Mädchen hat mir zu viel im Klopstock gelesen.' Though this is persiflage, the underlying truth is obvious.

Rhetoric haunts the play without respect of persons, but it is undeniable that it achieves its intensest passages on the lips of Karl Moor. Even before the fracture to his emotional life which Franz's false letter inflicts, Karl expresses himself in powerful rhythmic prose, full of antithesis, hyperbole, exclamation, and exaltation. When his emotions are stirred, as they are through most of the play, this language achieves a dynamism, a surging impulse, and a swift sequence of climaxes, now heavy like hammer-blows, now sharp like a whip-lash. The most striking examples of this angry, tempestuous speech are to be found in the first, fourth, and fifth acts, and have already been quoted in illustration of the elements of this vehement language. But a less sensational example, a passage which is reflective and elegiac and yet retains the rhetorical manner, its heightened language, its anastrophes, its variable pulse, and its series of climaxes and relaxations, will serve to demonstrate the unity of style in *Die Räuber*:

*Zeit* und *Ewigkeit* — gekettet aneinander durch ein einzig Moment! — Grauser Schlüssel, der das Gefängnis des Lebens hinter mir schließt, und vor mir aufriegelt die Behausung der ewigen Nacht — sage mir — o sage mir — *wohin* — *wohin* wirst du mich führen? — Fremdes, nie umsegeltes Land!                                                                     (IV. V.)

## 5. THE INCOMPATIBILITY OF AIM AND MEANS

The similarity of tone pervading *Die Räuber* can easily be interpreted as a fault. A play which sets out to reflect the real world falls short if it fails to reproduce the obvious divergences between human beings; mode of speech is an expression of character and should, we incline to feel, change from person to person. Schiller himself lends colour to the view that his aim was a reproduction of reality by the implication in the Vorwort to *Die Räuber* that he is copying the real world: 'Jeder Menschenmaler ist in diese Notwendigkeit gesetzt, wenn er anders eine Kopie der wirklichen Welt und keine idealische Affektationen, keine Kompendienmenschen will geliefert haben.' He goes on to assert of Franz Moor: 'Ich denke, ich habe die Natur getroffen.'[1] In the original, unpublished, Vorrede there occurs also a denial of caricature—'Ich wünschte zur Ehre der Menschheit, daß ich hier nichts denn Karikaturen geliefert hätte, muß aber gestehen, so fruchtbarer meine Weltkenntnis wird, so ärmer wird mein Karikaturenregister.'[2] There is, however, in these prefaces no indication (nor is there in the letters) that Schiller saw himself engaged on writing anything even remotely naturalistic. The very first words of the *Vorrede* to the first edition reveal that he is working at depths far below the surface: 'Man nehme dieses Schauspiel für nichts anders als eine dramatische Geschichte, die die Vorteile der dramatischen Methode, die Seele gleichsam bei ihren geheimsten Operationen zu ertappen, benutzt.' The dramatist, as Schiller conceives him (and therefore as he sees himself), 'muß das Laster in seiner nackten Abscheulichkeit enthüllen und in seiner kolossalischen Größe vor das Auge der Menschheit stellen — er selbst muß augenblicklich seine nächtlichen Labyrinthe durchwandern'.[3]

Schiller's aim, far from being realistic as the word is ordinarily understood, sets out to portray another plane of reality, the plane of the soul. At the depth to which he intends to probe, though differences subsist, yet similarities predominate. Schiller exhibits humanity with the lid off, and in the process the generic characteristics of human nature are mercilessly exposed. Fierce appetites, brutal impulses, violent desires, obscure perversions are revealed—and against them is set the concept of judgement, at once postulating the norm and providing the sanction against departure from it. The unity of tone in the language emphasizes the common elements, whilst still providing sufficient detailed points of differentiation. At the same time its elevated mood removes the work from any possibility of confusion with the play of realism as Schiller knew it in *Emilia Galotti* or *Götz von Berlichingen*.

Yet, wonderful as the achievement of the dynamic and violent prose of *Die Räuber* is, its separation from the language of every

---

[1] *NA* 3. 5.         [2] *NA* 3. 244.         [3] *NA* 3. 5.

day is both too great and insufficient; we are too much accustomed to expect of non-metrical speech the restraint and inhibition of conversation or disquisition. We instinctively feel that prose should never lose its self-control. Only when we cross the frontier fence which verse erects between itself and prose, are we ready to accept another set of conventions. Schiller's prose in *Die Räuber* adopts many of the features of verse, but it fails to warn us that we have crossed into the land of poetry. Historically we can understand that the choice of verse could hardly seem open to a beginner in the drama in 1779 and 1780. For the younger generation, Alexandrine tragedy was dead. The great plays of the day were *Ugolino*, *Emilia Galotti*, *Götz von Berlichingen*, *Julius von Tarent*, and *Die Zwillinge*, all in prose, which in some of them is decked up with poetic touches. *Nathan der Weise* was described, not as a drama, but as 'ein dramatisches Gedicht', and the verse *Iphigenie* was not yet written.[1] Klopstock's hexameters, too, so easily spoken as prose, had tended to blur the distinction between the two modes. Prose must have seemed to Schiller, not the better choice, but rather the only possibility. Moreover, if Schiller's roughly contemporary 'Operette' *Semele* offers us any criterion, the dramatic verse of which he was then capable would have brought a remedy worse than the disease. We are left with a language whose extraordinary tension, violence, and dynamism can easily estrange, and impose an obstacle to appreciation, which, for many, can only be surmounted, if at all, by a conscious effort of critical realignment. Yet it is worth the effort. For the power of the language gives us both an extraordinarily impressive vision of the human cauldron and an equally inspiring view of the power of the moral law.

[1] *Nathan der Weise* was published in 1779, when Schiller was already well advanced with *Die Räuber*. The *Iphigenie* of 1779 was both in prose and unpublished.

# II · *FIESCO*

### I. OBLIQUENESS AND IRONY

THE tremendous drama of *Die Räuber* had used a pattern of megaphonic voices to set forth plainly operations which unroll in silence in the recesses of the mind. Crime, conscience, and retribution had been its preoccupations. All these factors play a part in *Fiesco*, in which, correspondingly, many of the stylistic motifs and procedures of *Die Räuber* recur, though with differently placed emphasis. It may seem strange that *Fiesco*, the historical play focused on events occurring more than two hundred years before Schiller's day, should be closer to 'reality' than *Die Räuber* in its near-contemporary setting. Yet so it is. The earlier play is a magnified and distorted phantasmagoria imprisoned in an enclosed space. Nine of its scenes are set in rooms, the only function of which is to limit space; of the remaining six, two are enveloped in darkness as impenetrable as any wall, and in only one, the scene *Gegend an der Donau*, has the open-air setting any significance, leading the eye for a moment away from the central group of figures.

The eleven scenes of *Fiesco* have an even greater proportion of interior settings—eight against three. And its atmosphere, too, is not without a claustrophobic intensity. Nevertheless a shift towards the open and visible world takes place. Music offstage, curtains, furniture, become important. The action begins to take heed of its environment, which in three scenes is indicated with precision. In Act III. ii the rubric *Saal bei Fiesco* is amplified by the evocative direction: *In der Mitte des Hintergrunds eine große Glastüre, die den Prospekt über das Meer und Genua öffnet. Morgendämmerung.* Thus Schiller indicates visual factors which intervene in the action and, in so doing, takes the first steps towards an economy of speech which is to be one of the highest qualities of his mature dramatic style. Similar effects are achieved by the lighted windows in the wing overlooking the courtyard in Act IV. i, and by the bursting open of the 'Thomastor' (v. i) before the eyes of the audience, in which a new phase in the action is clearly signalled by visible means—*Das Tor wird gesprengt und öffnet die Aussicht in den Hafen, worin Schiffe liegen, mit Fackeln erleuchtet*. These are symptoms of a shift in outlook which is accompanied by a shift in style. But it is only a beginning, and the language of *Fiesco* will be seen to resemble at many points that of *Die Räuber* and, in any case, to reveal its descent from that play.

The historical episode in which Giovanni Luigi de' Fieschi, Conte di Lavagna, met his death in Genoa in 1547 seemed to offer Schiller a particularly congenial theme. The brilliant hero engages in circuitous and tortuous plottings to overthrow the existing usurping government and to establish himself as a new usurper in its place. In Schiller's first reference to this conspiracy Fiesco and Catiline are mentioned in the same breath,[1] and a sentence from Sallust's *De conjuratione Catilinae* appears on the title-page of *Die Verschwörung des Fiesco zu Genua*.[2] The translation by Rousseau, which first brought Fiesco to Schiller's notice, uses the expression 'erhabener Verbrecher'. A sublime criminal had already made his mark in *Die Räuber*, and it might have been expected that the story of Fiesco would result in a similar work. Yet the historical dimension introduces a new factor. Karl and Franz Moor were figments of the imagination independent of environment. Count Fiesco must be drawn to a scale which is incompatible with the magnifying impulse behind the earlier play.

[1] See Schiller's second and successful passing-out dissertation, *Über den Zusammenhang der tierischen Natur des Menschen mit seiner geistigen* (1780): 'Katilina war ein Wollüstling, eh er Mordbrenner wurde; und Doria hatte sich gewaltig geirret, wenn er den wollüstigen Fiesko nicht fürchten zu dörffen glaubte' (*NA* 20. 65).

[2] Nam id facinus imprimis ego memorabile existimo sceleris atque periculi novitate.

The rhapsodic drama of *Die Räuber* begins in muted, apparently tensionless, speech, which then quickly flares up into a language, giving in the mouth of Franz Moor no heat, but possessing a rhythmic intensity which burns brightly enough. This process is repeated in the scenes *Schenke an den Grenzen von Sachsen, Die böhmischen Wälder, Gegend an der Donau,* and indeed in almost every scene in *Die Räuber.* After a few cautious, ambling steps the language takes charge and bolts. The structure of the speech is simple and stark, the vocabulary limited but powerful, the tone in its climaxes one of wild intoxication.

In contrast to this, *Fiesco* begins in emotional turmoil. Leonore, in the opening scene, does not work up to her passion of jealousy and her anguish of humiliation; she is revealed to us at a moment when these passions are already at high pressure. A dramatic opening is attempted which makes considerable demand upon the language. Leonore begins with exclamations which are fully in keeping with the disturbance in her mind—'Nichts mehr! Kein Wort mehr! Es ist am Tag.... Vor meinen Augen!', etc.; she passes through the natural transition to self-pity—'und vor meinen weinenden Augen' (I. i). The two handmaidens, though sympathetic, are exempt from real participation. Their inadequate interjections evoke from Leonore an exclamatory argumentation—'Galanterie? — und das emsige Wechselspiel ihrer Augen? Das ängstliche Lauren auf ihre Spuren? Der lange verweilende Kuß auf ihren entblößten Arm, daß noch die Spur seiner Zähne im flammroten Fleck zurückblieb? Ha! und die starre tiefe Betäubung, worein er gleich dem *gemalten Entzücken* versunken saß . . .' At this point we pause, for simile is a retarding figure of speech which consorts ill with passion or at best suggests its abatement. It introduces elements from outside and is incompatible with complete single-mindedness. Yet a moment later Leonore addresses her much-loved Arabella as 'Geh, giftige Schwätzerin — komm mir nie wieder vor die Augen', which must be understood as showing that she is beside herself.

Schiller has here posed himself a problem which he is unable to solve. He seeks to unfold a passion, not in the free and unfettered style of *Die Räuber*, but in closely wrought interplay between characters, in which the passion is revealed indirectly and obliquely. It is a more difficult task precisely because it implies a more realistic approach to drama. For indirect communication is the idiom of the theatre, more especially since the launching of the realistic drama in Germany by Lessing. The persons of the play move and speak in their own world, and the spectator infers the course of events, the motives of the participants, and the moral, social, or philosophical content of the play.

The obliqueness of dialogue, as it is found in *Fiesco*, goes further, however. Verrina, for example, demands from Fiesco a statement of attitude: 'Ist das deine wahre, ernstliche Meinung?' To this Fiesco replies: 'Andreas erklärt seinen Neffen zum Sohn und Erben seiner Güter, wer wird der Tor sein, ihm das Erbe seiner Macht abzustreiten?' (I. vii). Here question is countered by question, and inference is demanded not only of the spectator, but also of the interlocutor on the stage.

Similarly, in the second act, when the Mohr asks what answer he shall return to the question where Fiesco stands, the latter gives him this enigmatic reply: 'Die Frucht ist ja zeitig. Wehen verkündigen die Geburt — Genua liege auf dem Block, sollst du antworten, und dein Herr heiße Johann Ludwig Fiesco' (II. xv). This passage of dialogue contains a clue to the significance of the numerous oblique replies; for the Mohr's question was: 'Werdet Ihr Eure Maske noch länger tragen, oder was soll ich antworten?' Masquerade, concealment, intrigue are at the centre of this play. G. Storz has shown that Schiller, in referring to 'der politische Held', means the hero of political intrigue,[1] and it is abundantly evident that intrigue is the mainspring of the actions of Gianettino, of Julia, of Verrina and his friends, of the Mohr, and above all of Fiesco himself, who characterizes his ambience with the words 'die Geheimnisse des Kabinetts stecken sich gern in die Falten eines Weiberrocks' (II. xv).

To this atmosphere of parade, pretence, and subterfuge

[1] Op. cit., pp. 74 f.

belongs also the frequent use of irony. *Die Räuber* had not been devoid of irony, but its employment had been restricted to a crass form of the dramatic type. So Karl Moor takes the fatal decision upon the evidence of the false letter and repents when it is too late; and Pastor Moser expounds the unforgivable sin, not knowing that Franz, whom he addresses, has committed it. These are ironies unintended by the speaker, or perceptible only to the spectator. Ironies of this kind occur in Fiesco also, for example when Fiesco murders his wife, mistaking her for Gianettino. Much more frequent, however, is the deliberate irony which one character exercises towards another. An extended instance of this occurs in the second act when Fiesco praises the sensuous beauty of Romano's depiction of Virginia, feigning to ignore the picture's heroic message. A similar deliberate ambiguity marks Fiesco's request to Gianettino in the matter of the galleys (III. x). Such uses of speech are not confined to Fiesco. Verrina replies to Fiesco's demand for absolute control with a comment which reserves its interpretation: 'Ein freies Leben ist ein paar knechtischer Stunden wert' (III. v). To Fiesco's 'Merkt Verrina keine Veränderung an seinem Freunde?', Verrina retorts with an inscrutable 'Ich wünsche keine' (V. xvi); and, when at the catastrophe he pushes Fiesco from the gangway plank, it is with the ironical comment; 'Nun, wenn der Purpur fällt, muß auch der Herzog nach.' The examples can be multiplied: Julia, Gianettino, Calcagno, Sacco, the Mohr, even Leonore, speak on occasion with conscious irony.

This frequent incidence of irony is closely bound up with the component of intrigue, deceit, and double-dealing. This is most clearly demonstrated in the scene of recruitment for the conspiracy (IV. i–vii). The very disguise is symbolical. The nobles of Genoa are summoned to 'eine Komödie', and Fiesco has already made play with the ironical possibilities of the word on taking leave of Julia (III. x–xi). As the nobles assemble to find the host absent and the exits guarded, the word *Komödie* is constantly repeated as a *Leitmotif*, until Zenturione refers to it in unmistakable irony: 'Mich deucht, es [das Lustspiel] fing schon an, und wir spielten die Narren drin.' This passage characterizes the play, underlining the element of pretence, masquerade, play-acting. *Fiesco*, indeed, may be interpreted as an ironical tragi-comedy, in which the hero's mask (the 'Purpurmantel' of the final scene) directly leads to his ignominious demise.

The simple structure of language seen in *Die Räuber* is replaced by an intricacy which often seems affected. Antithesis is rare. Repetition and accumulation, though present, are less obvious. They do not manifest themselves in urgent hammer-blows with the same word, in succeeding waves of verbal assault, but in cunning rhetorical basic patterns, as in Fiesco's triumphant revelation to the amateur conspirators of his completed plot:

Dächtet ihr, der Löwe schliefe, weil er nicht brüllte? Waret ihr eitel genug, euch zu überreden, daß ihr die einzigen wäret, die Genuas Ketten fühlten? Die einzigen, die sie zu zerreißen wünschten? Eh ihr sie nur fern rasseln hörtet, hatte sie schon Fiesco zerbrochen. *Hier* Soldaten von Parma — *hier* französisches Geld — *hier* vier Galeeren vom Papst. *Was* fehlte noch, einen Tyrannen in seinem Nest aufzujagen? *Was* wißt ihr noch zu erinnern? (II. xviii)

The pattern of repetition and accumulation is discernible, but it is overlaid by Fiesco's ostentation. The simple structures of direct expression do not suffice for the complex mental manoeuvres of a character who scarcely ever directly expresses himself, preferring obscure hints, sudden darts, and bold dramatic strokes, all calculated for effect. Fiesco needs the assistance of an audience, before which he can, peacock-like, display, and in whose astonished eyes he can observe his own reflection.

Display, ostentation, the maintenance of façade, the upholding of prestige characterize the tone of much of the language. The dialogue adopts a supposedly high social tone. Fiesco expresses his hospitable nature with:

Sollte mein guter Wille *einen* Genueser mißvergnügt weglassen? Hurtig, Lakaien! man soll den Ball erneuern und die großen Pokale füllen. Ich wollte nicht, daß jemand hier Langeweile hätte. Darf ich Ihre Augen mit Feuerwerken ergötzen? Wollen Sie die

Künste meines Harlekins hören? Vielleicht finden Sie bei meinem
Frauenzimmer Zerstreuung? (I. vii)
This is a clumsy attempt at the grand manner, a catalogue of
entertainment, listed without elegance or finesse and particularly crude in Fiesco's reference to his wife. The touch of
arrogance and ostentation serves, it is true, to characterize him,
but the comparative crudity of the speech accords ill with
Schiller's description of his hero in the list of 'Personen des
Stücks'.[1] This Fiesco is 'stolz' but without 'Anstand' and
cannot truly be described as 'höfisch-geschmeidig'.

On other occasions the dialogue aims at the elegant, but
achieves only a sense of strain:

FIESCO. ... Du auch da, teurer Bruder Verrina? Ich würde bald
  verlernt haben, dich zu kennen, wären meine Gedanken fleißiger
  um dich als meine Augen. Wars nicht seit dem letzten Ball, daß ich
  meinen Verrina entbehrte?
VERRINA. Zähl ihm nicht nach, Fiesco. Schwere Lasten haben indes
  sein grauses Haupt gebeugt. Doch genug hiervon.
FIESCO. Nicht genug für die wißbegierige Liebe. Du wirst mir mehr
  sagen müssen, wenn wir allein sind. (II. xvii)

The aim here is the expression of social ease in high circles, but
it is apparent that effort is expended in the search for the effortless. The overlapping and jointing of speech with speech is
laboured and affected. The attempt to reproduce patrician tone is
an essay in the realistic dimension. The involuntary, strained,
touches of exaggeration neutralize the realistic intention.

The tone, moreover, is far from consistent. Leonore comes
close to a genuine dignity of speech in her reproaches to Fiesco:
'Ihre Gemahlin zu sein, hab ich nicht verdient, aber Ihre Gemahlin hätte Achtung verdient...'—but, when she perceives that love
for her still lives in Fiesco's heart, she breaks into speech which
is an unconvincing hybrid between the language of social life and
the rhetorical gesture: 'Himmel, habe Dank! Das war wieder
echter Goldklang der Liebe. Hassen sollt ich dich, Falscher, und
werfe mich hungrig auf die Brosamen deiner Zärtlichkeit'

---

[1] 'Junger, schlanker, blühend-schöner Mann von dreiundzwanzig Jahren — stolz
mit Anstand — freundlich mit Majestät — höfisch-geschmeidig und ebenso tückisch.

(III, iii). This is a moment which demands the note of intimacy. It is not forthcoming.

This unskilfulness in the handling of polite dialogue turns out, however, to be a positive asset in the scenes in which Gianettino Doria and his sister Julia appear; for both are portrayed as coarse, vulgar, and rasping characters, whose true nature continually falsifies the tone of elegant conversation which they seek to maintain. Yet even here Schiller may be thought to overdo the crudity of speech. On the realistic plane of *Fiesco* we are justified in asking whether such a clumsy boor and such a coarse harlot are acceptable without further explanation as members of the oldest and highest nobility of Genoa, as well as favourite relatives of the wise and prudent Andrea Doria. It is not unreasonable to assume that the trend to exaggeration and to violence, which is so conspicuous a feature of Schiller's youth, led to the cruder utterances of these characters, and so produced a touch of parody. This dialogue is seen at its worst when Julia, paying a morning call on Leonore, criticizes her hostess's appearance:

Und wie sie sich tragen, Madam! Pfui doch! Auch auf ihren Körper wenden Sie mehr. Nehmen Sie zur Kunst Ihre Zuflucht, wo die Natur an Ihnen Stiefmutter war. Einen Firnis auf diese Wangen, woraus die mißfärbige Leidenschaft kränkelt. Armes Geschöpf! So wird Ihr Gesichtchen nie einen Käufer finden. (II. ii)

The content of the speech is vulgar, and the attempt to clothe it in terms of elegance miscarries. The polish which can expedite malice is intended; all that is achieved is grimacing affectation. Schiller seems particularly ill at ease in the confrontation of the sincere and the false, the ingenuous and the scheming, in this scene; and he is no more adequate when Leonore or Scipio Bourgognino are at grips with Fiesco.

On the other hand, when two intriguers come face to face, his manner is easier, his tone lighter and surer. One of the highlights of Schiller's dialogue is the exchange between Gianettino and Fiesco in Julia's palace:

GIANETTINO. Graf, Sie erinnern sich einer unangenehmen Geschichte, die neulich zwischen uns beiden vorfiel —

FIESCO. Ich wünschte, Prinz, wir vergäßen sie beide — Wir Menschen handeln gegen uns, wie wir uns kennen, und wessen Schuld ists als die meinige, daß mich mein Freund Doria nicht ganz gekannt hat? GIANETTINO. Wenigstens werd ich nie daran denken, ohne Ihnen von Herzen Abbitte zu tun — FIESCO. Und ich nie, ohne Ihnen von Herzen zu vergeben — GIANETTINO. Eben fällt es mir bei, Graf, Sie lassen gegen die Türken kreuzen? FIESCO. Diesen Abend werden die Anker gelichtet — Ich bin eben darum in einiger Besorgnis, woraus mich die Gefälligkeit meines Freunds Doria reißen könnte. (III. x)

In this dialogue, in which each participant conceals murderous plans against the other, the sense of strain, so obvious elsewhere in the 'elegant' language of the play, has vanished and the tone of insincere polite exchange is perfectly caught.

In his conduct of dialogue Schiller rarely apportions speech evenly between the characters. The typical scene resembles a solo instrument accompanied by one or more other parts. Fiesco, Verrina, and the three Dorias are necessarily in the forefront. When one or more of them appears, however, the same pattern is preserved. Andrea receives the lion's share in the presence of Fiesco or Gianettino, Fiesco leads in the presence of Verrina, until the very last scene, when the roles are reversed. Schiller uses language in this way to illustrate a scale of strength, while maintaining some flexibility to express shifting coefficients of power.

Yet, in the great scene of the fourth act (xiv), it is Leonore who takes the lead, while Fiesco meekly provides the accompaniment. The consequence, heavily reinforced by the unexpected power of her language, is that Leonore here appears as the figure of strength. It is possible that this arises from a temptation which the dramatist ought to resist. Has Schiller conceived a brilliant scene which does not fit his over-all pattern and found himself unable to resist its inclusion? Certainly the sense for the dramatic situation was strong in him.[1] Yet so, too, was his awareness of

---

[1] Cf. the pleasure with which Schiller writes to Reinwald of the 'Gelegenheit zu starken Zeichnungen und erschütternden oder rührenden Situazionen' on 27 March 1783 (Jonas, I. 108); the reference is to *Don Carlos*.

general dramatic structure. It is entirely consistent with the design that Fiesco, having inwardly debated and rejected the public objections to his policy, should be faced also with its personal difficulties, and that he should move to his end after declining all the available alternatives. That Leonore addresses Fiesco in language of power, rhetorically constructed, is not a proof of insincerity; it indicates that the tactical advantage has for the moment shifted in her favour. It is one further demonstration that the young Schiller tends not to differentiate his characters, that problem and situation interest him more than the individual human being.

The speech of the Mohr, however, is in a category of its own. He speaks with a verve common to many of Schiller's characters and with a terseness known to few, at least in the early plays. To Fiesco's instructions concerning the galleys he replies, 'Verstehe. Die Bärte der Beschnittenen liegen obendrauf. Was im Korb ist, weiß der Teufel'—which combines the laconically direct with the impudently oblique. He speaks frequently in brief, vivid, images, straightforward yet illuminating. His account of the murder of a messenger is put in grimly humorous shorthand: 'Ein Expresser sollte damit nach Levanto fliegen. Ich wittre den Fraß. Laure dem Burschen in einem Hohlweg auf. Baff! Liegt der Marder — wir haben das Huhn.' Similarly he underlines his usefulness to Fiesco, whom he had once attempted to murder, with 'Der Löwe hats doch so dumm nicht gemacht, daß er die Maus pardonnierte? Gelt! er hats schlau gemacht, wer hätt ihn denn sonst aus dem Garne genagt?' (III. iv).

These zoological images are quite different in quality from the ferocious allusions of *Die Räuber*; they are almost homely, with a touch of the Aesopian fable about them, the expression of the humorist in crime, offsetting the splendours and horrors of the magnificent criminal Fiesco. In the figure of this individualist Schiller has solved the problem of characterizing by means of oblique speech.

## 2. MONOLOGUE

If, in general, Schiller's dialogue in *Fiesco* must be subject to reservations, there are two varieties of dramatic speech in which he is unequivocally successful: in monologue, and in anonymous group scenes. There are only two important monologues in this play, both set at a critical point and both spoken by Fiesco. Indeed, though they are separated by Verrina's scene headed *Furchtbare Wildnis*, they ought to be regarded as virtually continuous, a process of thought broken by night and sleep, and resumed at sunrise. They reflect Fiesco's impulse to subdue his arrogant ambition and to obey the promptings of republican virtue, and his return to his original scheme for the seizure of power and the glorification of himself. Through the first of these soliloquies runs the theme of Heaven and Hell, God and the Devil. Fiesco begins with an admission of indecision, of inner turmoil—'Welch ein Aufruhr in meiner Brust?' He then sounds the characteristic note of conspiracy, concealment, sinister intent; the evil thoughts are 'gleich verdächtigen Brüdern, die auf eine schwarze Tat ausgehen, auf den Zehen schleichen, und ihr flammrotes Gesicht furchtsam zu Boden schlagen'. The plot is discovered, in the image of the lantern lifted to shine in the face of the conspirators and so to reveal their identity—'Haltet! Haltet! laßt mich euch ins Angesicht leuchten . . . Ha! ich kenne euch!' What is thus revealed is the livery of Hell: 'Das ist die Liverei des ewigen Lügners.' The confrontation of the plotters is seen by Fiesco as a heroic act—'heldenmäßig'; and it is significant that heroism, not virtue, is his justification. Now the language rises to the poetic mode, with inversions and a rhythmic pulse: 'Hier ist der gähe Sturz, wo die Mark der Tugend sich schließt, sich scheiden Himmel und Hölle'; the image of the hero returns insistently—'Eben hier haben Helden gestrauchelt, und Helden sind gesunken, und die Welt belagert ihren Namen mit Flüchen — Eben hier haben Helden gezweifelt, und Helden sind stillgestanden, und Halbgötter geworden.' The vision of power rises, alluring, beckoning: 'Daß sie *mein* sind, die Herzen von

Genua? Daß von *meinen* Händen dahin, dorthin sich gängeln läßt das furchtbare Genua?'—and the diabolical origin of the temptation is recognized anew: 'O über die schlaue Sünde, die einen Engel vor jeden Teufel stellt.' Fiesco, faced with the choice of the diabolical or the divine, opts for the latter: 'Ein Diadem erkämpfen ist *groß*. Es wegwerfen ist *göttlich*.' Perish the tyrant! Be free, Genoa! And with what result? That Fiesco shall be 'dein glücklichster Bürger!' In this climax of his speech the very words hint to us that Fiesco's decision is unsound, because it is in conflict with his nature. 'Glücklich' and 'Bürger' are both concepts that mean nothing to him. The whole speech, poetic and heroic, parading the images of glory, diabolical crime, and the sublimity of the great man ranked (maximal hybris) as God, ends on an unmistakable note of bathos; but this bathos is intended, subtly implying the falseness of Fiesco's resolution.

The second soliloquy is separated from the first in time only by a restless night. It is, so to speak, in four movements. After a brief prelude the note of grandeur (*groß*) is reintroduced, this time opposed, not to the divine, but to virtue. In this shift of words is revealed the change which the night of tormented reflection has wrought. The godlike could tempt Fiesco, for it elicits admiration and adoration. But virtue is merely a human quality and one, moreover, readily associated with the 'Bürger', the very word which had constituted the final false note of the first speech. It is already evident that Fiesco's 'virtuous' resolution is to be overthrown, and the substitution of 'erhaben' for 'groß' and of 'gemein' for 'Tugend' only confirms this.

In the second section, wrongdoing is admitted. But the valuation of crime is made to fluctuate with its scale. At the one extreme, 'Es ist schimpflich eine Börse zu leeren', at the other, 'es ist namenlos groß, eine Krone zu stehlen'. And, though a grain of irony in this utterance shows conscience not quite dormant, yet the note of cynicism is also audible. The direction in which Fiesco's mind is moving is illustrated by the images 'majestätisch' 'königlich', 'Monarchenkraft', 'mporzuflammen', and 'diesem grundlosen Ozean', all highly significant emotive words with Schiller.

From this Fiesco passes to the third movement, derived appropriately from the images of kingship. The contrast now appears in the stark antithesis of command and obedience ('Gehorchen — Herrschen!'), which is equated to non-existence and existence. Between them lies a dizzy gulf—'ungeheure, schwindligte Kluft'—and, since there can be no compromise, Fiesco must choose existence, command, imperial power.

The fourth section is a rhapsody on the pleasures of power, a pre-enjoyment of that which Fiesco has resolved to embrace. First and foremost is the ecstasy of the sublime height, the dizzy intoxication of the lonely eminence ('Zu stehen in jener schröcklich erhabenen Höhe'),[1] the pleasure of invulnerability, the joy of being above the law ('tief unten den geharnischten Riesen Gesetz am Gängelbande zu lenken'), the gratification induced by domination and control. In these imaginings Fiesco has worked himself into the situation of God, the maker of laws, the disposer of human kind. The voluntary submission, which on the previous evening had been 'godlike', is forgotten; 'godlike' is now the exercise of untrammelled power, the sense of omnipotence. And he intoxicates himself with ecstasies of power—'Ha! welche Vorstellung, die den staunenden Geist über seine Linien wirbelt'—and of violence—'Zerstücke den Donner in seine einfache Silben, und du wirst Kinder damit in den Schlummer singen; schmelze sie zusammen in *einen* plötzlichen Schall, und der monarchische Laut wird den ewigen Himmel bewegen.'[2] The tone is ecstatic, dithyrhambic, and the concluding gesture of 'Ich bin entschlossen' is simply the final chord in a key already established in this dynamic symphony of words.

[1] Cf. the following stanzas from Schiller's *Der Eroberer* (1777):

Ha! Eroberer, sprich: Was ist dein heißester,
Dein gesehntester Wunsch? — Hoch an des Himmels Saum
Einen Felsen zu bäumen,
Dessen Stirne der Adler scheut,

Dann hernieder vom Berg, trunken von Siegeslust,
Auf die Trümmer der Welt, auf die Erobrungen
Hinzuschwindeln, im Taumel
Dieses Anblicks hinweggeschaut.

[2] The use of *monarchisch* shows clearly the direction of Fiesco's thoughts.

The close association of these two monologues is indicated by the occurrence, in each, of the rare image 'gängeln', 'Gängelband', and its application in each instance to the control of the multitude by the ruler.

These two soliloquies are separated by the duologue between Verrina and Bourgognino; and this may justifiably be viewed as a disguised monologue. Bourgognino takes no significant part in this scene, merely miming his responses of astonishment and horror with the minimum of words. It is not necessary for him to learn Verrina's resolution; his knowledge of it has no bearing on the action. His function here is solely to turn a soliloquy into a dialogue without altering its essential nature. In a play which had an appreciable factor of realism, Schiller could not confront the spectator with a succession of three monologues. It is a curious irony that this concession to realism has produced one of the few ludicrously unrealistic scenes of the play. Verrina's sinister reflections would have been more readily acceptable in solo form. The long journey into the 'furchtbare Wildnis' with a companion, in order, not to act, but to impart a fearful communication, followed by a return with the same companion, has an absurdity which not even the verbal black magic of Schiller can save. The effort at reality here crumbles in Schiller's hands to unreality.

Verrina's speech, punctuated merely by conventional interjections such as 'Hören? Was? Ich beschwöre dich', detects Fiesco's far-reaching ambition and foresees his tyrannical goal, so providing a master-stroke of dramatic irony in its position immediately after Fiesco's false decision to renounce, and immediately before his true resolution to usurp. Its language is striking. Twice Verrina uses the image of night, each time in terms which arouse its maximal emotive power in the direction of horror—'doch *blühet* das, gegen die Nacht meiner Seele' (a characteristic hyperbole)—and on the second occasion 'grauenvoll wie die lichtscheue Nacht'. The speech falls into three sections, of which the first and longest is a passage of horrific, spine-chilling preparation. This is followed by the disclosure of intention, which is crystallized in three heavily weighted words

'*Fiesco muß sterben!*' The final section incorporates commentary
and explanation.

The flesh-creeping introduction throbs with images reflecting
the horror of corruption ('wo die Verwesung Leichname morsch
frißt, und der Tod seine schaudernde Tafel hält') and the ghastly
damnation which follows it ('wo das Gewinsel verlorner Seelen
Teufel belustigt, und des Jammers undankbare Tränen im durch-
löcherten Sieb der Ewigkeit ausrinnen'). In a brief parenthetic
passage Verrina laments the unsuitability of the youthful Bourgognino as a recipient for his messages of horror, and does so in
terms of a ghoulish sensuality as repulsive as his picture of decay:
'dein Blut ist rosenrot — dein Fleisch ist milde geschmeidig';
and he goes on to paint a repellent picture of old age: 'Hätte der
Frost des Alters, oder der bleierne Gram den fröhlichen Sprung
deiner Geister gestellt — hätte schwarzes, klumpigtes Blut der
leidenden Natur den Weg zum Herzen gesperret . . .'

The affinity of this passage to the horror elements in *Die Räuber*
is unmistakable,[1] just as the relationship of Fiesco's two soliloquies to the language of Karl and Franz Moor is obvious. The
interplay of Heaven and Hell, the repeated emphasis on grandeur
and majesty (Verrina also sees himself as 'der einzige große
Mann'), the image of divine judgement— 'sich keinem Menschen-
urteil mehr unterwerfen — nur den Himmel als Schiedsmann
erkennen'—all these elements of *Fiesco* are common also to *Die
Räuber*. And the scale of these three monologues brings this
phase of the play close to the preceding work, which had contained no fewer than thirteen soliloquies, many of them extensive
and most of them highly important. It is only at this point in
*Fiesco* that the language attains the dynamic power, the poetic
impetus, and the imaginative luxuriance which are the vital
qualities of the speech of *Die Räuber*. Here at the focus of the
play the pretence at realism is abandoned and the direct action of
the theatre of the mind is launched. The inference that this
phase of *Fiesco* fires Schiller's imagination, as no other part of it

---

[1] Cf. Franz's soliloquies in I. i and IV. ii and also his description of the moribund
syphilitic (I. iii).

does, seems inescapable. Here alone criminality, in Verrina as in Fiesco, is conceived in sublime terms.

## 3. GROUP DIALOGUE

*Fiesco* thus has a central point at which the colossal dynamic, poetic prose of *Die Räuber* is valid, and also considerable tracts of somewhat unsuccessful polite dialogue of realistic dimensions. These categories do not, however, exhaust its stylistic modes. Schiller's success with the speech of the soliloquizing character and that of the eccentric individualist, together with his partial failure in the dialogue of interplay, might suggest a serious inability to handle the speech of even small groups; such a fault would have a crippling effect upon the work of a dramatist. *Die Räuber*, however, had exhibited at least two instances of the effective conduct of concerted speech: *Schenke an den Grenzen von Sachsen* and *Die böhmischen Wälder*; and *Fiesco* also contains at least two brilliantly executed group scenes. These are the irruption of the indignant and excited nobles into Fiesco's palace after Gianettino's affront in the Signoria (II. v) and the assembly of the nobles in the courtyard for the 'Komödie' (IV. i–v). In the first of these the staccato utterances of the noblemen, the overlapping of their brief speeches, the repetitions used as the simplest expression of anger and consternation, stating and restating the fact as sufficient testimony without elaboration, all combine to produce the most convincing illusion of an agitation, in which individual distinctions are merged in group excitement. It affords a proof that the realistic mode is not denied to Schiller, that, at least in scenes of excitement, the ring of real speech reproduces itself easily for him. This view is supported by the second example, in which the individual identity of the speakers is unimportant; the scene would achieve its effect (and perhaps even more impressively) if played in complete darkness; it derives its power from the reactions and responses of a gathering group, not from the exhibition of character. It is a presentation of a mass. Between the solitary figure and the undifferentiated mass there still lay a tract of dramatic territory as yet inaccessible to Schiller.

## 4. THE EVIDENCE OF VOCABULARY

Schiller's choice of image, the recurrence of particular words, the use of certain associations is as significant in *Fiesco* as in *Die Räuber*. Indeed, the resemblances and distinctions between Schiller's first two plays emerge as clearly here as in the field of word-order, tempo, and figure of speech.

The words of freedom in *Fiesco* are less common than those of tyranny, and the word *frei* is, moreover, frequently used in contempt. Schiller is here more concerned with the decay and destruction of freedom than with its espousal. His positive preoccupation is with tyranny, which does not appear in this play as the hateful thing which Franz Moor and Kosinsky's prince make of it. In *Fiesco* it is an abstraction, isolated from social consequences, affecting only theoretical idealism on the one hand and *amour propre* on the other. So doctrinaire an idealist as Verrina only once uses the word 'free', and as he speaks it ('Ein freies Leben ist auch ein paar knechtischer Stunden wert') it is tinged with deceit and intrigue, for his plan for the eventual assassination of Fiesco is forming in his mind. On the other hand, Andreas Doria, expressly categorized as 'tyrant', is twice referred to as gentle (*sanftmütig*). The second tyrant, Gianettino, is merely a self-indulgent bully without real power. The sense which Schiller has found it necessary to give the word *Tyrann* has deprived the word *frei* of its urgency and impetus. One of Schiller's chief emotive word-groups is thereby sterilized, and he is left only with the associations of sublimity which attach to his conception of autocratic power, and these are plentifully conveyed by the words of kingship, *majestätisch*, *Monarch*, *Diadem*, *Krone*, *Thron*, *Purpur*. This neutralization of a set of significant words suggests one important reason for the diminished dynamism of this play when it is set against *Die Räuber*, where *frei* represented a real, deeply-felt, value and *Tyrann* stood for a dangerous and wicked enemy of mankind.

The devaluation of these normally powerful words is paralleled in other fields. The vocabulary of crime is here debased. Thefts are frequently mentioned. Fiesco lists three gradations of crime, and the most sublime of these involves the meanness of 'eine Krone zu stehlen' (III. ii). Even more notable is it that images of theft suggest themselves so readily to Schiller in the atmosphere of this play and are allocated for harmless purposes to highly respectable characters. Leonore, speaking of her girlhood when she and her friends adored Fiesco from afar, says, 'unsere Augen schlichen diebisch ihm nach und zuckten zurück, wie auf dem Kirchenraub ergriffen, wenn sein wetterleuchtender Blick sie traf' (I. i); and Romano, the painter, calls his trade 'Diebstahl an der Natur' (II. xvii). Even murder, which in *Die Räuber*, though terrible, is nevertheless allied to the sublime, is here a mean crime, and occurs mostly in the base and revolting form of *Meuchelmord*.

The importance of dissimulation in *Fiesco* has already been indicated. It manifests itself consistently through the play in the form of a vocabulary linked with acting, make-believe, concealment. The mask itself appears as a symbol in the first scene, *Saal bei Fiesco*. Leonore's first action is 'reißt sich die Maske ab', suggesting at once the equivocal atmosphere and her impatience with it. Gianettino and his adversaries, the three malcontents, all appear masked, making it clear that intrigue is the air both sides breathe, not the mark of the base tyrant. And *Maske* functions also as a word to denote the deceptive exterior. When the three masked malcontents encounter the maskless Fiesco, Verrina exclaims: 'Fiesco findet seine Freunde geschwinder in ihren Masken, als sie ihn in der seinigen.' The Mohr uses the word in the same symbolical way. *Heiligenmaske*, *Larve*, and *Fratze* all occur as synonyms, and related to these uses are Leonore's 'dem gemalten Entzücken gleich' and Julia's 'Einen Firnis auf diese Wangen'.

Equally insistent are the images and words of acting. The repeated emphasis on *Komödie*, *Lustspiel*, and *Schauspiel* in Act Four, Leonore's 'Wechselspiel ihrer Augen', Fiesco's 'Theaterschmuck' are all symbolical of simulation designed to dissimulate, a semblance to conceal the reality. And Fiesco refers to his equivocal role by such terms as *Schellenkappe*, *Hanswurst*, and *Harlekin*. All these theatrical terms accumulate to impose still more strongly upon the play the atmosphere of insincerity. And this is further reinforced by the use of the mirror, conveyed in a stage direction—*Fiesco tritt vor einen Spiegel und schielt über das Papier* (I. ix). A world of pretence and shams has supplanted the burning sincerity of *Die Räuber*, in which even Franz is sincere in his nihilism. The intriguers of *Fiesco* know no such integrity, and the recurrent notes of mask and comedy and mirror correspond to the shifting sands on which Fiesco and his fellows build their structure.

The note of insincerity is further stressed by the high incidence of metaphors of commerce. Gianettino, says the Mohr, 'traut meiner Jaunerparole ohne Handschrift', Sacco speaks of 'die feine Spekulation des Himmels' and of losing 'beim Schleichhandel'. Julia uses such expressions as 'einen Bruch in der Rechnung' and 'wohlfeiler markten', and later insults Leonore with 'So wird Ihr Gesichtchen nie einen Käufer finden'. Fiesco speaks of virtue falling in price ('die Tugend im Preis fallen'), he refers to Julia's *Negligé* as 'die Tracht seines [des Frauenzimmers] Gewerbes', and in his supreme monologue he reveals his fundamental insincerity by 'so adelt doch den Preis den Betrüger'. Lomellino, for his part, terms Fiesco 'den Wucherer mit den Herzen der Menge'. Even the fanatical Verrina draws liberally on the vocabulary of commerce with 'mit Taten zu bezahlen', 'Abrechnung gehalten', and '*Ehre* war unser einziges Kapital.' Most remarkable of all is the critical dialogue which leads to the catastrophe (v. xvi). Verrina adopts a metaphor of property— 'ich nehme mein Eigentum zurück'—, to which Fiesco responds with the crass utterance: 'Für ein Herzogtum wäre der Preis zu jüdisch.' Schiller demonstrates with this image that Fiesco is incapable of a genuine reaction. So deeply is he steeped in insincerity that its terms, the language of calculation and profit, infect even the moments in which he attempts sincerity.

In the closing stages of the play the words of commerce are
supplemented by images of gambling (*Spiel, Stichblatt, Würfel,
Wette*), emphasizing the motive of gain, yet suggesting the loss
of control, the failure of calculation. Most of these images are
used by Leonore and Verrina, both of whom, for different
reasons and in different ways, oppose Fiesco, and they therefore
represent a functional differentiation of speech; Leonore and
Verrina term gambling what Fiesco regards as calculation.

A considerable zoological vocabulary is apparent in *Fiesco*. Its
composition differs from that of *Die Räuber*. The ferocious yet
splendid beasts of prey, the lions and tigers, have become rare,
and their place is taken by cruder, clumsier killers such as the
bear and the elephant. The subtle and venomous serpent, the
(supposedly) poisonous toad, the stinging insects, the wasps and
scorpion, those patient and purposeful toilers the ants, these are
all symbols of treachery, heartlessness, concealed preparation, or
sudden attack. And the picture is completed by the animals of
craftiness, fox, stoat, and rat. The virtuous are represented by the
innocent and defenceless lamb or by the contemptible and
equally defenceless worm. This zoological selection has not been
determined by the desire to express majesty and a fearful beauty,
but by the need to convey a tone of cunning, intrigue, and
savagery; and its tendency towards realism is demonstrated by
its leaning towards simple fable, not only in the full-scale
political parable with which Fiesco persuades the workmen to
his view, but also in explicit references to wolf and lamb, to stoat
and fox and ant, all familiar creatures who populate the world of
Aesop.

The repeated emphasis on intrigue, dissimulation, deception,
which even affects the choice of animals, establishes the atmosphere of this play, distinguishing it from *Die Räuber*, which had
contained an element of deceit contrasted with a stronger
element of truth. But another factor emerges in the vocabulary of
*Fiesco*, which seems to bring us closer to the world of *Die Räuber*.
The expressions of brutality and violence are as abundant here as
in the earlier play. There are frequent references to *Qual* and

*quälen*; imagined throat-cutting is mentioned several times, always accompanied by the suggestively graphic word *Gurgel*. Though no one in the play, except for an insignificant, anonymous, messenger, is run through until the catastrophe, stabbing occurs several times as an image, reaching a maximum of crass and violent effect in the close linking of the sword thrust into and turned in Gianettino's heart and the kiss imprinted on the lips of the betrothed—'So gewiß ich dies Schwert im Herzen Dorias umkehre, so gewiß will ich den Bräutigamskuß auf deine Lippen drücken' (I. xii). Such savagery is not to be explained as the expression of a fierce or violent character, for these words are spoken by Bourgognino, the figure of youthful honour and chivalry, who may perhaps be regarded as an early study for Max Piccolomini. Fiesco, too, who according to his description in the list of persons in the play ought to be a focus of admiration and a model of elegance, uses language of remarkable crudity. Apostrophizing the temptation to sovereignty, he exclaims, 'der Tod sprang aus deinem kreißendem Bauche' (II. xix); but this is far surpassed by the wild and ferocious words he utters after the discovery of Leonore's death:

Ah, daß ich stünde am Tor der Verdamnis, hinunterschauen dürfte mein Aug auf die mancherlei Folterschrauben der sinnreichen Hölle, saugen mein Ohr zerknirschter Sünder Gewinsel.                    (v. xiii)

Verrina addresses his raped daughter in words of sadistic frenzy: 'Dein Leben sei das gichterische Wälzen des sterbenden Wurms'; and as if to prove that here is not a phrase adapted to a character, but a mode of feeling peculiar to the author, Fiesco uses a similar image: 'Schlugen sie nicht um gegen das Wörtchen *Subordination*, wie die Raupe gegen die Nadel?'

The element of horror is crystallized by Gianettino, who declares a programme of terror, which he likens to the head of Medusa, a symbol of paralysing horror:

Alltagsverbrechen bringen das Blut des Beleidigten in Wallung, und alles kann der Mensch. Außerordentliche Frevel machen es vor Schrecken gefrieren, und der Mensch ist nichts. Weißt du das Märchen mit dem Medusakopf?                    (III. ix)

The greater number of references to cruelty, horror, and violence, however, are connected with judicial procedures, so continuing a conspicuous feature of *Die Räuber*. The numerous words of torture ('Folter', 'Marter') are explicitly linked with legal processes—'peinlich verhören', 'inquirierte scharfe'. These are literal applications, but 'Folterbank,' used twice, is an image alluding to imaginary refinements of judicial torture. Verrina threatens to inflict appalling torments on his own daughter—'und sollt ich auf Martern raffinieren wie ein Henkersknecht'—and links this with: 'auf kannibalischer Folterbank zerknirschen' (I. xii). And Julia, avowing her humiliating passion for Fiesco, sensationally links private entreaties with judicial torture—'auf der Folterbank meinem Stolz nicht abdringen sollte' (IV. xii). Breaking on the wheel, dismemberment, and exhibition of mutilated bodies on pikes, the galleys, and the scaffold (*Blutgerüste*) all maintain the concentration on the bloodier or crueller aspects of legal violence. The most violent horrors are to be heard from Verrina, the most callous brutalities from the Mohr, and to this extent there is a variation of language in accordance with character. But the difference is little more than a slight lightening or darkening of the colours which give the whole picture its tone. If the revolting medical details are less frequent, they occur with at least as great a sense of shock, when Verrina talks of strangling himself with a rope made of his own entrails, or Calcagno describes himself and Sacco as 'Eiterbeulen'.

The language of love, too, exhibits a sadistic touch, when Leonore sees Fiesco's kiss leaving tooth marks on Julia's bare arm. Despite her purity Leonore recognizes the shadier side of sexual appetite. She frankly states the symptoms of sexual desire with 'zärtliche Augen brannten wilder' and 'sanfte Busen pochten stürmischer' (I. i); and in her imagination she visualizes her husband 'im schamlosen Kreis der Schwelger und Buhldirnen!' (I. i.)

The predominating picture of love in *Fiesco* is of a fever in the blood, senses roused, and pulses quickened. *Huren, Metzen, Dirnen* und *Töchter der Freude*, do not appear on the stage, but they hover in the background of the dialogue; and, however much their favours are accorded by calculation, they remain for the man symbols of sexual desire. It is especially in the scene of Julia's exposure and humiliation (IV. xii) that the words of desire, uncontrollably rising and breaking the surface, falter and plunge in a vivid realization of sexual experience—phrases like 'ein siedendes Blut', 'die verführerische Nacht', 'meine flammrote Wangen', 'dein Gesicht brennt fieberisch', 'schlägt wildes frevelndes Feuer', 'die aufgewiegelten Sinne' follow hot-foot upon each other. And the phantasy crystallizes in the vision of the desiring woman kneeling defenceless in the power of the successful yet spurning male—'dies dichte Dunkel ist zu licht, diese Feuersbrunst zu bergen, die das Geständnis auf meinen Wangen macht' (IV. xii).

Blood plays a conspicuous part in the language of *Fiesco*, as does also the closely associated word 'heart'. Even the literal uses are significant, since they are part of the author's shaping of this violent story. The true images, however, are more obviously symptomatic, as 'ins Heiligtum deines Bluts greifen' (I. x), 'Eh das Herzblut eines Doria diesen häßlichen Flecken aus deiner Ehre wäscht, soll kein Strahl des Tags auf diese Wangen fallen' (I. xii), 'ein schwaches Weiberherz zerfleischen' (III. iii), or 'Zuflucht zu Julias Blut' (IV. xii). Blood and the heart, its focus, are the meeting-points of the passions in *Fiesco*, the common ground of violence, cruelty, sexual desire, love, and friendship. The profusion of these references to *Blut* and *Herz* underlines an elemental quality in Schiller which expresses itself in forms, now attractive, now repellent. The conspicuous repulsiveness can easily colour one's impression and so lead to a rejection which is less than just to it as a whole.

## 5. BREVITY

The speech of *Die Räuber* had tended towards breadth. The characters mostly unfold their thoughts, expressing *themselves*; and when the expression is complete it is the turn of another character to elaborate his thought, emotion, or reaction. However swift the tempo in various individual speeches, the general effect is expansive and retarding. The change in *Fiesco* is complete. The dynamism of the individual is transformed into the dynamism of the drama.

The great increase in the number of short speeches[1] is symptomatic of the change of style in *Fiesco*. Where short utterances occur in *Die Räuber*, they are chiefly interpolations serving either to interrupt momentarily a long speech or to 'feed' the actor who holds the stage. In *Fiesco* substantial tracts are composed of swift interchange, in which staccato sentences answer each other. Karl Moor declaims, Franz Moor asserts and demonstrates; the characters in *Fiesco* clash in swift thrust and counterthrust.

The first example of this taut, sharp dialogue occurs in the second scene of the first act, in which Gianettino charges the Mohr to murder Fiesco:

GIANETTINO. Du hast mich verstanden.
MOHR. Wohl.
GIANETTINO. Die weiße Maske.
MOHR. Wohl.
GIANETTINO. Ich sage — die weiße Maske!
MOHR. Wohl! Wohl! Wohl!
GIANETTINO. Hörst du? Du kannst sie nur (*auf seine Brust deutend*) *hieher* verfehlen.
MOHR. Seid unbekümmert.
GIANETTINO. Und einen tüchtigen Stoß!
MOHR. Er soll zufrieden sein.

In these and the following lines appears something foreign to *Die Räuber*. Schiller has recognized the need for ellipsis and the value of terseness. His characters mean more than they say. Their laconic utterance is, in its way, as eloquent as the raging torrent of speech in the earlier play. The first step away from the over-obvious is taken, and with it the approach to a finer and more subtle irony.

---

[1] Compared with *Die Räuber*, *Fiesco* has nearly twice as many speeches consisting only of one sentence or a part of a sentence.

Dialogue of this kind is abundant in *Fiesco*, occurring notably in scenes six, seven, eight, and nine of the first act, and in every scene in which the Mohr appears. Indeed, the creation of this character, whose speech is always terse and usually ironical, is a sign of Schiller's developing power in dramatic language and of his new-found capacity for verbal economy. The pregnant brevity of the Mohr's speech might seem an instance of characterization through style; certainly no other figure speaks with quite this combination of oblique expression and direct meaning. Yet Schiller displays elsewhere in *Fiesco* a mastery of short, sharp, and incisive interchange. Act II. v is a remarkable example of terse dialogue subtly exploiting repetition. Three senators burst into Fiesco's room seething with indignation at the high-handed and ruthless behaviour of Gianettino; their anger is at such a pitch that articulateness is inhibited, and so they use the same simple construction (simple sentence in normal word order) and repeat a small stock of phrases:

ZENTURIONE. . . . Der ganze Adel ist in mir aufgefodert. Der ganze Adel muß meine Rache teilen. *Meine* Ehre zu rächen, dazu würde ich schwerlich Gehilfen fodern.

ZIBO. Der ganze Adel ist in ihm aufgereizt. Der ganze Adel muß Feuer und Flammen speien.

. . . . . . . .

ZIBO. . . . Achtundzwanzig Stimmen waren gesammelt. Vierzehn sprachen für mich, ebensoviel für Lomellino! Dorias und die seinige [Lomellinos] standen noch aus.

ZENTURIONE. (*rasch ins Wort fallend*) Standen noch aus. Ich votierte für Zibo. Doria — fühlen Sie die Wunde meiner Ehre — Doria —

ASSERATO. (*fällt ihm wieder ins Wort*). So was erlebte man nicht, solang Ozean um Genua flutet —

ZENTURIONE. (*hitziger fort*) Doria zog ein Schwert, das er unter dem Scharlach verborgen gehalten, spießte mein Votum daran, rief in die Sammlung:

ASSERATO. „Senatoren! Es gilt nicht! Es ist durchlöchert! Lomellin ist Prokurator."

ZENTURIONE. 'Lomellin ist Prokurator', und warf sein Schwert auf die Tafel.

ASSERATO. Und rief: 'Es gilt nicht!' und warf sein Schwert auf die Tafel.

This is the development of dialogue into an instrument reflecting exactly a situation. It makes no attempt to distinguish between characters, but, in its haste, concentration, and poverty of phrasing, it exactly reproduces the state of mind shared by the three speakers.

The third scene of the fourth act reveals equal skill in the handling of group dialogue, reflecting anxiety, agitation, and suspense. The repetitions which emphasized a congestion of mind, an inhibition by anger, are absent. The short staccato sentences interlock, but they do not form a continuous thread of sense; each interjection alters the course of the conversation and the result is the convincing portrayal of a group of men,[1] oppressed by a situation of menace and groping for a solution:

ZIBO. (*im Hereintreten*) Freund von Lavagna.
ZENTURIONE. Zibo, wo sind wir?
ZIBO. Was.
ZENTURIONE. Schau um dich, Zibo.
ZIBO. Wo? Was?
ZENTURIONE. Alle Türen besetzt.
ZIBO. Hier liegen Waffen.
ZENTURIONE. Niemand gibt Auskunft.
ZIBO. Das ist seltsam.
ZENTURIONE. Wieviel ist die Glocke?
ZIBO. Acht Uhr vorüber.
ZENTURIONE. Puh! es ist grimmkalt . . ., etc.

In these scenes Schiller's imagination is clearly working in a more dramatic mode than anywhere in *Die Räuber*. His style is flexible and adaptable, yet taut and economical. Credit has rarely been given for the original features of Schiller's style in *Fiesco* or even for the highly dramatic interlocking of much of the dialogue. The obstacles to recognition have been errors of taste

---

[1] Though only two voices are here quoted, the dialogue eventually involves five.

and a disparity of style. *Die Räuber* is superhuman in its scale, and its towering bombast matches its gigantic proportions. *Fiesco* is more nearly life-size, and the frequent exaggerations and crudities of its language, surviving from *Die Räuber*, are in crass contrast to its general proportions.

The relative unpopularity and neglect of *Fiesco* are linked also with another factor. Fiesco himself, like Wallenstein, is the hero from whom Schiller was detached. He, too, is a 'realist', an opportunist, and he may be seen as an early sketch for something achieved seventeen years later. In *Wallenstein* Schiller was able to infuse some warmth into the speech of his hero. The coldness of Fiesco's speech repels.

Incongruities in style and an unsympathetic hero damned the play in its original Mannheim performances, and they have continued ever since to militate against its acceptance. Yet it is certainly a far better stage-play than *Die Räuber*; and its picture of the political cauldron is powerful and convincing, thanks in part to the strong, rasping language in which it is presented. If we can succeed in ignoring the irrelevant crudities, we are astonished at the percipience and maturity of so young and politically inexperienced a man. Seen in the context of Schiller's development, *Fiesco* constitutes a fascinating intermediate phase, but it has not achieved a consistent style in its own right. Though its defects are out-weighed by its achievements, they are too considerable to be ignored.

# III · *KABALE UND LIEBE*

## I. REALISM

TRADITION[1] links the genesis of *Kabale und Liebe* with the fortnight's guard-room detention to which Schiller was sentenced by the Duke of Württemberg in person towards the end of June 1782. The story is no longer verifiable, and the plot of *Kabale und Liebe* has no connection with Schiller's personal experiences. Streicher provides some evidence, however, to support the view that the play may have already been in Schiller's mind before he fled from Stuttgart on 22 September 1782:

... so sei dem Leser schon jetzt vertraut, daß Schiller seit der Abreise von Mannheim mit der Idee umging, ein bürgerliches Trauerspiel zu dichten, und er schon soweit im Plan desselben vorgerückt war, daß die Hauptmomente hell und bestimmt vor seinem Geiste standen.[2]

If plans for this play (which Streicher tells us was *Kabale und Liebe*) were well advanced by the beginning of October, we can feel fairly sure that the mental processes shaping the work began much earlier. But whether it was before or during or after Schiller's brief period of incarceration we cannot know. We can regard it as certain that the arrest provided Schiller with a focal point on which his past anxieties were concentrated and reanimated. He experienced anew the loss of freedom and sense of confinement which, ten years before, seem to have impressed themselves so deeply on the 12-year-old's imagination as to fuse with his awakening sexual impulses, and to provoke fantasies of constriction and enclosure, which for years to come express themselves through the vocabulary of his plays and poems.

[1] Karoline von Wolzogen, *Schillers Leben*, 1830.
[2] Andreas Streicher, *Schillers Flucht von Stuttgart*, ed. P. Raabe, 1959, p. 138.

To the recollection of imprisonment, however mild, were added weeks of constant fear of re-arrest with much direr consequences than before. Schiller's apprehension pursued him even into his remote refuge at Bauerbach, which he reached on 7 December 1782, and it was some weeks before he felt fully secure. The most vital period in the shaping of *Kabale und Liebe* was probably the autumn spent apprehensively at Oggersheim near Mannheim (approximately from 13 October to 30 November) and the final form was given in the early weeks at Bauerbach. The whole history of the play belongs to a time of desperate need, repression, and anxiety. These factors have coloured the language, but they have not shaped it; for it comes from deep-seated impulses and well-established habit, newly directed by a powerful creative mind, alert to experiment.

The leap from *Fiesco* to *Kabale und Liebe* is bolder than that which took Schiller from *Die Räuber* to *Fiesco*. A principal aspect of the change, which will become fully apparent in later discussion, is well summarized by Professor Stahl:

> The lovers talk in an idiom different from that of their parents, and even within the aristocratic and the bourgeois groups Schiller differentiates between the language of the President and that of von Kalb and between the speech of the elder Millers.[1]

Whereas the earlier plays had displayed a scale of intensity, *Kabale und Liebe* exhibits a range of tones. Characterization is certainly one of the aims of its style, but its great variety is not exhausted by a single formula.

The play opens, before ever a word is spoken, with a point of social criticism. The stage direction, after giving the location and letting Miller rise and lean his cello against wall or chair, continues: *An einem Tisch sitzt Frau Millerin noch im Nachtgewand und trinkt ihren Kaffee.* The significant word is here the *noch*. In its light we understand her idleness, her slovenliness, and her indulgence in habits of luxury above her station. The *noch* asserts, moreover, a standpoint of the author; it places him in

[1] *Friedrich Schiller's Drama: Theory and Practice*, 1954, p. 28.

a clear-cut and negative relationship towards one of his characters. And, in so doing, it disposes in advance of the myth of naturalistic objectivity which has sometimes been allowed to gather round this play.

The realism of the dialogue in the first scene of *Kabale und Liebe* is nevertheless astonishing. Miller's first words are obviously a rejoinder to other words which must be imagined to have been spoken before the curtain rises; and so the opening words create, in a fashion not infrequent since the onset of the *Sturm und Drang*, the illusion of a continuing occurrence which all at once becomes apparent to our eyes and ears.

Miller begins with an ejaculated phrase and follows it with four terse simple sentences, all straightforward and uninverted in structure. Between the third and fourth a momentary pause interposes; Miller intends another remark, checks it, as the dash clearly shows, and concludes his speech with a sentence different from that which he had originally conceived: 'Der Präsident bekommt Wind, und — kurz und gut, ich biete den Junker aus.'

The tone thus set continues. Miller demonstrates a remarkable colloquial fertility. Graphic locutions such as 'alles Wetter kommt über den Geiger' or 'Wer einen Gruß an das liebe Fleisch zu bestellen hat, darf nur das gute Herz Boten gehen lassen' or 'das läuft dann wie spanische Mücken ins Blut' are strewn profusely throughout the scene, all of them given to Miller himself. He uses common turns of phrase, mostly with a touch of personal originality, as: 'Unterm Dach mags aussehen, wies will. Darüber kuckt man bei euch Weibsleuten weg, wenns nur der liebe Gott parterre nicht hat fehlen lassen' or 'Auf den Sack schlägt man. Den Esel meint man.' Sometimes he has recourse to plain traditional form, as in 'dem Major will ich weisen, wo Meister Zimmermann das Loch gemacht hat'. Miller talks inexaustibly, vividly, and often brutally. Sensational images tumble over one another ('und wenn du aus jedem Astloch ein Auge strecktest, und vor jedem Blutstropfen Schildwache ständest'); profane interjections leap constantly between the sentences ('der Henker weiß was' or 'Gott verdamm mich'); and coarse and crude expressions recur with equal frequency (e.g. 'eh will ich mein Violonzello zerschlagen, und Mist im Sonanzboden führen').

The affinity of Miller's speech to everyday language is obvious, Yet the people who speak in real life like Miller are few indeed.[1] He is a 'character' who takes pleasure in his rough, downright, and impetuous speech, a man whose loud and persistent bark precludes a savage bite, because it is the means by which he disposes of his anger and his anxiety. And so Miller's headlong language is a facet of his character, and Schiller has invented his speech, less to establish a tone of thoroughgoing and pervasive realism than to characterize an important figure.

How strongly Miller's speech is individualized becomes even clearer when the words of Frau Miller and of Wurm are examined. Miller's wife speaks to her husband in simple German, with none of the arabesques of language or florescence of images which mark his speech. At most she can rise to a simple proverbial expression ('Nur nicht gleich mit der Tür ins Haus' I. i). When she addresses Wurm, her language turns into a vulgar parody of fashionable speech, strewn with malapropisms ('Seckertare', 'barrdu'). Both modes of speech are quite different from Miller's, and, though both may be termed naturalistic, their primary function is to reveal and illustrate Frau Miller's character, her stupidity, and her social ambition.

Wurm, who has the smallest part in this opening scene, speaks usually in straightforward terms which are unobtrusively realistic. Even when he makes something approximating to a set speech, the logical order and fluency are not inappropriate to a man of his character, talent, and situation. Here, too, we see style serving the end of characterization, reflecting Wurm's clear head and frigid heart.

Moreover, these three characters maintain their separate modes of realistic speech through some of the varying situations

---

[1] In interpreting Miller's speech as establishing the 'bürgerlichen Pol', Wolfgang Binder ignores its highly idiosyncratic nature. *Das deutsche Drama*, ed. B. v. Wiese, i, 1960, p. 252.

in which they find themselves. Miller's rough-tongued eloquence persists in the presence of the angry Präsident and in conversation with the murderous yet tormented Ferdinand. Frau Miller speaks in the second scene as she has in the first. Wurm in his scenes with the Präsident does not swerve from his cool sober tone, demonstrating his self-control in touches of irony ('Ich mache hier gern den Bürgersmann, gnädiger Herr' and 'Wenigstens will ich den armen Schächer mit diesem zusammengeflickten Kobold durch ein Nadelöhr jagen', I. v and III i.).

## 2. EXALTATION

Up to the departure of Wurm the language of the first act, though showing important variation according to character, nevertheless preserves the tone of realistic speech. On the appearance of Luise it modulates into a remote key. Among her first words are 'O ich bin eine schwere Sünderin, Vater', and she goes on in terms which can only be described as literary. She, like her father, speaks in images; but where his were fresh and robust, if coarse, hers are the well-worn small change of literary commonplace—'Ich versteh Ihn, Vater — fühle das Messer, daß Er in mein Gewissen stößt' (I. iii). She expands and plays with images, some at least of which are outside the range of her own experience, indulging in poetic sophistry:

Wenn wir ihn über dem Gemälde vernachlässigen, findet sich ja der Künstler am feinsten gelobt. — Wenn meine Freude über sein Meisterstück mich ihn selbst übersehen macht, Vater, muß das Gott nicht ergötzen?

She indulges in a conceit— 'Dies bißchen Leben — dürft ich es hinhauchen in ein leises schmeichelndes Lüftchen, sein [Ferdinands] Gesicht abzukühlen'; and she continues with a conscious parallelism of construction and an artful use of the commonplaces of literary imagery, as they were current in the 1770s: 'Dies Blümchen Jugend — wär es ein Veilchen, und er träte drauf, und es dürfte bescheiden unter ihm sterben.' This speech concludes with a display of epithets which are quite unrelated to Luise's field of experience: 'kann sie das strafen, die stolze, majestätische Sonne?'

A brief and gentle remonstrance from her father only provokes her to higher flights. The vocabulary becomes exclusively poetic, the construction is varied by poetic inversion of word order:

Als ich ihn das erstemal sah — und mir das Blut in die Wangen stieg, froher jagten alle Pulse, jede Wallung sprach, jeder Atem lispelte: er ists, und mein Herz den Immermangelnden erkannte, bekräftigte: er ists, und wie das widerklang durch die ganze mitfreuende Welt. Damals — o damals ging in meiner Seele der erste Morgen auf. Tausend junge Gefühle schossen aus meinem Herzen, wie die Blumen aus dem Erdreich, wenns Frühling wird . . . .

Obviously these are not the words, the modes of expression, or the grammatical constructions of a sixteen-year-old girl[1] of humble circumstances and modest education. Her lover, it is true, is himself addicted to high-flown sentiments and has encouraged her to read sentimental literature.[2] It may be argued that Luise's speech reflects the imposition upon her simple and receptive mind of a mode of expression which she admires, because it resembles her lover's speech; that it thus demonstrates the extent to which she has become alienated from her own social environment.

In so far as it achieves this, however, it does so by symbolical means, not by reproduction of fact. For it would be difficult to credit that any young girl could absorb from her young man language such as Luise uses: 'Dieser karge Tautropfe Zeit — schon ein Traum von Ferdinand trinkt ihn Wollüstig auf.' Such speech, if factually interpreted, would turn Luise into a figure of comedy, which she assuredly is not.

It might be thought that Schiller, by this device, sought to demonstrate an opposition between simplicity and sophistication, that Miller reveals the down-to-earth freshness of the unspoiled

---

[1] Luise gives her age to Lady Milford as 'sechszehn gewesen', IV. vii.
[2] See Miller's serio-comic lament in I. i,

figure, contrasted in Luise with the shallow artificiality of the character infected by the vices of aristocratic society. This would mean that Luise is for Schiller an object of criticism, a symbol of that which he condemns. It is, however, only too obvious that she arouses his liveliest sympathy and participation; and that, whatever surface changes have been effected by Ferdinand, her honesty, modesty, and decency remain intact. Or can it be that the conventions are reversed: that realism indicates baseness, and elevation corresponds to purity? Miller himself refutes one arm of this proposition and Ferdinand the other. Perhaps we come closer to the matter if we consider Luise's position as the heroine of this tragedy. Wolfgang Binder has pointed out that Schiller's original title clearly stipulates her alone as the central figure;[1] the play was not *Ferdinand und Luise*, but plainly and unmistakably *Luise Millerin*.

It is her responsibility as heroine which turns Luise away from the realistic language which Schiller permitted himself in some secondary figures. The language of his heroes had so far been grandiose and he could not conceive it otherwise. The point is well illustrated in the scene in which Luise is induced to write the fateful letter by the mental torture imposed upon her by Wurm. The tone is set by Luise's first response to Wurm's entry, taking the form of a well-turned literary sentence: 'Meiner ängstlichen Ahndung eilt schon die unglückseligste Erfüllung nach.' There follows a swift dialogue in which Luise expresses herself in direct everyday language, passing presently into an interchange which, in its pithy, simple austerity, is almost stichomythic. Here the dramatist shows that he knows the importance of speed and how to achieve it. But, once the terrible truth is revealed, Luise is allowed to dilate in an exalted language, with which the author is clearly fully identified. 'Ihn vorzusingen', she cries, 'den Eulengesang, dabei zu stehn, wenn das blutende Herz am eisernen Schaft der Notwendigkeit zittert'. The fully stated image of butchery on such lips is suspect. When we listen a few minutes later to a speech of denunciation

---

[1] Op. cit., p. 250.

by Luise set in the macabre and ghoulish terms Schiller employs in *Die Räuber* and in some of his youthful poetry, we may well feel that we detect the *vox auctoris*:

Ich will ihm sagen, was Elend ist — will es ihm vormalen in allen Verzerrungen des Todes, was Elend ist — will es ihm vorheulen in Mark und Bein zermalmenden Tönen, was Elend ist — und wenn ihm jetzt über der Beschreibung die Haare zu Berge fliegen, will ich ihm noch zum Schluß in die Ohren schrein, daß in der Sterbestunde auch die Lungen der Erdengötter zu röcheln anfangen, und das jüngste Gericht Majestäten und Bettler in dem nämlichen Siebe rüttle.

It is obvious that the graveyard vocabulary, the hyperboles of horror, and the apocalyptic conclusion are couched in terms which, even in this terrible situation, cannot be 'natural' to Luise. The attempt at the characteristic gives way to the personal manner of the author.

This is a constantly recurring phenomenon in *Kabale und Liebe*. The mode of passion carries the author away; when the action is fully engaged his enthusiasm and exaltation, his anger and indignation, his own personal style, impetuously override the characterizing manner with which the play has begun.

Not only does Luise lean to heightened and literary vocabulary and uncharacteristic images; she is also greatly addicted to speaking in triadic constructions and so to following a formal principle. Thus three nouns successively depend upon one participle: 'abgeschält von allen Pflichten — und Tränen — und Freuden' (III. vi); three questions beginning with 'warum' occur in anaphorical sequence: 'warum mich zwischen zwei Schröcknisse pressen? Warum zwischen Tod und Schande mich hin und her wiegen? Warum diesen blutsaugenden Teufel mir auf den Nacken setzen?' Or she sums up under three heads the loss which Wurm has inflicted upon her: 'Es ist mein ehrlicher Name — es ist Ferdinand — ist die Wonne meines ganzen Lebens, was ich jetzt in Ihre Hände gebe ...'.

Such triple structure is familiar as a simple rhetorical device; it is hardly ever the natural expression of the mind. Its repeated incidence here points to the imposition upon this part of the play of a pattern of formal eloquence.

The pattern suggested here becomes obvious in the interview between Lady Milford and Luise in the fourth act. Luise's language rises to a new pitch of elaboration. She attacks Lady Milford with calculated eloquence, including in one short period a triad of subjects, two of them in balance, an allusion to the death of Cleopatra and a general moral reflection:

Stunden der Nüchternheit, Augenblicke der *Erschöpfung* könnten sich melden — Schlangen der Reue könnten Ihren Busen anfallen, und *nun* — welche Folter für Sie im Gesicht Ihres Dienstmädchens die *heitre Ruhe* zu lesen, womit die Unschuld ein reines Herz zu belohnen pflegt.

Luise formulates a series of rhetorical questions, compares cunning structures of interlocking clauses, and employs (for her) improbable images, in which whales and fleets of ships gambol; or she herself appears as an insect armed with a sting for its own protection. By this time Schiller has abandoned any effort to characterize Luise by her speech. The language is his own rhetoric, the images his own preferred images.

Luise is not the only character to speak in elevated style. Her mode of speech is matched by Ferdinand and by Lady Milford. The affinity of Luise's speech with that of her lover can, as we have seen, be in part interpreted realistically as an effect of his influence upon her. In Ferdinand von Walter the exalted mode is more truly in harmony with character. His first expression of his love is in a speech of most artful chiastic symmetry: 'Wenn ich bei dir bin, zerschmilzt meine Vernunft in einen Blick — in einen Traum von dir, wenn ich weg bin' (I. iv); or he declaims in parallel and with the help of a musical image on the impossibility of parting: 'Wer kann den Bund zwoer Herzen lösen, oder die Töne eines Akkords auseinanderreißen?'

The elaborate eloquence of his melting mood is, however, only one aspect of his exalted style. His ardour expresses itself in energetic language, turning quickly to hyperbole: 'Laß auch

Hindernisse wie Gebürge zwischen uns treten, ich will sie für
Treppen nehmen und drüber hin in Luisens Arme fliegen.' It is
a forcing of the tone which comes perilously near to bombast, and
even to bathos; for the 'Treppen' do not easily consent to the
magnification which Ferdinand seeks to impose upon them.
The crisp, ringing utterance of dramatic tone and antithetical
structure constitutes Ferdinand's third type of speech:

Ich bin ein Edelmann — Laß doch sehen, ob mein Adelbrief älter ist,
als der Riß zum unendlichen Weltall? oder mein Wappen gültiger als
die Handschrift des Himmels in Luisens Augen: Dieses Weib ist für
diesen Mann?

Here in two sharply focused parallel sentences Ferdinand speaks
with a touch of the imperious (thereby reminding us of his rank
at the very moment when he is deprecating hereditary nobility)
and emphasizes the force of his resolution and the scale of his
emotions by the two hyperbolical cosmic references (*Weltall* and
*Himmel*) which symbolize his love for Luise.

It seems clear that Ferdinand's stylistic exaggeration and
pretension is an aspect of his character. And this is confirmed in
his interview with his father (I. vii). Here, though his language is
less high-flown than when speaking to Luise (and this in itself is
a hint of character), he speaks in a manner very different from the
downright utterance of the Präsident. To a series of indignant
rhetorical questions from Ferdinand, culminating in an augmented triad, the father replies with blunt, contemptuous irony:

FERDINAND. ... Mit welchem Gesicht vor die Welt? Vor den Fürsten?
Mit welchem vor die Buhlerin selbst, die den Brandflecken ihrer
Ehre in meiner Schande auswaschen würde?
PRÄSIDENT. Wo in aller Welt bringst du das Maul her, Junge?

And earlier in the same scene the Präsident performs a similar
act of deflation in more polished fashion, but still with the same
contrast of style:

FERDINAND. ... Neid, Furcht, Verwünschung sind die traurigen
Spiegel, worin sich die Hoheit eines Herrschers belächelt —
Tränen, Flüche, Verzweiflung die entsetzliche Mahlzeit, woran

diese gepriesenen Glücklichen schwelgen, von der sie betrunken aufstehen, und so in die Ewigkeit vor den Thron Gottes taumeln — Mein Ideal von Glück zieht sich genügsamer in mich selbst zurück. In meinem *Herzen* liegen alle meine Wünsche begraben.

Thus Ferdinand not only expresses his self-righteous indignation with the help of an eschatological image (the sots of wickedness arraigned at the Last Day); he has also framed his speech in a balanced antithesis, embodying on each side a triad. The Präsident responds to this imposing indictment with unruffled, simple irony; and it is significant that he too begins with a triad, thus mocking the priggishly exalted style of his son: 'Meisterhaft! Unverbesserlich! Herrlich! Nach dreißig Jahren die erste Vorlesung wieder! — Schade nur, daß mein fünfzigjähriger Kopf zu zäh für das Lernen ist!'

Irony is indeed one of the basic springs of the Präsident's language. It flickers fitfully in this scene, it is employed against Ferdinand and Luise in the second act, and directed upon the Präsident himself in the third; but most of all it searches out Hofmarschall von Kalb. He counters Ferdinand's praise of the 'Hause der Unschuld' with 'Wo der Sohn Gehorsam gegen den Vater lernt?' He seeks to confound Luise with an ironical assumption that her favours are venially bestowed: 'Aber er bezahlte Sie doch jederzeit bar?' To Kalb's enthusiasm for the coming pyrotechnic display he retorts with a flash of self-irony: 'Ich habe Feuerwerks genug in meinem eigenen Hause.' And in this scene he punctuates von Kalb's account of the momentous catastrophe of Princess Amalie's garter with contemptuous interjections: 'Wer könnte so was vergessen?', 'Impertinent!', and so on. And he sums the chamberlain up in a *boutade* of withering sarcasm: 'Ein Bonmot von vorgestern. Die Mode vom vorigen Jahr.'

Irony is an expression of sophistication and superiority, and it is therefore a characteristic use of speech in aristocratic circles, both among equals and towards the 'lower orders'. Schiller uses this irony to mark the Präsident out as an epitome of his class. The third representative of the nobility, Court Chamberlain von Kalb, is also introduced in the first act. The complete emptiness of this outwardly important figure is indicated by the fatuity of what he says, but it is also underlined by the manner of his speech. His tautologisms point to his unclarity of mind, as in 'Wie geruht? Wie geschlafen?' His rapid succession of detached phrases mirrors the butterfly fluttering from flower to flower: 'dringende Geschäfte — der Küchenzettel — Visitenbilletts — das Arrangement der Partien auf die heutige Schlittenfahrt . . .'. And the frequency of his interjected exclamations and simple questions demonstrates his naïve self-importance and desire for approbation: 'Ich bitte Sie!', 'Was anzufangen?', 'Was fällt mir bei?', 'Was sagen Sie?', 'Was denken Sie' all occur in one quite short speech. The picture of the inflated inane is achieved as much by stylistic as by substantive devices.

When the first act closes, there is still one important character whose acquaintance we have not yet made. Lady Milford, unlike Frau Miller, is introduced in neutral language (II. i). A slight hint at character is given in the stage direction for her dress— *in einem freien aber reizenden Negligé, die Haare noch unfrisiert* — but this time the *noch* is factual, not condemnatory. Schiller despised Frau Miller's sluttishness, he does not react against Lady Milford's attractions. The Lady immediately speaks in brief, incomplete, and inconsequent sentences, which aptly convey agitation and may well represent a degree of realism, but her first short speech nevertheless ends in a touch of poetry: 'Menschen sehen und blauen Himmel, und mich leichter reiten ums Herz herum.' The lilting rhythm of the last six words, with its hint of the galloping horse, is a warning that the idiom of the opening is only apparently realistic.

It becomes quickly obvious that Lady Milford's speech is larger than life. She continues to Sophie (before whom, if nowhere else, we would expect her to be off duty) in a tone of hyperbole. 'Ich gebe dir', she says,' einen Demant für jede Stunde, wo ich sie mir vom Hals schaffen kann', an undertaking which is hardly to be understood literally. Her picture of the court circle is perceptibly exaggerated to produce caricature:

Das sind schlechte, erbärmliche Menschen, die sich entsetzen, wenn
mir ein warmes herzliches Wort entwischt, Mund und Nasen auf-
reißen, als sähen sie einen Geist — Sklaven eines einzigen Marionet-
tendrahts....

Thence she turns to full-flown oratory in her analysis of the
condition of the favourite and the powers of the prince. 'Unter
allen,' she exclaims 'die an den Brüsten der Majestät trinken,
kommt die Favoritin am schlechtesten weg', an image which
involves a curious reversal of sex (even though the feminine
'Majestät' does duty for the sovereign). The confusion arises
because rhetorical convention in this speech triumphs over
poetic precision. The pleasures which the prince procures for his
mistress are then enumerated in a series of periphrastic clauses in
bold hyperbole:

Wahr ists, er kann mit dem Talisman seiner Größe jeden Gelust
meines Herzens wie ein Feenschloß aus der Erde rufen. — Er setzt
den Saft von zwei Indien auf die Tafel — ruft Paradiese aus Wild-
nissen — läßt die Quellen seines Landes in stolzen Bögen gen Himmel
springen, oder das Mark seiner Untertanen in einem Feuerwerk
hinpuffen.

The style and gesture scarcely fit a woman, least of all a
woman whose heart of gold expresses itself in philanthropic
activity, and whose dream is a retreat into idyllic obscurity with
the man she loves. A moment later Lady Milford goes on to
sound trumpet-like the repeated notes of *groß* and *feurig* in a
sublime climax: 'Aber kann er auch seinem *Herzen* befehlen,
gegen ein *großes feuriges Herz groß* und *feurig* zu schlagen?' It is
at this point that it dawns on us that we are not listening to a
woman at all. The masculine attributes *groß* and *feurig* are the
natural expression of Schiller himself when roused to a pitch of
enthusiasm. For the moment Lady Milford's personality has
receded, and we are left with a mask, through which the *vox
auctoris* pours its exalted eloquence.

It is, moreover, not the elevated tone alone which suggests
Schiller's own personal note. The anatomical touch of 'sein
darbendes Gehirn' and the forthright sensuality of 'Wallungen

löschen' echo Schiller's language in the poems of the *Anthologie*, notably in the odes to 'Laura'. The expanded antithesis of '*Herrschen* und *Dienen*', too, sets out the relations of the sexes in terms which, in their hyperbolical generalization, can only be masculine: 'die höchste Wonne der *Gewalt* ist nur doch ein elender Behelf, wenn uns die *größere* Wonne versagt wird, Sklavinnen eines Mannes zu sein, den wir lieben.'

And the language of Schiller's early personal poetry recurs in the oxymoron 'Belogene Lügner!' and in the bold transformation of an intransitive into a transitive verb—'sie blitzen Höllenflammen in mein Herz'.

Lady Milford speaks from time to time a less elevated language. Some of her utterances to the footman who brings her the diamond tiara are simple, almost homely—e.g. 'Mann, was ist dir? Ich glaube, du weinst?' or 'Doch keinen Gezwungenen?' (II. ii). In her interview with Luise (IV. vii) an involved and elaborate locution is used to illuminate a facet of character, as the stage direction *geschraubt* indicates, but this dramatic exploitation of the tone of high society is merely a detached instance of sophistication. For the most part the eloquence arises from the personal participation of the author, and is a proof of his engagement in the social criticism with which the part of Lady Milford is linked.

Of course Lady Milford is a great lady at court. We know that pride and arrogance are the concomitant of rank and power, and so it might be held that the elevated style is appropriate as an expression of character. The Lady's interview with Ferdinand in Act Two proves it otherwise. The conversation begins in formal politeness, a realism of speech suited to the social situation:

FERDINAND. Ich bin ein Mann von Ehre.
LADY. Den ich zu schätzen weiß.
FERDINAND. Kavalier.
LADY. Kein bessrer im Herzogtum.
FERDINAND. Und Offizier.
LADY (*schmeichelhaft*). Sie berühren hier Vorzüge, die auch andere mit Ihnen gemein haben. Warum verschweigen Sie größere, worin Sie *einzig* sind? (II. iii)

Here the elegance of polite conversation does more than render the tone of a social milieu. The swiftness with which Lady Milford caps each point of Ferdinands' declaration betrays her anxiety. Thus general characterization and behaviour in a particular situation are simultaneously achieved.

This phase in the conversation is soon at an end. The transition to the rhetoric of Schillerian exaltation is made by Ferdinand with a triadic rejoinder:

LADY. Diesen Degen gab Ihnen der Fürst.

FERDINAND. Der Staat gab mir ihn, durch die Hand des Fürsten — mein Herz Gott — mein Wappen ein halbes Jahrtausend.

Ferdinand's hostility quickly evokes a response in Lady Milford. Her speech rises to systematic organization with a series of parallel sentences, as she addresses herself to her task, an extended essay in apologetics. It begins historically, with brisk, economical narration. She quickly warms to her work; almost imperceptibly the images acquire a tinge of exaggeration, as in the following account of her upbringing and accomplishments:

Ich hatte nichts gelernt, als das bißchen Französisch — ein wenig Filet, und den Flügel — desto besser verstund ich auf Gold und Silber zu speisen, unter damastenen Decken zu schlafen, mit einem Wink zehen Bediente fliegen zu machen, und die Schmeicheleien der Großen Ihres Geschlechts aufzunehmen.

Dramatic contrasts appear; to the 'verführenden Schimmer' of the new prospect is opposed the 'Schwarz wie das Grab' of her destitution and despair. So far the language, though it is perhaps not designed to characterize, is nevertheless appropriate to character. We recognize in Lady Milford the woman of intelligence and energy, possessed of histrionic instincts which enable her to exploit the advantages of her story and situation.

At this point her narration touches a general question—the social conditions of the land in which she has found herself in a position of simultaneous dependence, power, and privilege. At once the language swells to hyperbole: 'Die Wollust der Großen dieser Welt ist die nimmersatte Hyäne, die sich mit Heißhunger Opfer sucht.'

The image of ferocity, implicit in the hyena, is duplicated in that of the tiger ('ich stellte mich zwischen das Lamm und den Tiger'). An extraordinary violence pervades her speech; the deaths of girls by syphilis are thus portrayed: 'sterbende Schülerinnen schäumten den Namen ihres Lehrers unter Flüchen und Zuckungen aus.' The tyranny of Parisian mistresses (they are 'flatterhafte Pariserinnen') is expressed in an image of blood: 'das Volk blutete unter ihren Launen.' The gentle sway, which Lady Milford claims to have exercised, recalls the severities and cruelties of the preceding epoch: 'ich habe Kerker gesprengt — habe Todesurteile zerrissen, und manche entsetzliche Ewigkeit auf Galeeren verkürzt.'

Triad succeeds triad, as the eloquence rises in pitch, until finally all pretence at individual characterization is dropped and Lady Milford adopts the posture of the Schillerian hero. A significant symptom of this development is the shift, when speaking of herself, from the first person to the third; from 'den ich in brennender Sehnsucht im Traum schon umfasse' to 'Jetzt oder nimmermehr. Lange genug hielt die Heldin stand.' She speaks of herself (still in the third person) being 'heldenmäßig emporgehoben vom Rufe der Tugend', and the vocabulary of hyperbolical horror and frightfulness continues with 'dem fürchterlichen Ruf der Verzweiflung', 'in noch abscheulichere Tiefen des Lasters', and 'wo mein zerrissenes Herz an tausend Dolchstichen blutet'. From this point her statuesque pose declines under the deflation applied by Ferdinand's confession of his love for another. But it is noteworthy that she concludes the scene with a military image— 'Ich laß alle Minen sprengen'—so maintaining the masculine, heroic note.

The exposition of character is complete at the end of this interview between Lady Milford and Ferdinand von Walter. The language has served, in part, to characterize the persons, especially the secondary, environmental, figures: Miller and his wife, the Präsident, and Wurm. With Ferdinand and Luise, and, in her curious detached role, Lady Milford, characterization, though not unimportant, is overshadowed by another function.

The exalted speech of these three shifts the conflict to the lofty atmosphere of pure tragedy, which Schiller evidently deemed unattainable on the level of verisimilitude and individualization at which the early scenes had operated. Luise and Ferdinand and Lady Milford speak a lingua franca which makes them intelligible to each other across the barriers of class, precisely because it has, when under tension, nothing to do with characterization; indeed, it erases distinctions. This common speech of the three principal figures is itself, however, not fully homogeneous. It is compounded of two diverse elements: on the one hand the structural element of rhetorical speech, with its antitheses and parallelisms, its triads and extended periods; on the other a vocabulary and range of image at once bold and violent, which reveals the author himself. The spiritual exaltation of the man Schiller, plainly visible in these three characters, is a prime unifying factor in some of the most important scenes in the play. Two widely differing styles sometimes conduce to an over-all unity. But in *Kabale und Liebe* the styles seem to have no common ground.

Characterization, as we have seen, is one of the aims of Schiller's realistic dialogue. And this distinguishing function acts simultaneously on two different levels. It separates classes and differentiates individuals. The speech of the Millers is *bürgerlich*, that of the Präsident and Hofmarschall aristocratic; Wurm's speech is a hybrid of the two, as also, in a more tentative and uncertain way, is Luise's in her moments of relaxation. Yet Miller is clearly differentiated from his wife, and the Hofmarschall from the Präsident.

There is, however, another and equally important aspect of the speech. The apparently realistic style exhibits a constantly recurring satirical twist. This is most obvious in the speech of Hofmarschall von Kalb; his share of the dialogue is carefully designed to evoke from his interlocutors retorts which hold him up to general ridicule. But there are also less obvious examples. Millers's naïve delight at the gold which Ferdinand gives him ('Und auf dem Markt will ich meine Musikstunden geben, und

Numero fünfe Dreikönig rauchen, und wenn ich wieder auf den Dreibatzenplatz sitze, soll mich der Teufel holen', v. v) is also satirically barbed, though the shaft is directed at the social circumstances which have made him what he is, rather than at Miller himself. The lifelike does not satisfy Schiller in *Kabale und Liebe*. Touches of exaggeration transform reality into satire and caricature. Even the portrayal of the Präsident, that figure of the realist, is weighted towards caricature, as his touch of tyrannical bombast demonstrates: 'Wenn ich auftrete, zittert ein Herzogtum' (I. vii).

Indeed, the prevalence of hyperbole through large tracts of the play is a clear indication that Schiller has not ceased to be himself in *Kabale und Liebe*; though new paths are explored, the familiar gait is maintained. When Ferdinand exclaims to Luise, 'Dein Fußtapfe in wilden sandigten Wüsten ist mir interessanter, als das Münster in meiner Heimat', or, in solitary fury, damns Luise's supposed action as 'ein unerhörter Betrug, wie die Menschen noch keinen erlebte!' we recognize the compulsively magnifying mind which was manifest in *Fiesco* and even more throughout *Die Räuber*.

### 3. UNITY BY STRUCTURE AND RHYTHM

A striking feature of the linguistic structure of *Kabale und Liebe* is the abundance of triple (and occasionally quadruple) grammatical forms. These are a development of the accumulation and augmentation which are so conspicuous an element in Schiller's early style. This form of repetitive grouping, already noticed in the elevated eloquence of Ferdinand and Lady Milford, recurs whenever the tone is exalted and the situation 'strong', as in the Lady's 'Gehoben das furchtbare Hindernis, zerbrochen alle Bande zwischen mir und dem Herzog, gerissen aus meinem Busen diese wütende Liebe!' (IV. viii). Here the triple structural rhythm is enhanced by the inverted order, in accordance with which each phrase begins, instead of ending, with the participle. Luise, too, uses such a triple form on completing the fateful letter to Wurm's dictation. Her language, though less ornate, is equally elevated: 'Es ist mein ehrlicher Name — es ist Ferdinand — ist die ganze Wonne meines Lebens, was ich jetzt in Ihre Hände gebe.' Schiller here blends the formal with the realistic, for it is noteworthy that the omission of the *es* as subject of the third clause suggests a catch in the throat and so tinges Luise's rhetoric with a natural and spontaneous expression of emotion.

Here lies the clue to one of the elements which give unity to the language of *Kabale und Liebe*, in spite of evident diversity. The triple structure is a formal pattern occurring in clear and pointed form over and over again in the passages of elevated feeling and exalted expression in the second half of the play. But it is not limited to these. The realistic and characteristic style of the early Miller scenes has as its basic pattern a triple rhythm. In his first speech Miller explains the seriousness of the situation in a triad of terse sentences: 'Meine Tochter kommt mit dem Baron ins Geschrei. Mein Haus wird verrufen. Der Präsident bekommt Wind...'. He follows this with three parallel sentences: 'Ich war Herr im Haus. Ich hätte meine Tochter mehr koram nehmen sollen. Ich hätt dem Major besser auftrumpfen sollen...'. And when he rehearses his intended audience with the Präsident he expresses himself in a 'syllogistic' triad, in which the third element relates the first two: 'Dero Herr Sohn haben ein Aug auf meine Tochter; meine Tochter ist zu schlecht zu Dero Herrn Sohnes Frau, aber zu Dero Herrn Sohnes Hure ist meine Tochter zu kostbar.'

The Präsident's speech also frequently displays a similar pattern. In his first interview with Ferdinand three clauses beginning 'Wem zu lieb...?' occur in succession. And a moment later there comes another quasi-anaphorical sequence: 'Lohnst du mich *also* für meine schlaflosen Nächte? *Also* für meine rastlose Sorge? *Also* für den ewigen Skorpion meines Gewissens?' No sooner are these words uttered than a fresh triad appears: 'Auf mich fällt die Last der Verantwortung — auf mich der Fluch, der Donner des Richters.'

Even Frau Millerin, whose utterances are mostly too short to permit a threefold pattern, nevertheless speaks a triad when her anxiety stimulates her eloquence: 'Der Präsident wird hieher kommen — Er wird unser Kind mißhandeln — Er wird uns mißhandeln...'. It is truly striking that this deft touch of egotism is conveyed in the triple rhythm which is the prevailing pattern of the play.

This structure naturally occurs most frequently in the speech of the most articulate characters, and above all with the most passionately eloquent. Nevertheless, every character of substance, including even Wurm, on occasion employs the triple pattern, which thus becomes a unifying factor linking the realistic, characterizing speech and the high-pitched eloquence that are the two contrasting stylistic modes of this play.

This binding element, though common to both tones, is itself rhetorical, and its pervasiveness points to the importance of the elevated type of speech, which becomes increasingly dominant as the play proceeds.

Not only is the triadic form rhetorical, however; it suggests also a rhythmic quality of speech. Of concealed blank verse, such as we find in Goethe's *Egmont*, *Kabale und Liebe* has little. The rhythm of the elevated tracts is not the even iambic pulse, which later seems to be Schiller's natural element, but the more wayward and variable measure of magniloquent prose.

We see it in the subtle tempo of Luise's vision of heaven:

Ich werde dann reich sein. Dort rechnet man Tränen für Triumphe, und schöne Gedanken für Ahnen an. Ich werde dann vornehm sein, Mutter — Was hätte er dann noch für seinem Mädchen voraus?

(I. iii)

It emerges even more clearly in her harrowing speech of renunciation in Act III. iv:

*Verlieren!* — O ohne Grenzen entsetzlich ist der Gedanke — Gräßlich genug, den unsterblichen Geist zu durchbohren, und die glühende Wange der Freude zu bleichen — Ferdinand! dich zu verlieren! — Doch! Man verliert ja nur, was man besessen hat, und dein Herz

gehört deinem Stande — Mein Anspruch war Kirchenraub, und
schaudernd geb ich ihn auf.

The subtlety of this passage lies in the temporary abandonment
of the rhythm in the short centre section, in which all trace of
the beat is lost. The psychological possibilities of this device
for expressing shock or bewilderment or sudden resolution are
obvious, and one of them is clearly illustrated here.

A more complex rhythmic structure underlies Miller's
anguished address to Luise in Act Five:

Zieh hin! Lade alle deine Sünden auf, lade auch diese, die letzte, die
entsetzlichste auf, und wenn die Last noch zu leicht ist, so mache
mein Fluch das Gewicht vollkommen — Hier ist ein Messer —
durchstich dein Herz und das Vaterherz.

Three times the rhythm surges forward, each time with stronger
pulse, only to be arrested at a long *fermata*. Then swiftly, irresistibly, the psychological blow is struck.


## 4. VOCABULARY

In view of the realistic tone of the opening, it is not surprising that colloquialisms occur with greater vigour and intensity than in any other play of Schiller. Miller's speech in the
first two acts is full of them. 'Herumschwänzen', 'das Geklatsch',
'obenaus wollen', 'in jeder Suppe zu fressen kriege', and 'wutsch'
are random examples. Miller, even when in Act Five his language
takes on a rhetorical tinge, makes no use of the words which are
regarded as characteristically Schillerian—*stolz, unendlich, groß,
Held*, and *golden*. But Luise, when she enters the colloquial first
scene, immediately introduces 'die stolze, majestätische Sonne'
and 'Der Riß zum unendlichen Weltall'. For the moment, these
remain sporadic.

The second act sees Schiller's personal symbols re-established.
Lady Milford, even before her encounter with Ferdinand
heightens the tension, uses the familiar range of exalted words.
With 'kann er auch seinem *Herzen* befehlen, gegen ein *großes*

*feuriges Herz groß* und *feurig* zu schlagen?' she combines the sublime significance which *groß* has for Schiller with the cherished image of fire. Two more favoured words, *Herz* and *frei* are conjoined in 'Mein Herz habe ich frei behalten'; and shortly after there occurs Schiller's emphatic denotation of 'always', with a characteristic stress achieved by repetition. 'Ja! es auf ewig zu trennen! auf ewig diese schändliche Ketten zu brechen!' In Ferdinand's presence this range of vocabulary proliferates. 'Die freigeborene Tochter des freiesten Volkes unter dem Himmel', 'zu stolz', 'als größer und kühner Britanniens Adern schlagen', 'eine große Seele', 'die Heldin', 'heldenmäßig emporgehoben'— all these and many other similar expressions establish a link with the elevated vocabulary of *Die Räuber* and *Fiesco*. Yet for all the evocative words of idealism ('goldene Bilder der Liebe', 'goldne Jahrtausende') and heroism ('Heldin', 'Heldenmut', 'Sieger'), for all the vehemence of the images of fire ('voll glühender uner- schöpflicher Liebe', 'jede feurige Wallung'), the incidence of elevated vocabulary has diminished in *Kabale und Liebe* when it is set against the two earlier plays. The verbal dualism of collo- quialism and exaltation persists and the harmonization is left to the rhythm.

On the other hand, the words of violence, horror, and cruelty have held their own. Particularly numerous are the words relating to sharp stabbing weapons. When the Präsident uses the phrase 'uns beide ans Messer liefern' or the Hofmarschall exclaims 'Sie stoßen mir ein Messer ins Herz' our first reaction may be that these are conventional expressions, images from which the colour has faded. But, seen in the context of the whole dialogue, they prove to be something much more significant; they acquire an ironic force as echoes, spoken by the heartless, of words which are repeatedly and vividly on the lips of others possessed of sensitive and quivering hearts.

Lady Milford powerfully uses such an image in one of the interludes of deep sincerity interspersed between her rhetorical tirades: 'In diesem entsetzlichen Augenblick nicht, wo mein zerissenes Herz an tausend Dolchstichen blutet.' But it is Luise, the character of pure love and devotion, who reiterates the image of the stabbed and wounded heart. To her father's gentle reproaches she replies with 'Ich. . . fühle das Messer, das er in mein Gewissen stößt'. The threat of separation with its consequent agony of suffering appears to her as 'Ein Dolch über dir und mir! — Man trennt uns!' When the threat becomes a searing reality, her use of this image becomes more original and more expressive. To Wurm she speaks terrible words of anguish: 'wenn das blutende Herz am eisernen Schaft der Notwendigkeit zittert.' The gruesome violence of this phrase is then surpassed by her words to Lady Milford: 'den Mann, den man mit Haken der Hölle von meinem blutenden Herzen riß.' The point of these terrible images is the exposure to view of the human suffering normally concealed and dampened by literary and social convention. The realism and the rhetoric both operate on one plane, the suggestive images on another. That Schiller sometimes overreaches himself in the exhibition of horror is true. His poetic purpose was liable to be intensified and even distorted by the attraction that images of pain and blood held for him.

The motif of death reinforces the vocabulary of suffering. Ferdinand's 'In meinem Herzen liegen alle meine Wünsche begraben' is an unconscious prophecy of the outcome of the tragedy. For Lady Milford the future is 'schwarz wie das Grab'. But the characters dwell more readily on the pangs of dissolution than on the image of death itself. 'Daß in der Sterbestunde auch die Lungen der Erdengötter zu röcheln anfangen', exclaims Luise; and Lady Milford renounces Ferdinand, who has become for her 'das Geschenk deines [Luisens] Sterberöchelns'. Luise achieves a dreadful confrontation of horror and laughter with 'das schwarze Ungeheuer Verwesung drücken wir im Spaß in die Arme'.

As in the previous plays there is a predilection for words of horror associated with judicial processes, especially real or imagined judicial torture. Every attempt by Luise to escape from the hideous impasse in which she is trapped is countered by Wurm with the repeated vision of the executioner—'An den

Henker Ihres Vaters'—achieving here a triad of horror. There is in this a significant parallel with Ferdinand's words in Act Three: 'Der Sohn wird den Vater in die Hände des Henkers liefern.' Ferdinand's bitter sarcasm, pillorying his father—'aus *vollkommenen Henkersknechten schlechte Minister* machte' (II. vii) —suggests the savagery behind the façade of decorum which is a part of the temper of this tragedy.

The most telling symbols of this contrast are provided by the vocabulary of torture. Almost all of them concern Luise, the victim whom passion, prejudice, and intrigue crush and destroy. Luise herself twice refers to breaking on the wheel, and once explicitly refers it to herself (III. vi). Her image 'mich zwischen zwei Schröcknisse pressen' evokes a *peine forte et dure*. In her anguish she uses a verb which doubles the vividness of the image of torment: 'du verstehst dich darauf, Seelen auf die Folter zu schrauben' (III. vi). Twice Ferdinand, in his murderous agony, alludes to torture, each time with reference to Luise ('erspart mir die Folterung' and 'Auch die Unschuld bekennt sich auf der Folterbank zu Freveln, die sie nie beging'). The most horrifying of all these allusions is made by Luise herself: 'das Eisen erst langsam-bedächtlich an den knirschenden Gelenken hinaufzuführen, und das zuckende Herz mit dem Streich der Erbarmung zu necken.' It needs strong nerves to read this sentence without flinching. Clearly Schiller was more concerned to create a symbolism for his purpose than to write a piece of dialogue suiting the speaker. That the image could be executed with such an eye (or ear) for detail as the word *knirschend* betrays indicates an alertness and direction of Schiller's mind which are foreign to usually accepted views.

All this judicially imposed cruelty underlines the point that the sufferings in the play are inflicted by society. The contrast between temporal and divine judgement is implied in Luise's words to Lady Milford: 'Die arme Sünderin auf dem berüchtigten Henkerstuhl lacht zu Weltuntergang.' If the judgement of the world is arbitrary and cruel, there is another plane of judgement which is repeatedly on the lips of the characters and, indeed, constantly in Schiller's mind. The Präsident twice implies his conviction of the reality of divine justice, on his first ('Auf mich fällt der Donner des Richters') and on his last appearance ('Von mir nicht, von mir nicht, Richter der Welt, fodre diese Seelen von diesem!'). Miller invokes the divine judge twice in the last act, and Luise exclaims, 'wenn ... das jüngste Gericht Majestäten und Bettler in dem nämlichen Siebe rüttle' (III. vi). Ferdinand deals even more frequently and urgently in divine judgement, as something present here and now. 'Ich will sie führen vor des Weltrichters Thron', he says of Luise. In the blackest moment of his murderous resolve he thrice addresses God as 'Richter der Welt', twice repeating the phrase 'das Mädchen ist mein!', and demonstrating his metaphysical megalomania with 'Ich einst ihr Gott, jetzt ihr Teufel'. Ferdinand sees himself as the instrument of God, executing His punishment; for, though His justice, in contrast to that of men, is not cruel, yet God is a severe and stern avenger: 'Die Rache des Himmels unterschreibt, ihr guter Engel läßt sie fahren.' The insistence with which Gott and Teufel, Engel and Teufel, Himmel and Hölle recur antithetically in the play is a reminder that Schiller's world, even in this play, is a religious one. Moreover, it is a world of metaphysical conflict; the hosts of light and the powers of darkness wage a fierce and protracted battle which, though it destroys the human protagonists, yet ends in the victory of the divine.

Yet, if Kabale und Liebe is concerned with man in his relationship to God, it is also a play in which the shortcomings and the hollowness of the social structure are repeatedly suggested by a pattern of words. The mirror[1] is a symbol of insincerity, an image without reality. Its fullest social significance is seen in the striking stage direction in Act Four, according to which Lady Milford intentionally views Luise in her mirror before she turns to address her. And a similar purpose is served, especially from the fourth act on, by the proliferating words of disguise, suggesting the concealment of a sinister or repulsive reality. The characteristic word is Larve with its derivative entlarvt, already

[1] The image occurs six times.

familiar from *Fiesco*; these are plentifully supplemented by *Grimasse*, *Schminke*, *Firnis*, *Hülle*, *Farbe*, and *Puppe*.

The zoological vocabulary, too, has affinities with *Fiesco*. The noble predators, except for the isolated mention of the tiger, are absent. The subtle serpent and the insidious insect prevail in a play in which evil pursues a sinuous course and approaches unperceived. *Natter*, *Schlange*, *Skorpion*, *Insekt*, and *Spinne* populate the literary vivarium of *Kabale und Liebe*; *kriechen* is conspicuous as a verb, and even the innocent are represented by the *Wurm*, trodden beneath the heel of the aggressor. It is not chance either that one of the characters, a creature subtle, ingenious, and deadly, should bear the name 'Wurm', which has here its other sense, of the serpent going upon his belly.

## 5. FORMS OF ADDRESS

*Kabale und Liebe* contains a huge number of forms of address[1], and their abundance stresses an important aspect of the play. Address emphasizes human relationships and points to the social structure. Thus Lady Milford observes punctiliously the conventions, addressing Ferdinand as 'Herr Major', 'Walter', and 'Herr von Walter', indicating by these variations shifts of mood and stance, but preserving the framework of decorum intact. Miller, on the other hand, maintains the forms (or what he takes to be the forms) towards his superiors, but lets himself go without a trace of inhibition within the four walls of his family life. 'Infame Kupplerin', 'du Rabenaas', 'blaues Donnermaul', and 'alte Heulhure' are among the choicer appellations which he directs at his wife. Wurm's familiar address in Act Five, in which he speaks to the Präsident as 'dummer Bösewicht', 'Kamerad', and 'Bube', represents the breakdown under stress of the social boundaries, which have hitherto fenced apart noblemen, agent, and humble musician.

The commonest forms of address, however, are those involving the relationship of parent and child. 'Vater', 'mein Vater', 'meine Tochter', and minor variants of these occur in great profusion;

---

[1] There are approximately 550 of them.

and the insistence with which Ferdinand, Luise, and Miller insert one or more in almost every speech they make forcefully and repeatedly reminds the spectator of the importance which the family relationship has for them. The actively unsatisfactory parent, the Präsident, is much more sparing with expressions such as 'mein Sohn', preferring 'Junge', 'junger Mensch', even 'vorlauter Knabe', or no address at all. He opts for 'mein Sohn' only when he is simulating a solicitude he does not feel.

Besides revealing character and expressing temper and mood, address can sometimes serve to underline the shift to exalted speech. When Lady Milford addresses Ferdinand as 'Jüngling', when Luise interpolates 'Unbesonnener' in speaking to her lover, or says to Wurm, 'Geh, Barbar!', it is clear that we have withdrawn from the sphere of realistic language. And Ferdinand reinforces the point in retorting to her with 'Schlange' and addressing her father as 'Graukopf'. Such appellations are in harmony with the passages of rhetoric. These instances of poetic address are, however, remarkably few, and the familiar 'mein Vater' or 'meine Tochter' occurs again and again in elevated speeches. These simple forms seem to act as an element of unity, persisting even when the style sweeps upward.

It is Schiller's feat to have endowed the divergent types of speech in *Kabale und Liebe* with sufficient common elements to ensure its ability to function as a unity. He achieves it by a strain of exaggeration in the realistic passages, by the persistence of certain patterns such as triadic structures, by the pervasiveness of the rhythm, and, lastly, by the predominantly realistic forms of address, which unify the tone.

It is the remarkable verve of Schiller's colloquial dialogue, especially in the opening scene, that has attracted understandable attention from many commentators.[1] In *Die Räuber* and *Fiesco* he had written occasional touches of common speech, but these are embedded in longer stretches of conventional or elevated language. In *Kabale und Liebe* he writes in certain scenes a continuous dialogue of realistic idiom with such skill that it

[1] Cf. especially Erich Auerbach, *Mimesis*, 3rd edn., 1964, pp. 404–12.

could easily be imagined to be a climax of long experience, instead of a sudden unprepared début. The *tour de force* is truly astonishing. Its brilliance can divert the eye from other even more important aspects. One must resist the temptation to see the linguistic shift from realism to rhetoric as a derogation from the original design, or to interpret Schiller's tragedy as a failure to write the powerful realistic play of social conflict a century before its eventual emergence. Can it really be thought that Schiller, in *Kabale und Liebe*, missed the chance to create a new drama ? The historical perspective makes it clear that he did not. The favourable ambience was lacking. And the two truly European literatures of that time, English and French, give no support to the view that a drama of class struggle in realistic terms was conceivable. What is even more certain is that it was not open to a dramatist of Schiller's temperament and gifts to write a realistic tragedy. Realism was for him a subsidiary adjunct. If treated in prolongation it became a distraction; it focused attention on irrelevancies, as he could see only too well in the plays of Lenz.

The tragedies Schiller admired, *Julius von Tarent* and *Emilia Galotti*, restricted their realism to deft touches, employing an over-all style which, though not attaining Schiller's heights of rhetoric, is elevated above the plane of everyday speech. Lessing's play must certainly have haunted the background of Schiller's mind at this time, for at least four reflections of *Emilia Galotti* are discernible in *Kabale und Liebe*. The unmistakable resemblance of Ferdinand's progressive 'Gezwungen, Lady? Gezwungen gab? und also doch gab?' (II.iii) to Odoardo's 'Schlimmer? schlimmer als tot — Aber doch zugleich auch tot?' (*Emilia Galotti*, IV. vii) has been remarked by H. O. Burger and W. Höllerer, who have also pointed out the close resemblance between Wurm's 'Ich werd einmal eine fromme christliche Frau an ihr haben' (I. ii) and Appiani's 'Ich werde eine fromme Frau an Ihnen haben' (*EG* II. vii).[1] To these must be added Wurm's 'wenn Sie mir freie Hand lassen wollen' (III. i), which is too

---

[1] *NA* 5. 222; the resemblance has since also been noted by G. Storz, op. cit., p. III.

similar in situation as well as phrasing to Marinelli's 'Wollen Sie
mir freie Hand lassen, Prinz?' for the likelihood of a reminiscence
to be discarded. And Luise's description of 'Die Paläste gewisser
Damen' as 'die Freistätten der frechsten Ergötzlichkeit', though
remote in phrasing, also suggests an echo of Emilia's misgivings
(*EG* v. vii).

Schiller's aim in *Kabale und Liebe* was an intense and violently
cathartic tragedy, and the means available to him were winged
rhetoric and strong emphasis. The unadulterated realism of the
opening is a setting of tone, a piece of genre painting which could
be indulged in only at this point, when the tension is not yet
engaged. Once the drama is fully in motion, the realistic speech
occurs either as a useful auxiliary and foil (in II. vi and vii) or at
a static moment as in Act Five. Far from losing his way in
*Kabale und Liebe*, Schiller has contrived a masterpiece of stylistic
counterpoint. That in doing so he gratified his own impulse
towards exaltation of language is certain; but this does not
detract from the achievement.

The language in this play also serves a purpose which is new
to Schiller's dramatic work. In *Die Räuber* the scene had ranged
from room to forest to river bank and back again; in *Fiesco* the
characteristic townscape of Genoa, the port, had played its
part in the action; scenic mobility had kept both plays open.
*Kabale und Liebe* is totally enclosed. Every scene takes place
within four walls. These man-made barriers are a symbol of
society, which confines each one of the characters, even the
prosperous. But the play must find some way of reaching beyond
the walls, some means firstly of establishing the extension of
society beyond these cabined limits and secondly of asserting the
higher standard of right and wrong which are Schiller's constant
preoccupation. Language is the instrument by which this extension is attained, in repeated extramural reference, the crass-
ness of which ensures that it is heeded, in the repeated association
of the divine and the judicial, and above all in the disconformity
between the rhetorical tone and the visual realism of costume and
furniture.

# IV · DON CARLOS

## I. THE CHANGE TO VERSE

FROM prose to verse, from the Germany of Schiller's own day to the Spain of two centuries earlier—it seems a far cry. Yet *Kabale und Liebe* and *Don Carlos* are at least closely linked in time. When Schiller arrived in Bauerbach in December 1782 his *Luise Millerin* was still in the making and two months of writing went by before he was ready to suggest to his correspondents that the work was finished (in reality he did not complete it until late July 1784). Yet, as early as 9 December 1782 he had written to Reinwald, the Meiningen librarian, asking for the loan of a life of Don Carlos. Since Schiller had contemplated this subject five months before[1] as the subject for a possible future tragedy, it is virtually certain that this request represents a stage in the germination of *Don Carlos*. By March 1783 he had discarded two other ideas[2] with which he had toyed, and by mid April he was rapturously committed to Carlos. Thus, Schiller's social drama, with its doses of crude realism, and his first essay in historical verse tragedy were for a time bedfellows.

This remarkable overlap is offset by the unusually protracted duration of the writing. In the *Briefe über Don Carlos* Schiller claimed that plays should be written straight through in a concentrated burst of a few months: 'ein dramatisches Werk kann und soll nur die Blüte eines einzigen Sommers sein.' In fact, *Don Carlos* had taken him four years. The long span and piecemeal publication resulted in a play of complex, overloaded action. He conceded that he had kept at it too long—'Der Hauptfehler war,

---

[1] Letter to Dalberg, 15 July 1782 (Jonas, 1. 63).
[2] Imhof and Maria Stuart (Letter to Reinwald, 27 March 1783, Jonas, 1. 107).

ich hatte mich zu lange mit dem Stücke getragen'— and he acknowledged the deviations of plan—'es kann mir begegnet sein, daß ich in den ersten Akten andere Erwartungen erregt habe, als ich in den letzten erfüllte.' Schiller's disarming frankness stops short of admission that the play had lost its coherence and the *Briefe über Don Carlos* are a spirited defence of its essential unity, which, however, has not found universal acceptance.[1] Some have gone so far as to view the work as a group of magnificent but inadequately integrated scenes.[2]

It is no use pretending that the inconsistencies are not there,[3] or that the completed *Don Carlos* is what a reader of the scenes in *Die Thalia*[4] could reasonably expect. Yet, when all the admissions have been made, the impact of the play remains so strong that it must clearly be something better than a great design vitiated by inadequate linkages and faulty motivation. Though the faults are detected, they are not keenly felt. The shift is perceived as a widening rather than as a change of course.

What holds *Don Carlos* together and unifies its apparently divergent elements is something which, surprisingly, has never had its full due—Schiller's verse. Almost every interpretation pays brief tribute to it, praises its *élan* or its beauty, notes its rhythms, its sweep, or its terseness, shaking perhaps a reproving finger at its repetitive loquacity.[5] The verse figures as a minor aspect of studies which are chiefly occupied with ideas, characters, or conflicts. No one will deny the value of these, but Schiller's verse deserves also to be treated as an essential and significant feature of *Don Carlos*.

In the three preceding prose plays, rhythm had played its part. But it had inevitably been irregular, fitful, and spasmodic. Through *Don Carlos* there runs for the first time the measured beat of an iambic pulse. The metre was not there from the start.

[1] Cf. G. Storz, op. cit., p. 147.
[2] Cf. W. Witte, *Schiller*, 1949, p. 146.
[3] They are well analysed in L. Bellermann, *Schillers Dramen. Beiträge zu ihrem Verständnis*, 1891, i. 252–70.
[4] Nos. 1 and 2.
[5] Cf. K. Berger, *Schiller*, 1905, i. 256; G. Storz, op. cit., pp. 132–3; B. v. Wiese, op. cit., p. 277; W. Witte, op. cit., p. 138.

When Schiller wrote to Reinwald on 9 December 1782 asking for de Saint-Réal's *Histoire de Dom Carlos* he undoubtedly contemplated writing the new play in the vigorous prose which he knew how to handle with such ease and skill. The first evidence of a change to verse is contained in Schiller's letter of 24 August 1784 written to Wolfgang Heribert von Dalberg: 'froh bin ich, daß ich nunmehr so ziemlich Meister über den Jamben bin; Es kann nicht fehlen, daß der Vers meinem Karlos sehr viel Würde und Glanzgeben wird'.[1] This enthusiastic adherence to iambic verse follows upon equally ardent applause for 'die hohe Tragödie' as his own proper field in preference to the prose domestic drama which he now slightingly terms 'die Schranken des bürgerlichen Kothurns'.

The impulse to this new attitude and declaration of faith is believed to have come from Wieland in his *Briefe an einen jungen Dichter*,[2] to which Schiller refers in the 'Vorrede' in *Die rheinische Thalia*. Here Schiller accepts Wieland's demand for verse, while decisively rejecting his championship of rhyme. And *Don Carlos* is in fact written in what Schiller calls in this preface 'reimfreien Jamben'.

When Schiller began to write *Don Carlos* in verse, he had few models before him. Oddly enough, in view of Wieland's espousal of rhyme, one of the few blank-verse plays was Wieland's *Lady Johanna Gray*, published in 1758; the outstanding example was Lessing's *Nathan der Weise*, which had appeared in 1779. Schiller does not seem to have owed anything to Wieland's and Lessing's blank verse except the stimulus to adopt the form. His mind was doubtless poised for this step and needed nothing more than an impulse from without. The resultant verse is highly distinct and idiosyncratic. In its power, eloquence, and flexibility, it is little short of miraculous. For Schiller's verse, as revealed up to this point in his poetry, is harsh and congested, whilst the available blank-verse models are pedestrian.

The first characteristic of Schiller's verse in *Don Carlos* is its

---

[1] Jonas, 1. 208.
[2] Published in *Der teutsche Merkur*, 1782,

disregard of the line as a rhythmic unit. Periods begin or end without apparent reference to the pentametric structure. The pattern is set in the opening lines:

Die schönen Tage in Aranjuez
Sind nun zu Ende. Eure königliche Hoheit
Verlassen es nicht heiterer. Wir sind
Vergebens hier gewesen. Brechen Sie
Dies rätselhafte Schweigen. Öffnen Sie
Ihr Herz dem Vaterherzen, Prinz.... (ll. 1–6)

The succession of simple sentences slurs the 'natural' ending of the lines, setting the visual and aural patterns at variance. Aware that such rhythmic waywardness could develop into an irritating mannerism, Schiller then allows the next period to reassert the linear structure:

Zu teuer
Kann der Monarch die Ruhe seines Sohns —
Des einzgen Sohns, — zu teuer nie erkaufen. (ll. 6–8)

This opening passage is devoid of emotional tension. Much greater flexibility marks the passages of stress. Carlos, having confessed to Posa his love for his stepmother, expresses his agony of hopeless commitment and anguished self-accusation with

Nein! Diese Schonung will ich nicht. Sprichs aus,
Sprich, daß auf diesem großen Rund der Erde
Kein Elend an das meine grenze — sprich — (ll. 272–4)

Here the triple articulation of the first line and the framing of the long impetuous clause between the retarding repetitions of *sprich* impart to the verse an impressive range of tempo.

The divergence between line and period, and hence between metre and rhythm, underlies the dialogue between Posa and Carlos in the Charterhouse, where information is sought and given, and emotions, though ardent, are tautly restrained:

CARLOS. Ach endlich einmal, endlich —
MARQUIS.                                    Welche Prüfung
Für eines Freundes Ungeduld! Die Sonne
Ging zweimal auf und zweimal unter, seit

> Das Schicksal meines Carlos sich entschieden,
> Und jetzt, erst jetzt werd ich es hören — Sprich,
> Ihr seid versöhnt?
> CARLOS.                    Wer?
> MARQUIS.                        Du und König Philipp;
> Und auch mit Flandern ists entschieden?
> CARLOS.                                    Daß
> Der Herzog morgen dahin reist? — Das ist
> Entschieden, ja.                              (ll. 2265-73)

The natural phrasing here so completely overrides the linear grouping that at three points not a vestige of pause at the end of a line is possible. Indeed, twice the monosyllabic conjunction ('seit, daß') strikes in on the final stress and demands the instant entry of the subject.

Similar 'irregular structure' permeates the verse in which Carlos arraigns his king and father after the murder of Posa (v. iv) and Posa's elegiac parting from the Queen:

> Den König geb ich auf. Was kann ich auch
> Dem König sein? — In diesem starren Boden
> Blüht keine meiner Rosen mehr — Europas
> Verhängnis reift in meinem großen Freunde!
> Auf ihn verweis ich Spanien — Es blute
> Bis dahin unter Philipps Hand!               (ll. 4317-22)

Equally heedless of the linear units are the passages of rapid dialogue, in which the speech is distributed in fragments among two or more interlocutors.

The predominance of interrupted lines, of elided line endings, and of periods apparently heedless of the basic pattern provokes the question of why Schiller bothered to adopt the metrical form; why he should have had these irregular groupings printed in a regular design which they appear to violate. There would, indeed, have been no point if irregularity had been universal. The basic pattern proves not to be irrelevant, and the irregularity would lose its potency if it were not perceptibly the variation of a regularity. This is the function of the perfect line-units which occur in some number throughout the play. Thus Domingo, in his opening speech, follows his sequence of cross-rhythms with the couplet:

> Wär noch ein Wunsch zurücke, den der Himmel
> Dem liebsten seiner Söhne weigerte? (ll. 9–10)

And Carlos's passionate eloquence interpolates in a passage of irregularity a complete line of rapid speech:

> Was du mir sagen kannst, errat ich schon. (l. 275)

Moreover, from time to time groups of two to four lines of polished rhetoric intervene to provide a reminder of the underlying pattern. So Posa exclaims:

> Auf Kaiser Karls glorwürdgem Enkel ruht
> Die letzte Hoffnung dieser edeln Lande.
> Sie stürzt dahin, wenn sein erhabnes Herz
> Vergessen hat, für Menschlichkeit zu schlagen. (ll. 164–7)

Or Philipp similarly addresses Posa with

> Ich will den Jüngling, der sich übereilte,
> Als Greis und nicht als König widerlegen. (ll. 3265–6)

Such touches of regularity serve to insist upon the basic underlying pattern, asserting its continuing validity beneath the kaleidoscopic variations of shifting word-groups. In thus maintaining the interplay of regularity and irregularity, of law and freedom, Schiller has provided a potent unifying factor. The basic pulse confers on the play a sense of unity which persists even when the action is confused, the utterances of the characters contradictory, and their motives obscure. It is a pattern which holds together and harmonizes the diversities of the play.

## 2. DECLAMATION AND CONVERSATION

Though the verse of *Don Carlos* can express lofty rhetoric, it can also reproduce the inflections and the terseness of ordinary speech. It is ruled throughout by an assured tact. For all the elevation, the inflation of bombast hardly occurs. It may be that when Philipp exclaims,

> Ich heiße
> Der reichste Mann in der getauften Welt;
> Die Sonne geht in meinem Staat nicht unter,                    (ll. 861–3)

we hear the attitudinizing of the stage tyrant rather than the living Philipp that Schiller has otherwise so subtly drawn. And there are perhaps one or two other similarly flawed passages,[1] but these are negligible blemishes in this immense play of more than 5,000 lines.

The most consistent executant of lofty speech is Posa. And here we detect one of Schiller's most subtle stylistic devices for characterization. The pulse of rhythm unifies the work, the tone distinguishes the characters. The verse spoken by Posa repeatedly reveals a dramatic attitude, a mind leaning towards statuesque posture, conscious noble bearing, and even to acting a part. This note is heard as soon as he begins to touch the political theme. Hardly has he met Carlos and exchanged a few private words than he bursts into a set speech:

> Das ist
> Der löwenkühne Jüngling nicht, zu dem
> Ein unterdrücktes Heldenvolk mich sendet —
> Denn jetzt steh ich als Roderich nicht hier,
> Nicht als des Knaben Carlos Spielgeselle —
> Ein Abgeordneter der ganzen Menschheit
> Umarm ich Sie — es sind die flandrischen
> Provinzen, die an Ihrem Halse weinen
> Und feierlich um Rettung Sie bestürmen.                    (ll. 152–60)

The same elevated tone pervades the climax of Posa's audience with Philipp, beginning:

> Geben Sie,
> Was Sie uns nahmen, wieder. Lassen Sie,
> Großmütig wie der Starke, Menschenglück
> Aus Ihrem Füllhorn strömen — Geister reifen
> In Ihrem Weltgebäude....

[1] Perhaps the tub-thumping lines finishing 'Dies Blutgericht soll ohne Beispiel sein' (ll. 895–9) might be reckoned a further example.

and culminating with

> Werden Sie uns Muster
> Des Ewigen und Wahren!                    (ll. 3195–209)

It is the eloquence of the gifted speaker carried away by the flood of his own oratory. The refrain 'Geben Sie...', occurring three times, is not a calculated stroke, but the predominating motif in a torrent of enthusiasm. 'Great' words with intoxicating associations for Schiller abound—'Großmütig', 'Menschenglück', 'Weltgebäude', 'dieser großen Stunde', 'Des Ewigen und Wahren'. Sublime numbers, 'Millionen', 'Tausende,' add their weight and are reinforced by the magically evocative words of Schiller's rhetoric, 'Strahl' and 'Flamme'. This compendium of Schiller's exalted speech is perfectly placed in the mouth of this enthusiast, whose raptures are political and idealistic.

A warmer, more emotional rhetoric pervades the utterances of Carlos. It is characterized by speed and impetuosity, which, however, are often checked by the semblance of a sob or a catch in the throat. It maintains its elevation by the discreet use of 'poetic' phrasing and familiar formal patterns, such as the triad, as is apparent in the following address by Carlos to the Queen:

> Ein Wink,
> Ein halber Blick, ein Laut aus Ihrem Munde
> Gebietet mir zu sein und zu vergehen.
> Was wollen Sie, daß noch geschehen soll?
> Was unter dieser Sonne kann es geben,
> Daß ich nicht hinzuopfern eilen will,
> Wenn Sie es wünschen?                       (ll. 644–50)

Here the formality is blended into a flexible pattern of crescendo and diminuendo, of accelerando and rallentando, with pauses in which the heart is too full to speak.

Though the tone in which Carlos attempts to storm the remote fortress of his father's suspicion is more exalted, the general characteristics are similar, with the refrain of 'Jetzt oder nie!',

the variations of tempo, and the beloved image of the 'Sonnen-
strahl':

> Jetzt oder nie! — Wir sind allein.
> Der Etikette bange Scheidewand
> Ist zwischen Sohn und Vater eingesunken.
> Jetzt oder nie! Ein Sonnenstrahl der Hoffnung
> Glänzt in mir auf, und eine süße Ahnung
> Fliegt durch mein Herz.                    (ll. 1057–62)

The note of impassioned rhetoric, of inspired exaltation
infusing these passages, is the most familiar aspect of Schiller's
verse. It is less often realized that he is in this, his first attempt,
a master of the difficult art of using colloquial language in verse.
In almost every scene we hear at some point the accents of
ordinary speech, yet these touches of realism are perfectly
integrated in the flow of the verse.

The simplest case is the communication of fact. Posa puts his
plan to help Carlos to a tête-à-tête with the Queen in straightforward, almost commonplace, terms:

> Wie man sagt,
> Will der Monarch zur Stadt zurücke kehren.
> Die Zeit ist kurz. Wenn Sie die Königin
> Geheim zu sprechen wünschen, kann es nirgends
> Als in Aranjuez geschehn.                    (ll. 363–7)

The simple syntax, the plain vocabulary of these lines, could pass
as prose if printed as such—or almost; only two slight details
(*Monarch* for *König* and the third syllable of *zurücke*) hint at a
process of transformation. The other two brief sentences are
impeccably colloquial.

Sometimes the touch of every day appears faintly and casually
as in the 'sehr viel' of Carlos's

> ich habe sehr viel Unglück
> Mit meinen Müttern.                    (ll. 30–1)

The tone is ironical and such expressions are particularly potent
in colloquial form, as in Carlos's reserved 'Glauben Sie?' in
reply to Domingo's 'Die Nachricht würde schmerzen'. Even

more obviously colloquial is the emphasized demonstrative pronoun in Carlos's words to Princess Eboli:

Auch sogar *der*? Ja, freilich, gute Fürstin,
Für *den* besonders war das nicht.                    (ll. 1704–5)

And Carlos, in addressing Domingo, gives his irony aggressive point with an interjection:

Also geben Sie
Mich lieber auf. Sie sind ein heilger Mann,
Das weiß die Welt — doch frei heraus — für mich
Sind Sie bereits zu überhäuft.                    (ll. 99–102)

Yet irony alone does not account for the striking incidence of colloquial phrasing. The Duchess Olivarez raises the question of Princess Eboli's marriage in two lines of virtual prose:

Prinzessin Eboli, Sie haben uns
Noch nicht gesagt, ob Gomez hoffen darf? —

and the Queen responds a moment later with

Ja! Gut, daß Sie uns mahnen, Herzogin.                    (ll. 434–7)

Posa, as he is introduced into the audience chamber, addresses Alba in speech of a negligence which expresses contempt:

Mich will er haben? Mich — Das kann nicht sein.
Sie irren sich im Namen — Und was will
Er denn von mir?                    (ll. 2941–3)

The impatient garrulity of Princess Eboli, irritated at the silence of the page Henarez, pours itself out in a torrent of the simplest everyday sentences:

Du sprachst mit ihm? Heraus damit! Was sprach er?
Wie nahm er sich? Was waren seine Worte?
Er schien verlegen, schien bestürzt? Erriet
Er die Person, die ihm den Schlüssel schickte?
Geschwinde — oder riet er nicht? Er riet
Wohl gar nicht? riet auf eine falsche? — Nun?
Antwortest du mir denn kein Wort? O pfui,
Pfui, schäme dich.                    (ll. 1472–9)

And in calmer conversational tones she devises her part in the plot:

> In eingen Tagen werd ich krank; man trennt mich
> Von der Person der Königin — das ist
> An unserm Hofe Sitte, wie Sie wissen.
> Ich bleibe dann auf meinem Zimmer. (ll. 2210–13)

Carlos, for his part, evades the princess's too impetuous intrusion into his secret life with the dignified, remote, and yet colloquial

> Sie tun mir Unrecht, Fürstin. Das war Andacht. (l. 1720)

And Alba comments on Domingo's political astuteness with

> Ihre Blicke reichen
> Sehr weit. (ll. 2038–9)

Here the colloquial realism, emphasized by the conjuncture of the two unaccented syllables at line ending and beginning, momentarily deranges the rhythm of the verse.

Simple everyday language is often used to express the upsurge of emotion. Phillipp, when deeply moved by Posa's pleading, responds in short, gradually expanding sentences:

> Nein!
> Nein, Marquis! Ihr tut mir zu viel. Ich will
> Nicht Nero sein. Ich will es nicht sein — will
> Es gegen Euch nicht sein. (ll. 3272–5)

Earlier, Carlos, faced with Elisabeth's determined and dignified resistance, replies in broken phrasing which corresponds to his inner turmoil:

> Das ist was anders — Dann — ja, dann Vergebung.
> Das wußt ich nicht, daß Sie den König lieben. (ll. 710–11)

Conversational, too, are many of the quick interchanges, such as the high-speed dialogue at the climax of the chapter of misunderstandings between Carlos and Princess Eboli:

> EBOLI.    Meinen Brief
> Und meinen Schlüssel geben Sie mir wieder.
> Wo haben Sie den andern Brief?

CARLOS. Den andern?
Was denn für einen andern?
EBOLI. Den vom König.
CARLOS. Von *wem*?
EBOLI. Den Sie vorhin von mir bekamen.
CARLOS. Vom König? und an wen? an Sie?
EBOLI. O Himmel!
Wie schrecklich hab ich mich verstrickt! Den Brief!
Heraus damit! ich muß ihn wieder haben. (ll. 1867–74)

The dialogue between Carlos and Lerma (IV. iv), in which Lerma tries to warn the prince against the supposed machinations of Posa and encounters almost hostile politeness, is a perfect reproduction of dignified and haughty real utterance:

CARLOS. Von wem
Ist denn die Rede?
LERMA. Marquis Posa —
CARLOS. Nun?
LERMA. Wenn etwa mehr, als jemand wissen darf,
Von Eurer Hoheit ihm bewußt sein sollte,
Wie ich beinahe fürchte —
CARLOS. Wie Sie fürchten?
LERMA. — Er war beim König.
CARLOS. So?
LERMA. Zwo volle Stunden
Und in sehr heimlichem Gespräch.
CARLOS. Wahrhaftig?
LERMA. Es war von keiner Kleinigkeit die Rede.
CARLOS. Das will ich glauben.
LERMA. Ihren Namen, Prinz,
Hört ich zu öftern Malen.
CARLOS. Hoffentlich
Kein schlimmes Zeichen. (ll. 3526–36)

And perhaps even more striking than this disdainful stonewalling is Carlos's rejoinder, made a few moments before, to Lerma's reference to a friend:

Den ich
Nicht wüßte! — Wie? Was wollen Sie damit? (ll. 3520–21)

Here is all the terseness and ellipsis of idiomatic speech.

Equally impressive is the almost photographic realism of the dialogue of evasion and suspicion between Carlos and Posa in the next scene (IV. v). In embarrassed fragmentary phrases Posa gives a misleading and evasive summary of his momentous interview with Philipp:

> Der? Nicht viel. — Neugierde,
> Zu wissen, wer ich bin — Dienstfertigkeit
> Von unbestellten guten Freunden. Was
> Weiß ich? Er bot mir Dienste an.          (ll. 3574–7)

His speech is monosyllabically reluctant: twice a belated *ja*; a *Der*, echoing Carlos, gives him time for thought; 'ziemlich gut' and 'Doch ja. Im allgemeinen' enable him to retreat into vagueness. This dialogue, if printed in prose, could do duty in a naturalistic play, and yet it maintains throughout the regular iambic rhythm. The colloquialism of all these examples brings no interruption; it is fully integrated into the metrical pattern. Its purpose is to distribute through the play points of realistic reference.

### 3. THE MEDIAL TONE

Rhetoric and common speech belong to different, even opposed, conceptions of art. It might seem that here the familiar dualism of Schiller's creative imagination manifests itself. These two contrasting elements do not, however, stand out detached, they are carried along in the continuous medium of the play, the iambic verse. And this fluid element has not only subdued the starkness of the stylistic contrast between the rhetorical and the realistic; it has led to the development of a third and fully harmonious tone in which the apparently discordant factors are merged and transformed into a style of speech which simultaneously has touches of elevation and traces of actuality.

I call this important fusion 'the medial tone'. It occurs both in calm and in emotional passages. It can correspond to great self-control, as when Carlos denounces Alba's political cruelty and does it with studied and purposeful moderation:

Gott oder Teufel, gilt gleich viel! Sie waren
Sein rechter Arm. Ich weiß das wohl — und jetzt
Nichts mehr davon. Ich bitte. Vor gewissen
Erinnerungen möcht ich gern mich hüten. —
Ich ehre meines Vaters Wahl. Mein Vater
Braucht einen Alba; *daß* er diesen braucht,
Das ist es nicht, warum ich ihn beneide.
Sie sind ein großer Mann — Auch das mag sein;
Ich glaub es fast. Nur, fürcht ich, kamen Sie
Um wenige Jahrtausende zu zeitig.                (ll. 1430–9)

Here the style is not far removed from the colloquial. The
sentences are brief and plain. The language is bare of images.
Yet signs of elevation are identifiable—in the numerical concept
of 'Jahrtausende', in the careful choice of vocabulary, which,
though simple, is also refined. It could be considered common
speech turned by discipline into an art form. The successful
fusion is perhaps epitomized by the two lines which follow:

Ein Alba, sollt ich meinen, war der Mann,
Am Ende aller Tage zu erscheinen!                (ll. 1440–1)

In this the elevated, eschatological, note is expressed with perfect
simplicity.

Domingo unveils to Alba his misgivings and apprehensions for
the future, using the 'poetic tone' in a passage of improvised, yet
measured, dialectic:

Und Sie so ruhig? so gelassen? — Kennen
Sie diesen Jüngling? Ahnen Sie, was uns
Erwartet, wenn er mächtig wird? — Der Prinz —
— Ich bin sein Feind nicht. Andre Sorgen nagen
An meiner Ruhe, Sorgen für den Thron,
Für Gott und seine Kirche.                       (ll. 2009–14)

The shaping and movement reveal colloquial patterns, but the
vocabulary ('mächtig wird' for 'come to power', 'Thorn', 'Gott',
'Kirche', 'rasenden Entwurf') discreetly elevates it.

Frequently the measured or medial manner employs the
techniques of rhetoric, yet its controlled rhythm, even tone, and
simple moulding differentiate it from the passages of soaring

eloquence. So Philipp, speaking to Posa, combines the colloquial
with a chiasmus:

> Euch ziemt
> Es, so zu denken, so zu handeln, mir.                    (ll. 3822–3)

And he continues with antitheses and parallelisms, yet the scope,
restraint, and directness of his words reveal pure communication, not the gesture before an onlooker, not even before
himself:

> Was Ihr in wenig Stunden mir gewesen,
> War er in einem Menschenalter nicht.
> Ich will nicht heimlich tun mit meinem Wohgefallen;
> Das Siegel meiner königlichen Gunst
> Soll hell und weit auf Eurer Stirne leuchten.            (ll. 3824–8)

It seems likely that the bold inclusion here of an iambic hexameter heightens the impression of purposeful adaptation.

It is in the emotional passages that Schiller's 'medial tone' attains
its most winning and persuasive eloquence. Here he underplays
his hand, achieving concentrated expression by short pregnant
sentences, clear formulation, and a careful vocabulary, almost
devoid of images:

> Jetzt gib mir einen Menschen, gute Vorsicht —
> Du hast mir viel gegeben. Schenke mir
> Jetzt einen Menschen. Du — du bist allein,
> Denn deine Augen prüfen das Verborgene —
> Ich bitte dich um einen Freund; denn ich
> Bin nicht, wie du, allwissend.                           (ll. 2809–14)

This prayer of Philipp's has the slow tempo of the man. Carlos,
with his more volatile temperament and in a more urgent
situation (v. i) expresses himself in a style of similar fusion:

> Du selbst wirst jetzt vollenden,
> Was ich gesollt und nicht gekonnt — Du wirst
> Den Spaniern die goldnen Tage schenken,
> Die sie von mir umsonst gehofft. Mit mir
> Ist es ja aus — auf immer aus. Das hast
> Du eingesehn — O diese fürchterliche Liebe
> Hat alle frühe Blüten meines Geistes
> Unwiederbringlich hingerafft . . . .                     (ll. 4506–13)

The tempo is at once swift and broken; the pauses and the precipitate utterance both testify to the fullness of the heart. The syntax is simple and straightforward. The poetic heightening of the passage comes from the *élan* of the tempo and from the use of evocative words ('vollenden', 'die goldnen Tage', 'umsonst gehofft', 'fürchterliche Liebe', 'unwiederbringlich'. The eloquence of Schiller's 'medial tone' is poised midway between the note of every day and the rhetoric of display. These provide patches of variation, moments of exaltation, and reminders of reality. But the over-all tone of the play is determined by the poetic style which has acquired nobility and yet not lost the common touch.

The perfection of this fluid continuum, which holds *Don Carlos* together, was not achieved immediately. It is the outcome of a maturing process in Schiller himself. Schiller began with a highly developed rhetoric of display, which can still be seen in the first act as it was originally published in *Die rheinische Thalia* in 1785. The taciturn, suspicious Carlos of the completed play, almost as silent and secretive as Hamlet, indulges, in the earliest version, in tirades of impassioned eloquence such as this, which refers to his relations with his father:

> Fließt mir deswegen eine einzge minder?
> Heilt dieses Herz vielleicht, wenn seines blutet?
> Nur Tränen hat er für den einzgen Sohn? —
> Die gibt auch wohl ein Bettler seinem Kinde.
> Er presse doch nur einen Tropfen Mohn
> Aus seines Perus unerschöpften Schachten,
> Den Schmerz in seinem Busen einzuschläfern; —
> Er biete doch den prahlenden Tribut,
> Den ihm sein furchtbarer Vasall, das Meer,
> Aus beiden Indien herüberfrönt,
> Ob er vielleicht den Henker seines Karls
> Damit bestechen kann?[1]

The triple question, neither pausing nor, indeed, wishing for any answer but the speaker's own, and the twin adhortatives with

[1] Schiller, *Sämtliche Werke*, ed. G. Fricke and H. G. Göpfert, Munich, 1958–9, ii. 1102.

their oblique (and only remotely relevant) allusions to Spanish colonial power are typical of a type of dramatic verse in which the fusion between the author and his character is incomplete. Schiller, imperfectly disguised as Carlos, yields to a temptation to harangue and perhaps secretly listens with some self-satisfaction to the tones in which he does it.

This style occurs only in the original first act of *Don Carlos*. By the time the second act appeared in *Die Thalia* (1786) the tones of the verse as we know it had brought a new tone of integrity to the language of the play. When, a year later, the whole work was published in book form, the first act had undergone a drastic revision. The first scene, especially, was reduced to little more than a third of its original length. No doubt it was dramatically out of balance, and the whole play was certainly too long; but the reduction was achieved by eliminating all that overpowering rhetorical language which Schiller, a master in the art of cutting,[1] could now see was not the true speech of the Carlos he had created, but a product of a temporary state of exaltation, felt in the solitude of Bauerbach and, in the play, irrelevant to character and situation.

Yet, in itself, rhetoric was far from unsuitable for this scene. What Schiller exercised was the impure speech in which the author, not Carlos, was implicated. Where rhetoric corresponded to character and situation it could be retained, as in the extended period in which Carlos's repressed emotions burst free from the torment of self-restraint:

> O zu gut,
> Zu gut weiß ich, daß ich an diesem Hof
> Verraten bin — ich weiß, daß hundert Augen
> Gedungen sind, mich zu bewachen, weiß,
> Daß König Philipp seinen einzgen Sohn
> An seiner Knechte schlechtesten verkaufte
> Und jede von mir aufgefangne Silbe
> Dem Hinterbringer fürstlicher bezahlt,
> Als er noch keine gute Tat bezahlte.          (ll. 107–15)

---

[1] Cf. H. B. Garland. 'Schiller the Revisionist—the poet's second thoughts', in *Reality and Creative Vision in German Lyrica Poetry*, ed. A. Closs, London 1963.

Apart from two minor verbal alterations, this passage from the *Don Carlos* of 1787 is identical with the corresponding lines in *Die Thalia*. The original then continued with a duplicating rhetorical speech, repeating with elaborations the pattern of 'Ich weiß, daß,...'. With one masterly stroke Schiller, in the final version, cuts this short, and interpolates a short passage which is both appropriate to character and related to real speech:

Ich weiß — O still! Nichts mehr davon! Mein Herz
Will überströmen, und ich habe schon
Zu viel gesagt.                                    (ll. 116–18)

Schiller was able, in his new feeling for stylistic relevance, to retain other passages, so long as their rhetorical mechanism gave a true instead of a distorted image of passion.

### 4. TOWARDS STICHOMYTHIA

The strongly developed dualism of Schiller's creative imagination expresses itself not only in the firm shaping of drama, but also in the ability to present the clash of character in terms of swift, aggressive dialogue. The gift was not apparent in *Die Räuber*, it began to develop in *Fiesco* and came into its own in *Kabale und Liebe*, achieving its first climax in the Präsident's invasion of the Millers' dwelling (II. vi and vii). That scene is a *tour de force* in which five conflicting voices are blended. In *Don Carlos*, more stylized in its general conception, Schiller preferred the form of the duel.

The distinct, clear opposition of single voice against single voice presents conflict in its purest form. The sharp, ringing interchange, the swift assertion, and immediate rejoinder are seen in the tormented dialogue between Carlos and the Queen (I. v):

KÖNIGIN. Er ist Ihr Vater.
CARLOS.                    Ihr Gemahl.
KÖNIGIN.                                      Der Ihnen
    Das größte Reich der Welt zum Erbe gibt.
CARLOS. Und *Sie* zur Mutter.                      (ll. 675–7)

The sharp clash, the rapier-like thrust, and counter-thrust

suggest the stichomythia of classical drama, even though the formal symmetry is absent. And one fundamental of the Greek device is fully realized. Pointed though the opposition is, the passage is a concerted movement, to which both parties contribute, as in a ballet or the art of fence. Formality and flexibility successfully co-exist.

Nowhere in *Don Carlos* does stichomythia appear in its pure form, but again and again approaches are made towards it. Thus we find in the same scene (I. v) a passage of 'unilateral' stichomythia, in which Carlos attacks, whilst the queen parries and evades, retreating before his onset:

CARLOS. Das wußt ich nicht, daß Sie den König lieben.
KÖNIGIN. Ihn ehren ist mein Wunsch und mein Vergnügen.
CARLOS. Sie haben nie geliebt?
KÖNIGIN.                           Seltsame Frage!
CARLOS. Sie haben nie geliebt?
KÖNIGIN.                           — Ich liebe nicht mehr.
CARLOS. Weil es Ihr Herz, weil es Ihr Eid verbietet?

(ll. 711–15)

At this point the one-sided fencing-match glides smoothly back into normal dialogue. There are several short passages of such duel-like character, and a very extensive and flexible one between Carlos and Lerma in Act IV. iv. The fullest use of stichomythic altercation occurs, however, in the fifth act, in the interview between Philipp and the Großinquisitor. After various onsets of contentious speech, which appear to shape for stichomythia only to recede again, the dialogue reaches a point of formal interchange, in which, however, question and answer replace thrust and counter-thrust:

KÖNIG. Kannst du mir einen neuen Glauben gründen,
    Der eines Kindes blutgen Mord verteidigt?
GROßINQUISITOR. Die ewige Gerechtigkeit zu sühnen,
    Starb an dem Holze Gottes Sohn.
KÖNIG.                           Du willst
    Durch ganz Europa diese Meinung pflanzen?
GROßINQUISITOR. So weit, als man das Kreuz verehrt ....

(ll. 5267–72)

In this passage Schiller adapts stichomythia to a new role, creating, by the deliberate abuse of the technique of catechism, a militant and formidable ritual. The clash of rapier against rapier is exchanged for the rhythm of hammer upon anvil. Repeatedly the alterations and arguments hover close to stichomythia, yet they never actually settle on the form. And the reason is plain. Of all Schiller's verse plays, *Don Carlos* is the one in which flux is most important. It is not only a matter of the great surges and tides; the flexible verse must conform to the little eddies and ripples, too, and this was the task of the 'poetic' tone, with which pure stichomythia, however impressive, was not compatible.

## 5. MEMORABILITY

Not all dramatic verse is memorable, but the potentiality to stamp itself indelibly upon the mind is an aspect in which it scores decisively over prose. This quality of impressing the memory may arise from perfection of form, economy of utterance, pregnancy of meaning, or incantatory phrasing. All these factors play their part in *Don Carlos*, which attains a remarkable standard of memorableness, literally from the first line to the last.

What is easily remembered must be short; and, for all the length of *Don Carlos*, Schiller achieves his individual effects by striking compression. So Posa exclaims,

> Mein Gebäude stürzt
> Zusammen — ich vergaß dein Herz,     (ll. 4526–7)

achieving pregnancy by a significant ellipsis. He uses two disjoined simple sentences, passing without transition from a common image to a statement charged with emotion. A similar suggestive juxtaposition is seen in Posa's assertion of his political power:

> Ich führe seine Siegel,
> Und seine Alba sind nicht mehr.     (ll. 4305–6)

These examples are open, causing resonances and revealing vistas. On the other hand, many of the most memorable lines are complete, rounded, balanced, implying nothing beyond their own limits. These often occur in couplet form, as in

> Ein Augenblick, gelebt im Paradies,
> Wird nicht zu teuer mit dem Tod gebüßt          (ll. 639–40)

or

> Die Wahrheit ist vorhanden für den Weisen,
> Die Schönheit für ein fühlend Herz.          (ll. 4364–5)

Such brief passages often have the character of *sententiae*, cogent and apposite formulations of moral truths. In the same category is the lapidary summarization of Posa:

> Der Freundschaft arme Flamme
> Füllt eines Posa Herz nicht aus. Das schlug
> Der ganzen Menschheit.          (ll. 5060–2)

A third source of memorable verse is the full and striking image, cunningly and compactly constructed of commonplace material. So Posa fixes Philipp's rigid opposition to change under the image of a vain attempt to check the impetus of a rolling wheel:

> Sie wollen —
> Allein in ganz Europa — sich dem Rade
> Des Weltverhängnisses, das unaufhaltsam
> In vollem Laufe rollt, entgegenwerfen?
> Mit Menschenarm in seine Speichen fallen?          (ll. 3166–70)

And Philipp's use of the bow has equally plastic quality—

> Ich bin der Bogen, bildet ihr euch ein,
> Den man nur spannen dürfe nach Gefallen.          (ll. 2771–2)

Lastly there is the crisp revelatory phrase, in which a terse and arresting group of words crystallizes a facet of character. Such lapidary fragments gleam through the rhythmical texture of every act. So Carlos's

> Wenn
> Sie Dank erwarten, gehen Sie zum König          (ll. 73–4)

suddenly focuses a light on the depth of his suspicions. His majesty and pride emerge in his imperious reproof to Alba:

> Meinen Degen
> Nehm ich aus solcher Hand nicht an. (ll. 4580–1)

Or Posa's infectious and irresistible confidence is perfectly compressed in

> Ein Federzug von dieser Hand, und neu
> Erschaffen wird die Erde. (ll. 3214–15)

Schiller displays a particular gift for bold ellipsis, reducing the formulation to a barest yet pregnant minimum, as we see when Philipp turns from Domingo to Alba:

> Toledo!
> Ihr seid ein Mann. Schützt mich vor diesem Priester. (ll. 2741–2)

Alba achieves powerful and memorable understatement in his

> Unterdessen geb ich
> Madrid den Frieden. (ll. 4880–1)

And the totality of Philipp's collapse is vividly conveyed in two terse and unforgettable sentences:

> Gib diesen Toten mir heraus. Ich muß
> Ihn wieder haben. (ll. 5016–17)

## 6. THE HELP OF SYNTAX

The most obvious syntactical feature of *Don Carlos* is the abundant repetition. This has sometimes been interpreted as the manner of a beginner, a device by which metrical correctness can be achieved when the sentences only partially fill out the pattern of the blank verse. This seems inadequate to account for a device which, in its emotive power, is so uniformly successful. Still, it is possible that Schiller did find the repetition of words the easiest, and sometimes the only, way of shaping his sentences into blank verse. But if so, he developed it into something much more vital and subtle than technical in-filling. For repetition, always a feature of Schiller's mental process in drama, becomes in *Don*

*Carlos* a powerful and flexible instrument of expression. Through all the revisions—and Schiller was savage in his cuts—the repetition has come through unscathed.

*Don Carlos* contains literally hundreds of instances of repetition.[1] They are least common in the third and fifth acts, most abundant in the second and fourth; the figures for the first act lie roughly in the middle. The number in the fourth act slightly exceeds that in the second. Since, although the acts were written in their proper order of succession, the fourth act shows the highest incidence of repetition, it is unlikely that this frequency was simply the consequence of unskilled workmanship. Moreover, in the first act the repetitions in the final book form are more numerous than in the original version in *Die rheinische Thalia*.

What then did Schiller gain by repeating so many words and phrases? Firstly the device gave him a means of emphasis. In Domingo's opening speech, in which all is calculation and the emotional temperature at zero, twice a repetition achieves an apparently spontaneous, but in truth deliberate, emphasis, so underlining the oblique subtlety of the priest's mind:

>                       Zu teuer
> Kann der Monarch die Ruhe seines Sohns —
> Des einzgen Sohns — zu teuer nie erkaufen.       (ll. 6–8)

This is to be quickly followed by:

> Und jetzt in *einem* — *einem* Niederfall.       (l. 14)

Any stylistic device can decline into a habit and eventually degenerate into a mannerism, and the frequency of the duplicated negative 'Nein, nein' may perhaps be explained in this way, since the simple 'Nein' is no less emphatic than the double form. Yet emphasis is not all, and the form 'Nein, nein', occurring many times, gives a note of impetuosity or agitation, which the single 'Nein' does not convey.

It is beyond doubt that the repetitive form of speech was

---

[1] Even if trivial or accidental recurrences are disregarded, there are still upwards of 300 instances in the play.

especially congenial to Schiller, a part, indeed, of his mental structure, something which corresponded to the vehemence which was an essential feature of his make-up. This habit of expression was then made to serve many purposes. Foremost among these are the expression of agitation, anxiety, urgency, mental disturbance of all kinds. We see it (in triple form) in Carlos's animated rejoinder to Posa's 'Auch meine Stunde schlägt vielleicht':

> Jetzt, jetzt —
> O zögre nicht — jetzt hat sie ja geschlagen. (ll. 263-4)

It sounds in Posa's more restrained excitement:

> jetzt, erst jetzt werd ich es hören. (l. 2269)

We hear it in the anguished urgency of Philipp's

> Ich schlage
> An diesen Felsen und will Wasser, Wasser
> Für meinen heißen Fieberdurst. (ll. 2515-17)

or in his insistent, panic-stricken triad:

> Stehn Sie auf.
> Erholen Sie sich! Stehn Sie auf! Man kommt!
> Man überrascht uns — Stehn Sie auf! (ll. 3803-5)

Repetition also provides Schiller with an indication of emotional stress. It expresses the fullness of the heart inhibiting fluent speech, so that the words come hesitantly and are interrupted by pauses suggesting a sob:

> Ja, es ist aus. Jetzt ist
> Es aus — Ich fühle klar und helle, was
> Mir ewig, ewig dunkel bleiben sollte.
> Sie sind für mich dahin — dahin — dahin —
> Auf immerdar. (ll. 745-9)

In Posa it appears as a catch in the voice, when, thrust for a moment from the pinnacle of his self-confidence, he exclaims:

> Nein! Das,
> Das hab ich nicht vorhergesehen — nicht
> Vorhergesehn, daß eines Freundes Großmut.... (ll. 4522-4)

And with Carlos overbrimming emotion checks the words he
speaks to the faithful Lerma:

> Nicht also —
> Nicht also, Graf — Sie rühren mich — Ich möchte
> Nicht gerne weich sein. (ll. 4941–3)

Sometimes the distraught mind uses the repetition at one and the
same time as a form of self-torment and an incitement to action.
This is especially conspicuous in Princess Eboli's long monologue in Act II. ix. It is first evident on the discovery that her
love is spurned:

> — verstoßen —
> Verworfen — Nein! Verdrungen nur, verdrungen
> Von einer Nebenbuhlerin. (ll. 1888–90)

It recurs when suspicion of the queen becomes conviction:

> Das sollte ungerochen
> Der Gauklerin gelungen sein? gelungen,
> Weil sich kein Rächer meldet? (ll. 1942–4)

And from this fury it is but a step, in the next scene, to the
concentrated anger and bitter resentment of

> da glaubte ich im Besitze
> Der schönsten Königin ihn *glücklich* — glaubte
> Die treue Gattin meines Opfers wert.
> Das glaubt ich damals — damals. Freilich jetzt,
> Jetzt weiß ichs besser. (ll. 2127–31)

Repetition serves, too, to denote preoccupation, as in the word
which Carlos, on his way to what he believes to be an assignation
with the queen, addresses to the importunate Alba:

> Mir?
> Mir ganz und gar nicht — mir wahrhaftig nicht.
> Sie reisen — reisen Sie mit Gott! (ll. 1359–61)

The device serves also to convey surprise, as in Posa's reaction
to Philipp's summons to an audience:

> Mich will er haben? Mich — Das kann nicht sein. (l. 2941)

Or with immense power it reflects the incredulous astonishment
and rising tension as the queen listens to Princess Eboli's confession of guilt:

EBOLI. ... Ich — ich war der Dieb,
Der Sie bestohlen.
KÖNIGIN.          Sie?
EBOLI.          Und jene Briefe
Dem König ausgeliefert —
KÖNIGIN.          Sie?
EBOLI.          Der sich
Erdreistet hat, Sie anzuklagen —
KÖNIGIN.          Sie —
Sie konnten —                              (ll. 4173-7)

Here the shifting significance of each repetition is carefully
pointed by the punctuation. When Posa draws his dagger on the
princess, her surprise is linked with panic by a repetition:

Mich? Mich?
O ewige Barmherzigkeit! Was hab
Ich denn begangen?                         (ll. 4122-4)

Repetition may mark concentrated cogitation in Eboli's

Wie kam es,
Das seine strenge Tugend hier verstummte?
Hier? eben hier?                           (ll. 1900-2)

or embarrassment in her

Nicht doch! Nein! Das war —
Das war von etwas anderm.                  (ll. 2199-200)

Carlos, in a combination of frustration and confusion, stumbles
over and repeats his words:

Prinzessin —
Verzeihen Sie, Prinzessin — ich — ich fand
Den Vorsaal offen.                         (ll. 1541-3)

And Philipp, when the queen is announced at an unpropitious
moment, expresses his utter consternation with a fivefold 'jetzt':

Jetzt?...
.................. Jetzt aber? Jetzt?
In dieser ungewohten Stunde? — Nein!
Jetzt kann ich sie nicht sprechen — jetzt nicht —   (ll. 3663-6)

Not all the uses of repetition, however, reflect emotional disturbance. Often enough it fulfils the obvious function of emphasis. Unexpectedly it reveals at one point, in a speech of the princess, pose and insincerity:

> Längst hätt ich diesen Hof
> Verlassen, diese Welt verlassen.                    (ll. 1801–2)

And once, on the lips of the Grand Inquisitor, it conveys a searing sarcasm:

> Leidenschaft? — Antwortet
> Mir Philipp der Infant? Bin ich allein
> Zum alten Mann geworden? — Leidenschaft!          (ll. 5188–90)

More subtly Posa suggests by a hesitation and a repetition his momentary contempt for Carlos's frailty:

> was haben
> Entweihungen des königlichen Bettes
> Mit deiner — deiner Liebe denn zu schaffen?       (ll. 2403–5)

And, especially in Posa's last interview with the queen, it is used in quasi-ritualistic fashion to establish a note of solemnity.

For all these expressive uses of repetition there is a basis in everyday speech. Embarrassment, surprise, sarcasm, grief, agitation, panic, and haste commonly provoke a recurrence of words. But there is a stylistic, as well as a psychological, value in repetition. Reiterated words, phrases, or sentences can be deployed as a pattern or employed as a refrain. At its simplest it is used anaphorically to balance and link two clauses:

> Dreimal wiesest du
> Den Fürsten von dir, dreimal kam er wieder
> Als Bittender . . . .                              (ll. 230–2)

Similarly the two prongs of a dilemma are both connected and distinguished in Carlos's

> O, in diesem
> Gefühl liegt Hölle — Hölle liegt im andern.        (ll. 750–1)

Here the chiastic conjuncture of the repeated *Hölle* suggests a
symmetrical pattern, branching out in two directions from a
central point.

Schiller's most powerful stylistic repetitions occur where the
recurrence is distributed in the interchange of dialogue. Here, for
instance, Carlos repeats Posa's own phrase to reject his impassioned plea:

POSA. . . . . . . . .
 Auf Kaiser Karls glorwürdgem Enkel ruht
 Die letzte Hoffnung dieser edeln Lande.
 Sie stürzt dahin, wenn sein erhabnes Herz
 Vergessen hat für Menschlichkeit zu schlagen.
CARLOS. Sie stürzt dahin.                                    (ll. 164–8)

An echo such as this takes effect not only as a simple, though
oblique, statement; it also implies the warnings, conditions, or
statements associated with the first use of the phrase. It is an
aspect of Schiller's dramatic economy.

The stylistic use of repetition is not always in the rhetorical
mode. It occurs also in highly emotive laconic form, as in Posa's
poignant final leave-taking:

KÖNIGIN.    Marquis!
 Ist keine Rettung möglich?
MARQUIS.                     Keine.
KÖNIGIN.                            Keine?
 Besinnen Sie sich wohl. Ist keine möglich?
 Auch nicht durch mich?
MARQUIS.                     Auch nicht durch Sie.
KÖNIGIN.                                    Sie kennen mich
 Zur Hälfte nur — ich habe Mut.
MARQUIS.                     Ich weiß es.
KÖNIGIN. Und keine Rettung?
MARQUIS.                     Keine.             (ll. 4389–94)

The recurring sound of the *nein* tolls like a bell, reinforcing the
finality of its burden. At the same time line 4392, the first
trimeter Schiller ever wrote in his plays ('Auch nicht durch

mich / Auch nicht durch Sie / Sie kennen mich'), retards with its measured pace the tempo and strengthens the funerary note.

It seems likely that repetition fulfils another important role in the economy of this play. The basic impulses underlying poetry are largely repetitive. A regular recurrent impulse provides its fundamental pattern; strophic form, refrain, rhyme, and alliteration come to the support of rhythm. Schiller rejected rhyme, and alliteration plays at this stage only a subsidiary role in his verse. He uses repetition, however, as a surrogate for rhyme. In a fitful and varied way it traces patterns, avoiding monotony and abstaining (and this was important for Schiller) from emphasizing line-endings as rhyme does. The whole scheme of Schiller's verse in *Don Carlos* runs contrary to such pointing of regular units of given length. Repetition was perfectly adapted to support the flexible structure of his verse.

A notable development of syntax in *Don Carlos* is the recession of antithesis, which had provided an underlying pattern for the dramatic prose. The shrivelling away of a favourite device, which, moreover, clearly corresponded to an aspect of Schiller's mental structure, must be explained by the supervention of another impulse, which is, at least for the time being, of greater import to him. The antithetic urge is countered by an impulse to harmonize. In *Don Carlos* the trend to harmony is, for the first time in the plays, victorious over the vision of duality. The flow of the verse unites and binds, bridging gaps, smoothing roughnesses, overcoming the old dichotomy, of which antithesis is an expression.

## 7. THE ROLE OF VOCABULARY

The imagistic vocabulary of *Don Carlos* is simultaneously significant for the tenor of the play and for Schiller's development. The words of fire—*Feuer, feurig, Flammen, glühen, entglühen, entzünden*—occur more frequently than any other group of symbolical words. They appear, however, much more often in the first three acts than in the remaining two. This suggests a correspondence with the mood in which the earlier part of the play was written. In the letters which Schiller wrote to Reinwald in the early months of the year 1783 there is frequent mention of *Don Carlos*, and the words *Feuer* and *feurig* emerge in this context with almost monotonous regularity. This inflammatory vocabulary serves first as an accompaniment to the consuming and destructive ardour of Carlos's passion for the queen; then it becomes less immediate, denoting with Domingo the prince's former political fervour, or conforming with Princess Eboli to the conventional language of love. In the third act it shifts appreciably to mark, not the youthful ardour of Carlos, but the slow destructive and corrupting internal fires which torment King Philipp. Thereafter the words of burning recede. The mood to which 'fire' and 'flame' and 'glow' corresponded appears to have burned itself out, and this must have happened about 1786. The contrast between the earlier abundance and the later sparseness is striking. 'Meine feurigsten Erwartungen', 'Mit jugendlicher Glut', 'Mein Herz, das feurig fühlt' are characteristic utterances from the first act; whilst the second adds such expressions as 'Feuerküsse' and 'Sein Herz entglüht für eine neue Tugend'. In the third act *glühen* and *brennen* replace the *Feuer* and *Flammen*, corresponding to a suggestion of subterranean fires. The fourth and fifth acts make their occasional references to fire in terms of dispraise or rejection—'Der Freundschaft arme Flamme' or 'wie Flammen / Der Hölle schlägt sie brennend mein Gewissen'.

The images correspond on the one side to Carlos's ardour, on the other to Philipp's smouldering resentment and hatred; and as the play proceeds they come also to be associated with Posa's political zeal. Commonplace though the metaphor of fire was in the late eighteenth century, it almost always appears in *Don Carlos* fresh-minted, immaculate, and shining. Only once, in its application to Alba, does it become a mere cliché:

wie voll Eifer dort
Der Herzog brennt, der Gunst zuvorzueilen,
Die meinem Sohn beschieden war.          (ll. 2766–8)

Elsewhere the conventional recedes and fire plays its part as a significant image and a purposeful motif. As it had opened

Carlos's career in this play, so it closes it in the last scene, making retrospective allusion to evoke similarity and to establish change:

> Ein reiner Feuer hat mein Wesen
> Geläutert —                                        (ll. 5316–17)

Compared with earlier plays, the vocabulary of *Don Carlos* is functional. The prominent words are there because the matter requires them. *Traum* must clearly often recur in a play so deeply concerned with the advocacy and betrayal of political ideals; *Gift* is appropriate in a plot which turns on intrigue, rancour, and hatred. The oscillation between the polar concepts of *Himmel* and *Hölle* corresponds to the intensity and mobility of the emotions of the principal character. The words of buying and selling denote the cold and calculating character of the world which opposes Carlos.

In view of the trend towards harmony in *Don Carlos* it comes as no surprise to find that the territory of the vocabulary of horror has contracted. It still occurs in two contexts, one peripheral, the other focal. The words of the first group centre on religion, as it is exemplified by the Roman Catholic Church. Even into the idyllic peace of Aranjuez the shadow of horrors inflicted in the name of religion extends. We learn in an oblique reference of a 'promised' burning at the stake:

> Und ein Autodafe hat man uns auch
> Versprochen . . . .                                   (ll. 418–19)

It is a harmless pleasure because

> Es sind ja Ketzer, die man brennen sieht.             (l. 421)

Alba boasts that his sword is the plough of the Faith:

> zeichnete dem Samenkorn des Glaubens
> Auf diesem Weltteil blutge Furchen vor.               (ll. 1427–8)

Princess Eboli compares Carlos in his moment of confusion to a heretic arraigned before the Inquisition:

> Gleich einem Ketzer vor dem heilgen Amte.             (l. 1713)

And Posa describes in gruesome terms the scenes he has witnessed in Flanders:

> Da stieß
> Ich auf verbrannte menschliche Gebeine —
>
> .    .    .    .    .    .    .    .
>
> O schade, daß, in seinem Blut gewälzt,
> Das Opfer wenig dazu taugt, dem Geist
> Des Opferers ein Loblied anzustimmen!          (ll. 3141–8)

All these examples, though products of a mind dealing readily with the violent and the horrible, are here canalized and concentrated in the service of one element in the play. They are all part of the assault on the bloodthirsty, cruel, and treacherous conduct of the Inquisition, as Schiller by Protestant upbringing and historical study had learned to conceive it. The vehemence of this vocabulary is a relic of the importance which this element in the play at first had for Schiller. That it was originally more central to the play is shown by his reference to the Inquisitor ('eines grausamen heuchlerischen Inquisitors') as one of the four principal characters,[1] and further supported by a passage declaring a clear hostile intention:

> ich will es mir in diesem Schauspiel zur Pflicht machen, in Darstellung der Inquisition, die prostituirte Menschheit zu rächen, und ihre Schandfleken fürchterlich an den Pranger zu stellen.[2]

Though this aim has been thrust on one side, the fierceness of the language remains as a token of its former significance.

A more central feature is the use of the words of murder. The first appearance of the word takes place with something like the force of an apocalyptic vision. Carlos, driven to extremity by Philipp's cold and suspicious rejection of his request for the Flanders command, makes a last despairing attempt to sway the king's determination:

> Ich soll und muß aus Spanien. Mein Hiersein
> Ist Atemholen unter Henkers Hand —
> Schwer liegt der Himmel zu Madrid auf mir,
> Wie das Bewußtsein eines Mords.          (ll. 1223–6)

---

[1] Letter to Reinwald dated 27 March 1783 (Jonas, I. 108).
[2] Letter to Reinwald dated 14 April 1783 (Jonas, I. 115).

Here *Mord* and *Henker* appear in close conjunction at a moment
when Carlos's extremity of distress has broken down the last
remnants of his reticence. These words echo the apprehension of
his dilemma:

> Dieser Weg
> Führt nur zum Wahnsinn oder Blutgerüste;                    (ll. 280–1)

and they hint ominously at the earlier utterance:

> O Roderich, wenn ich den Vater je
> In ihm verlernte — Roderich — ich sehe,
> Dein totenblasser Blick hat mich verstanden —
> Wenn ich den Vater je in ihm verlernte,
> Was würde mir der König sein?                    (ll. 353–7)

The linking of *Mord* and *Henker* in the audience scene, in front
of Philipp, is an unwitting disclosure, rent from Carlos by the
agony of his failure, of the desperate thoughts which his conscious
self seeks to conceal and repress. It is a telling and penetrating
stroke in the portrayal of character. Its greatest significance,
however, is symbolic—it sounds the note of Carlos's own doom,
determined in this moment of crisis.

The word *Mord* next occurs in the great audience scene of Act
Three. Here it is set in the mouth of Philipp, who to Posa's 'Ich
genieße die Gesetze' replies 'Dies Recht hat auch der Mörder'
(ll. 2985–6). Again the image reveals a feature of character; and
again the words are prophetic, foreshadowing Posa's assassination and Carlos's execution at Philipp's behest.

In the fifth act the words of murder fall thick and fast. Now
that Posa lies dead, the word is in its place and its repetition
inevitable. Nevertheless the power and emphasis with which it is
invested give it the force of a solemn and sinister motif. It
occurs obliquely in a reference to Cain:

> Seht ihr
> Das Brandmal nicht an seiner Stirne? Gott
> Hat ihn gezeichnet.                    (ll. 4746–8)

But, for the rest, it is spoken in the simplest, starkest form—
'Dein / Geruch ist Mord', 'Mord ist jetzt die Losung', 'Es ist

noch kein Mord geschehn, / Als heute', and 'Sie konnten nichts, als ihn ermorden'.[1] The austere simplicity and absence of elaboration hammer home the double accomplishment of the long prefigured murder.

Beyond the images which, by single words, almost imperceptibly touch in motifs, *Don Carlos* contains a number of more extensive metaphors, frequently employed to underline human loneliness. So Carlos, with a cosmic image, achieves without extravagance of language a sublime presentation of the situation of utter remoteness in which he and his father find themselves. It is an image invoking the inter-stellar spaces:

Hier, Roderich, siehst du zwei feindliche
Gestirne, die im ganzen Lauf der Zeiten
Ein einzig Mal in scheitelrechter Bahn
Zerschmetternd sich berühren, dann auf immer
Und ewig auseinander fliehn.                       (ll. 341–5)

The comparison is quickly followed by another, this time turned inward, suggesting the hopeless solitude of total enclosure and the frustration of every effort to escape from it. It is the image of the labyrinth:

Durch labyrinthische Sophismen kriecht
Mein unglückselger Scharfsinn, bis er endlich
Vor eines Abgrunds gähem Rande stutzt.           (ll. 350–2)

The vivid appropriateness of the labyrinth to this tangled and obscure web of human relationships is further underlined by its recurrence in the third act, this time in the mouth of Philipp—

Ihr sollt
Aus diesem dunkeln Labyrinth mich führen.        (ll. 2696–7)

The labyrinth stands for a confused and hopeless groping in isolation. The same sense of human beings lost and barred from each other is pointed by another symbolic image, the lock which will not yield to the keys the princess possesses:

Ich stehe
Vor einem zauberisch verschloßnen Schrank,
Wo alle meine Schlüssel mich betrügen.           (ll. 1743–5)

---

[1] All between l. 4741 and l. 4822.

It is a confession of frustrated communication, which Carlos underlines with 'Wie ich vor Ihnen'.

Yet human loneliness is only one side of *Don Carlos*. Schiller's imagination functions always in strong oppositions. The silence of utter solitude is countered by the musical image of human harmony, delicate, exquisite *Saitenspiel*, an image which is used three times at critical moments. Carlos, in the reunion with Posa, speaks of 'Unsrer Seelen zartes Saitenspiel' (l. 199). And Posa at his final leave-taking lyrically extends the image in his tribute to the Queen:

> Gehört die süße Harmonie, die in
> Dem Saitenspiele schlummert, seinem Käufer,
> Der es mit taubem Ohr bewacht? Er hat
> Das Recht erkauft, in Trümmern es zu schlagen,
> Doch nicht die Kunst, dem Silberton zu rufen
> Und in des Liedes Wonne zu zerschmelzen. (ll. 4358–63)

It is a motif which Schiller specifically points by adding the complement of a memorable double *sententia*:

> Die Wahrheit ist vorhanden für den Weisen,
> Die Schönheit für ein fühlend Herz.

And the image recurs a third time in vivid antithesis in Carlos's contemptuous reproach to Philipp the murderer:

> Dies feine Saitenspiel zerbrach in Ihrer
> Metallnen Hand. (ll. 4821–2)

Even the motif of dark threatening storm is accompanied in this play by images of serenity. When Posa uses it in extended form, he combines it with the brightness of day:

> Warum
> Dem Schlafenden die Wetterwolke zeigen,
> Die über seinem Scheitel hängt? — Genug,
> Daß ich sie still an dir vorüberführe,
> Und, wenn du aufwachst, heller Himmel ist. (ll. 3648–52)

The image of the storm is in *Don Carlos* not only a neighbour to serenity; it is also beneficent, bringing cleansing rain ('Wie deine Wetter reinigen die Welt', l. 2819) and quickening the growth of plants. This proximity to Nature with its element of gradualness heralds a new tone and atmosphere. The jerkiness and violence of Schiller's mental movement had been reflected in the earlier plays by the words of fury and horror, and the over-powering use of antithesis. In *Don Carlos* these elements fade, especially from the third act onwards; where they still occur, it is with obvious psychological or dramatic appropriateness, for instance in Philipp's almost insane, destructive paroxysm in the last act. They are replaced by a whole range of images drawn from plant life. This change betokens that shift from the abrupt, staccato mode of thought to the process of progressive gradual-ness and regular development which is symbolized by the rhythmic movement of the verse. Here is perceptible the first step in that long journey towards the outlook of Goethe, to which Schiller refers in his letter of 23 August 1794:

> Lange schon habe ich, obgleich aus ziemlicher Ferne, dem Gang Ihres Geistes zugesehen und den Weg, den Sie sich vorgezeichnet haben,mit immer erneuerter Bewunderung bemerkt.... Von der ein-fachen Organisation steigen Sie Schritt vor Schritt, zu den mehr verwickelten hinauf, um endlich die verwickeltste von allen, den Menschen, genetisch aus den Materialien des ganzen Naturgebäudes zu erbauen.[1]

Many of these images of growth are used negatively, expressing the arrest, the crushing, the withering of growth. Carlos tells, in one of the few occurrences of this image in the earlier part of the play, how his upbringing stamped on the tender plant: 'Der Liebe zarten Keim zertrat' (l. 311). Posa boldly reproaches Philipp:

> Sie wollen pflanzen für die Ewigkeit
> Und säen Tod? (ll. 3181–2)

And Philipp recognizes the blighting effect of his policy in the wistful words:

> Nicht alle
> Glückseligkeit soll unter mir verdorren. (ll. 3275–6)

[1] Jonas, 3. 472.

In the utter depression of the first scene of the fifth act we find Carlos's mind ranging back to the image of a tender growth destroyed, which he had already used in Act One:

O, diese fürchterliche Liebe
Hat alle frühe Blüten meines Geistes
Unwiederbringlich hingerafft. (ll. 4511–13)

And Philipp, at a later stage of the final crisis, can find no more powerful way to express his reborn nihilism than the image of a scorched earth:

Ich will
Ihn nützen, diesen Abend, daß nach mir
Kein Pflanzer mehr in zehen Menschenaltern
Auf dieser Brandstatt ernten soll. (ll. 5083–6)

That this image should occur most often in negative form was inevitable in this tragedy. The noblest growths are here cut down, the tougher are distorted by a harsh environment. At one vital point of the play, however, affirmation replaces denial. When the Queen and Posa, the two foremost representatives of a humane and harmonious future into which mankind will grow, meet in the poignant leave-taking scene of Act Four, the image of growth recurs insistently and in a mode which emphasizes hope in defiance of the negative form, in such phrases as 'Von meiner schönen Pflanzung abzurufen' (l. 4263) or 'In diesem starren Boden / Blüht keine meiner Rosen mehr' (l. 4318–19). Here another more fertile soil is implied, and when Posa refers directly to Carlos he does so with a positive form of a related image of growth—'In seinem Herzen Wurzel fassen' (l. 4329).

The concept *Natur* is closely related to this group of images. It may seem at first sight surprising that the queen only once uses the word *Natur*, for she of all characters in this play seems the most 'natural.' Her single reference to nature is in the line

Hier grüßt mich meine ländliche Natur. (l. 398)

And, though it is quickly apparent that she employs the word to denote the landscape, she emphasizes by the *mein* how completely she identifies herself with Nature. Of the four central figures she refers to Nature least, and clearly one who is so harmonious, so at one with herself, so unerring in her perception of the true and the false, is to be seen as a representative of Nature, of the laws of natural growth and development, of the inherent rightness of the natural order. Being Nature, she has no need to invoke it.

If we disregard Princess Eboli, who twice uses the word as an instrument of flattery and therefore misuses it in the cause of artificiality, we find three characters who not only refer to Nature, but invest it with significance: Posa, Carlos, and Philipp. For Posa the word serves two senses which are linked by the principle of free growth. *Natur* is the element which creates affinities;

> Nie hat zwei schönre Herzen die Natur
> Gebildet für einander                                   (ll. 563-4)

is the phrase expressing the spontaneous love of Fernando and Mathilde in the parable of Mirandola. And this conception of *Natur* is a moral one; for the sexual attraction which Guelpho feels for his nephew's bride is seen as an impulse *contrary* to Nature:

> Die neue Regung
> Erstickt die leise Stimme der Natur.                     (ll. 580-1)

*Natur* has, however, also a political sense, the free development of man and his institutions; so Posa in the great audience-scene condemns Philipp's view as 'Unselige / Verdrehung der Natur' (ll. 3118-19) and prophesies the failure of the policy of repression, claiming that Philipp has worked in vain:

> umsonst
> Den harten Kampf mit der Natur gerungen.               (ll. 3184-5)

A few moments later the identification of *Natur* with freedom is made completely explicit:

> Sehen Sie sich um
> In seiner herrlichen Natur! Auf Freiheit
> Ist sie gegründet — und wie reich ist sie
> Durch Freiheit!                                          (ll. 3217-20)

*Natur* is for Posa a principle commanding ardent admiration; he nevertheless views it from outside.

Philipp's attitude to Nature is more complex. At his whim he assumes its identity with himself, or denies its validity. As he broods, worn and sleepless, in the small hours, he exclaims:

> Ich bin um meinen Schlummer. Nimm
> Ihn für empfangen an, Natur.                    (ll. 2479–80)

He thus displays himself as the despot accustomed to service from his environment, viewing Nature as an adjunct to his state and court. Nowhere is his arrogant and fatal misunderstanding of it more sharply outlined than in this prayer of thanks to Nature for preserving his strength for the destructive fury of the evening of his life:

> Habe Dank, Natur! Ich fühle
> In meinen Sehnen Jünglingskraft. Ich will
> Ihn zum Gelächter machen. Seine Tugend
> Sei eines Träumers Hirngespinst gewesen.
> Er sei gestorben als ein Tor. Sein Sturz
> Erdrücke seinen Freund und sein Jahrhundert!      (ll. 5076–82)

Here, with sinister irony, Nature is commended for assistance in destroying Nature. Suspicious always, Philipp intersperses his praise of Nature with distrust. Beset by doubts and evil imaginings about the queen, he exclaims:

> Kann die Natur mit solcher Wahrheit lügen?        (ll. 3654)

Though the question is rhetorical, the fact that he can frame it in this way betrays the mistrust which, a moment later, emerges in unmistakable terms. And this instability of attitude, this questioning of the principle he has once taken to be his servant, becomes clearer in the fifth act, where he attributes to *Natur* the unnatural enmity and murderous thoughts of Carlos:

> Ich will doch erwarten,
> Zu welcher Schandtat die Natur — . . .            (ll. 4764–5)

Twice Philipp mentions the 'voice of Nature', each time to reject it. In his violent quarrel with the Queen he utters the words

> ich ehre keine Sitte
> Und keine Stimme der Natur, (ll. 3789–90)

and of the Inquisitor he demands immunity from this same voice of Nature:

> Ich frevle
> An der Natur — auch diese mächtge Stimme
> Willst du zum Schweigen bringen? (ll. 5272–4)

Philipp's conception of *Natur*, swerving between admiration and hate, expresses the disunity of his character, the degree to which he has lost touch with Nature. Yet he is no true enemy of Nature either, and the use, in this utterance to the Grand Inquisitor, of *frevle* and the admission which is contained in *mächtig* prove that deep down in Philipp *Natur* still maintains a foothold. Philipp's tragedy is contained in the ebb and flow of his attitude to Nature. The importance of this persisting shred of loyalty to Nature is antithetically underlined by the Inquisitor, who, secure, remote, and inhuman, counters in words of dogmatic intransigence:

> Vor dem Glauben
> Gilt keine Stimme der Natur. (ll. 5274–5)

In Philipp's unconscious attachment to Nature can be discerned the quality which enabled Schiller to treat with sympathy this figure, whose opinions and policies he condemned. Philipp's final tragedy is consummated as he stamps out within himself the last faint embers of *Natur*.

Carlos, in contrast, is animated by a deep respect for Nature. For him, as for Posa, it creates affinities:

> Wenns wahr ist, daß die schaffende Natur
> Den Roderich im Carlos wiederholte. (ll. 197–8)

Even though his desires run counter to the law of Nature, he recognizes its moral sanction:

> Weltgebräuche,
> Die Ordnung der Natur und Roms
> Gesetze verdammen diese Leidenschaft. (ll. 276–8)

Virtuous purity is for him the quintessence of Nature:

> Dir, Mädchen, dir entdeck ich mich — der Unschuld
> Der lautern, unentheiligten Natur
> Entdeck ich mich. (ll. 1844–6)

And the voice of Nature, which his father ignores, he reveres:

> Er hat noch nie die Stimme der Natur
> Gehört — laß mich versuchen, Roderich,
> Was sie auf meinen Lippen wird vermögen! (ll. 916–18)

It is Carlos's tragedy, as it is also his father's, to see the respect and reverence for *Natur*, the symbol of harmony and integration, crushed within him. Twice in the last act he mentions *Natur*, each time to reject it. 'Natur? / Ich weiß von keiner' (ll. 4765–6), he exclaims to Philipp; and to the Queen he declares:

> Ausgestorben ist
> In meinem Busen die Natur. (ll. 5341–2)

But, though in the hearts of the chief protagonists *Natur* is defeated, the principle of growth is maintained. This is the symbolical significance of the proliferating plant imagery. It is this, even more than Posa's eloquent declaration of faith, that gives the play the sense of a promised land some day to be inhabited.

The greatest threat to the beckoning future is embodied in the motif of sacrifice, recurring in the words *Opfer* and *opfern* with ever greater frequency as the play approaches its catastrophe. *Opfer* is man's perversion of *Natur*. It is exemplified in the sacrifice imposed upon the Queen—

> Es ist
> Ein hartes Schicksal, aufgeopfert werden — (ll. 452–3)

and reiterated in the voluntary effort which she in turn demands of Carlos:' . . . opfern Sie, was keiner opferte' (l. 777). It is represented by Posa's urgent reference to the victims of Spanish repression in the Netherlands, and underlined by Philipp's

> Er brachte
> Der Menschheit, seinem Götzen, mich zum Opfer;
> Die Menschheit büße mir für ihn! (ll. 5086–8)

The final embodiment of sacrifice is the Grand Inquisitor himself, the personification of the unnatural. Though he uses the word *Opfer* only once, the whole scene in which he appears is drenched with the spirit of cruel, ruthless sacrifice which was suggested at the beginning of the play by the 'promised' *auto da fé*. Whether it is expressed in generous renunciation or in harsh coercion, the *Opfer* is a consequence of man's denial of Nature.

At first impression *Don Carlos* appears to end in the extinction of hope and the blight of promise. Yet the sensitive reader is aware of something beyond. The impact of the catastrophe is at first paralysing, but as the mind slowly collects itself, a note of assurance survives. What outlasts the shock of disaster is a feeling of harmony; and this is the achievement, not of the brave words, which, alone, might seem to mock themselves, but of the movement of Schiller's verse, which, while allowing the tragedy its full effect, asserts an over-all pattern of harmonious persistence.

# V · WALLENSTEIN

## I. WALLENSTEINS LAGER

THE *Lager* is one of the great surprises of Schiller's career. Since 1787 he had written nothing for the stage, and now more than ten years later the impassioned and fluent verse of *Don Carlos*, which had once promised a new epoch in his development, seemed to have been a dead end. When it became known in the 1790s that Schiller was working on a play about Wallenstein, whose story he had already dealt with historically in *Die Geschichte des dreißigjährigen Kriegs*, it must have seemed that the new work must be either in the blank verse of *Don Carlos* or in the prose of the earlier plays. Yet, when *Wallensteins Lager* was first performed on 12 October 1798 it proved to be in neither one nor the other, adopting instead the rough and ready jolting metre to which Germans give the name *Knittelverse* and which they associate with Hans Sachs.

Schiller had no need to go back to the sixteenth century for his models. Since *Satyros* and *Pater Brey* Goethe had made the *Knittelvers* peculiarly his own. He had used it extensively and brilliantly in *Faust* (important parts of which were generally accessible since the appearance of Volume Seven of Goethe's *Schriften* in 1790), and he had published in *Der teutsche Merkur* in 1786 an outstanding poem written in this archaic metre—*Hans Sachsens poetische Sendung*.

It was not, then, an unknown form which Schiller chose for his 'prologue', as he termed *Wallensteins Lager*. But, for a dramatist who had last written in a style characterized by magnificent eloquence, broad sweep, and subtle flexibility, it was a most unexpected choice. The broken rhythms of *Knittelverse* are not the telling pauses of the blank verse of *Don Carlos*; the lines stumble and recover, skip and hop, and in this unforeseeable waywardness is a predisposition to the comic. It is true that the genius of Goethe had adapted the form in *Faust* to serious purposes, yet in the tensest or tenderest moments he abandoned it for blank verse, free rhythms, or even the prose of *Kerker*.[1]

For Schiller it is a verse of comedy; and, indeed, he uses it for a comedy new in his work, serene and balanced, remote from the savage parody and satire of *Kabale und Liebe*. Yet the world of Wallenstein's camp is at least as brutal as the society in which Ferdinand and Luise perish. Schiller, however, denies it both the hyperbole of satire and the fluency of blank verse, preferring the short-winded and rhyming lines of the *Knittelvers*.

So unusual was this choice that he felt it necessary to essay a defence. The Prolog, spoken that evening, concludes with these words:

> Und wenn die Muse heut,
> Des Tanzes freie Göttin und Gesangs,
> Ihr altes deutsches Recht, des Reimes Spiel,
> Bescheiden wieder fordert — tadelts nicht!
> Ja danket ihrs, daß sie das düstre Bild
> Der Wahrheit in das heitre Reich der Kunst
> Hinüberspielt, die Täuschung, die sie schafft,
> Aufrichtig selbst zerstört und ihren Schein
> Der Wahrheit nicht betrüglich unterschiebt.
> Ernst ist das Leben, heiter ist die Kunst.

The contrast, in these rather self-consciously elevated lines, between the earnestness of life and the serenity of art goes beyond a view that art is a refined, decorated, or bowdlerized version of life. It implies awareness of reality, of its urgency, its grimness ('das düstre Bild') and its immediacy; at the same time it interposes a distance, separating the observer from the observed, the poet from his creatures. For the first time Schiller appears as the manipulator, who directs and moves his puppets. His relationship to them is not that of the passionate participant who identified himself with his Carlos; instead he is the cool, collected creator and controller. This distance from his figures, the source of the

---

[1] The transposition of this scene into verse is subsequent to 1798.

irony which infuses *Wallensteins Lager*, as it has pervaded no earlier work of Schiller, is intimately linked with the form of verse which Schiller has chosen for the play.

The salient characteristics of Schiller's *Knittelverse* are the rapidly recurring rhyme (though Schiller does not always employ it in couplets) and an irregular rhythm, now crudely heavy and emphatic, now scampering over syllables with an elephantine agility. Both factors act as constant reminders of artifice. But, if their purpose is to destroy an illusion of reality, that postulates its previous creation.

Indeed, if the rhyme and the rhythm are used constantly to assert the puppet status of the figures, other aspects of the language serve to emphasize their lifelikeness. The greater part of the speech of the *Lager* is basically the language of everyday. We see it in the first line, 'Vater, es wird nicht gut ablaufen', a simple, natural sentence, achieving a rhythmic quality, it seems, only by accident. And the second line, completing the couplet, parallels it—'Bleiben wir von dem Soldatenhaufen'. Yet, though each line by itself is impeccably realistic, the conjunction of the two, rhythmically parallel and linked by rhyme, plays deliberation off against spontaneity. The interplay leans to the comic by virtue of its incongruity.

More than half of the verse in *Wallensteins Lager* is composed of such direct, unaffected speech. Taken alone, countless lines would seem the baldest prose, as in 'Geb dir dafür das Paar Terzerolen' (l. 92) or 'Was für Grünröck mögen das sein' (l. 120) or 'Der Piccolomini, der junge, tut sie jetzt führen' (l. 676). But as line is added to line, and a rhythmic pattern becomes apparent, and the rhyme chimes in, a pleasure is aroused by juxtaposition; an element of play arises from the interpolation into the purest naturalism of non-realistic, formal features.

A cruder comedy irrupts into the play with the entry of the Kapuziner. Serious though the message of his camp sermon is, its vehicle is a sequence of homely images, backed by outrageous puns. 'Die Arche der Kirche schwimmt in Blute' (l. 513) puts a point forcefully in a robust and simple image. But the puns introduce an element of buffoonery, expressly performed to flash out an unexpected truth:

Und das römisch *Reich* — daß Gott erbarm!
Sollte jetzt heißen römisch *Arm.* (ll. 514–15)

These features of the sermon are borrowed, as is well known, from Abraham a Santa Clara[1] and Schiller has made what may be called either a bold plagiarism or a documentary adaptation. But in moulding the original prose to his *Knittelverse* he has compressed it to heighten its grotesque comedy; and has by his ribaldry set the religious element (and the Thirty Years War was allegedly a war of religion) on the very lowest rung of the soldiers' crude and distorted scale of values.

Altogether, in his handling of *Knittelverse* Schiller shows the same formal skill, without noticeable signs of apprenticeship, which he had exhibited in the blank verse of *Don Carlos*. Frequently the lines, short though they are, comfortably embrace two sentences, as in 'Was ists für einer? Es ist kein Böhm' (l. 673) or 'Nicht wir wir alle! das wißt Ihr schlecht' (l. 858). Names provide no obstacle, as the *Marketenderin* in nine lines includes 'Temeswar', 'den Mansfelder', 'dem Friedländer', 'Stralsund', 'Mantua', 'Feria', and 'Gent', adroitly using five of them for rhyme (ll. 139–47). The brusque curtness of soldierly speech comes off again and again in phrases such as:

Kürassiere, Jäger, reitende Schützen,
Sollen achttausend Mann aufsitzen, (ll. 692–3)

or

Was will der Bauer da? Fort, Halunk! (l. 49)

And the verse reproduces just as readily the Wachtmeister's pompousness:

So sagt er, ich hörts wohl einigemal,
Ich stand dabei. 'Das Wort ist frei,
Die Tat ist stumm, der Gehorsam blind',
Dies urkundlich seine Worte sind. (ll. 338–41)

---

[1] It is drawn mainly from *Auff, auff, Ihr Christen.*

All the while rhythm and rhyme maintain the distance between the poet and the spectator on the one hand and the poet's creatures on the other, so that the realism is, as it were, presented in a frame and proclaimed as a brilliant counterfeit, instead of pretending to be the thing itself. The verbal presentation of *Wallensteins Lager*, though complicated by the interplay of metre and rhyme, is nevertheless direct. The vocabulary is straightforward, serving primarily to characterize the soldier's life. Military words, such as 'Soldatenhaufen' 'Schwert', 'Beut', 'das resoluteste Korps', 'aufsitzen', 'Klinge', 'Fahne', and so on abound. This inevitable professional vocabulary is complemented by another range of words unconnected with the soldier's desperate and dangerous life in action. The importance of food and drink is stressed by the recurrence of such motifs as 'saufen und fressen', 'mit gutem Schluck und gutem Brocken', 'Soff', or 'das lustige Leben' (which also include 'Spiel und Mädels die Menge'). The direct, utilitarian character of the language is underlined by the paucity of images of violence, abundant in Schiller's early plays and still in some degree active in *Don Carlos*. The pre-occupation with the macabre has vanished in *Wallensteins Lager*, the ferocity of the wild beast and the violence of the criminal no longer appear as important symbols, and the depredations of the soldier—surely a subject which the Schiller of 1782 would have treated with vehement language, garish images, and surrealist detail—are indicated, not by murder and destructive brutality, but in terms of economic pillage and sexual vitality. In the rendering of the mercilessness of war, slaughter is replaced by the less blood-thirsty motif of rape:

Es sträubt sich — der Krieg hat kein Erbarmen —
Das Mägdlein in unsern sennigten Armen.          (ll. 224–5)

And the trail of devastation left by Holk's armies is marked, not by mutilated corpses and smoking ruins, but by a generation of thriving illegitimate grandchildren; for the motif of rape just mentioned is followed by these lines:

Wo wir nur durchgekommen sind —
Erzählen Kinder und Kindeskind

Nach hundert und aber hundert Jahren
Von dem Holk noch und seinen Scharen.                    (ll. 228–31)

In sum, not only is the language functionally concerned with the
matter in hand; it goes even further, deliberately neglecting
opportunities where the vocabulary of violence would be relevant.
A disciplined, if slightly stylized, realism has gained the day, at
any rate in the earlier part of the *Lager*.

As the play goes on, touches of the old violence in vocabulary
are detectable, but they remain scarce and are associated with a
shift in style. Flood and flame, for instance are used by the
second Holkischer Jäger when he boasts of the dash and menace
of his corps; but the style has changed, the rhythm no longer
stumbles or hops, but is swift and smooth, with here and there a
dactylic hint at the galloping rhythm; at the same time a perceptible heightening of vocabulary takes place:

Ziehen frech durch Feindes und Freundes Lande,
Querfeldein durch die Saat, durch das gelbe Korn —
Sie kennen das Holkische Jägerhorn! —
In einem Augenblick fern und nah,
Schnell wie die Sündflut, so sind wir da —
Wie die Feuerflamme bei dunkler Nacht
In die Häuser fähret, wenn niemand wacht.              (ll. 215–21)

This is the voice of the familiar Schiller, with the impetuous
movement, the repeated simple antitheses (*Feind — Freund,
fern — nah, Flut — Flamme*), the eye for the obvious, and the
courage to say it.

The question must immediately be asked whether this inter-
position of another style is a defect, the unconscious back-
sliding into a habitual manner, or whether on the other hand it
has a recognizable part in the pattern of the work.

It is not an isolated occurrence. No sooner has the second
Jäger concluded his eulogy (which has about it a faint tang of the
glory in crime which Karl and Franz Moor and other figures in
the early plays plainly exhibit), than his companion takes up the

theme of the soldier's life, at once expressing himself in obviously
poetic terms:

> Flott will ich leben und müßig gehn,
> Alle Tage was Neues sehn,
> Mich dem Augenblick frisch vertrauen,
> Nicht zurück, auch nicht vorwärts schauen —       (ll. 242–5)

The galloping rhythm, the image 'dem Augenblick vertrauen',
and the antithesis of the last line are part of Schiller's poetic
style; the real speech of the soldier has been abandoned. Yet the
last of these four lines is halting; try as one will, it cannot be read
with the same verve as the rest. It makes a transition to a line of
pure realism:

> Drum hab ich meine Haut dem Kaiser verhandelt.       (l. 246)

Immediately the Jäger climbs back to the poetic and continues
with exalted fervour: 'Führt mich ins Feuer frisch hinein
. . .' (ll. 248 ff.). This rapid fluctuation of style cannot be
accidental, especially in a self-conscious writer such as the thirty-
eight-year-old Schiller had become. Clearly there was an aim.
Schiller knew that the soldier's life was largely made up of food
and drink, of being flush and hard-up, of crude and fleeting
pleasure with dice and women. These aspects of military life
are mirrored in the realistic tones of the *Knittelverse*. The rare
moments of exaltation, devotion, and glory, on the other hand,
attract to themselves Schiller's fluency and elevated rhetoric, and
at once the style rises correspondingly. It is in this manner that
the first Jäger expresses his enthusiasm:

> Und der Geist, der im ganzen Korps tut leben,
> Reißet gewaltig, wie Windesweben,
> Auch den untersten Reiter mit.       (ll. 309–11)

The fluctuation between realistic and exalted speech is not
controlled by the rank, standing, or character of the speaker, and
so the appearance of the two Pappenheim Cuirassiers, the most
resolute and honest figures in the whole prologue, does not of
itself heighten the tone. They, too, begin with colloquial speech:

Von dem Friedländer lassen,
Der den Soldaten so nobel hält,
Mit dem Spanier ziehen zu Feld,
Dem Knauser, den wir von Herzen hassen?
Nein, das geht nicht! Wir laufen fort.　　　　(ll. 702–6)

The everyday language corresponds to the financial motive. And the tone rises only when the vision of the army as a whole (as symbolized by this motley assemblage of carabineers, cuirassiers, Jäger, harquebusiers, etc.) begins to comprehend its true function. The cue is provided by the Wachtmeister with the question 'Aus welchem Vaterland schreibst du dich?', to which the Erster Dragoner replies, 'Weit aus Hibernien her komm ich' (l. 786). The recondite proper noun (less familiar in German than in English) translates us to a land of poetry, and other answers, such as 'Hinter Wismar ist meiner Eltern Sitz', with its anastrophic genitive, maintain the new key. At this point the language of the Wachtmeister, which has hitherto been the most consistent instance of characteristic realism, glides on to a loftier plane:

Nun! und wer merkt uns das nun an,
Daß wir aus Süden und aus Norden
Zusammengeschneit und -geblasen worden?
Sehn wir nicht aus wie aus *einem* Span?
Stehn wir nicht gegen den Feind geschlossen;
Recht wie zusammengeleimt und -gegossen?
Greifen wir nicht wie ein Mühlwerk flink
Ineinander, auf Wort und Wink?
Wer hat uns so zusammengeschmiedet,
Daß ihr uns nimmer unterschiedet?
Kein andrer sonst als der Wallenstein!　　　　(ll. 797–807)

The repeated couplings with *zusammen*, the polar use of *Süden* and *Norden*, and the structure by a series of rhetorical questions all indicate the key of Schiller's elevated style. And yet, by the use of expressions such as 'wie aus einem Span' and 'auf Wort und Wink', and by the tautologism of 'Kein andrer sonst', Schiller maintains the consistency of the Wachtmeister's speech. This speech is the first step towards the poetic coda.

The vision of the united army, which the Wachtmeister has evoked, fades for a moment, and the individual voices are again heard wrangling about selfish interests in terms of realistic speech. But the mean squabble about pay is cut short by the brisk voice of the first Cuirassier. His speech on the theme of the soldier's lot begins in homely fashion but soon swells to an eloquence which belongs to rhetoric and has nothing more in common with realism. Parallel phrases appear, inversions, characteristic generic groups such as 'der Städte Glanz'; and, most important of all, the tempo becomes at once quicker and smoother, until it reaches a provisional climax with

> Frei will ich leben und also sterben,
> Niemand berauben und niemand beerben,
> Und auf das Gehudel unter mir
> Leicht wegschauen von meinem Tier.          (ll. 954–7)

Once again the individual voices reassert themselves and the vision of unity threatens to be lost in bickering and private interest; and the language, like a sensitive barometer, swings back to the realistic and homely. But this phase is succeeded by another wave of unity embodied in a simple device, the strophic song with which *Wallensteins Lager* ends.

The cue for the song is given by a couplet in which the whole army and its general are associated:

> Die Armee soll florieren!
> Und der Friedländer soll sie regieren.          (ll. 1050–1)

Swift movement and galloping rhythm carry it along. The vocabulary is simple and obvious: 'Feld' and 'Freiheit' and 'Herz', 'Herren und Knechte' and 'Dem Tod ins Angesicht schauen.' All this is the common currency of popular rhetoric, the elements of which are so often used to furnish platitudes and empty phrases. Yet the effect of this song as a conclusion to *Wallensteins Lager* is neither platitudinous nor empty. Its success is partly due to the impetus of Schiller's rhythm and to his gift for using well-worn words as if he had just heard them for the first time. Yet these qualities would not have sufficed to redeem the poem from banality. The real key is its place and function in the dramatic scheme. Firstly it is sung, secondly it is sung in company and part of it is choral, and thirdly it expresses group unanimity. In such a situation, simplicity and obviousness are in their place. Individual thought is subordinated to common emotion.

To say that the *Lager* provides the background to the tragedy is to state the baldest of commonplaces. Schiller himself refers to it as an explanation ('Sein Lager nur erkläret sein Verbrechen').[1] What it explains is the simultaneous diversity and unity of the army, its immense, yet capricious, potentiality for loyal support or treacherous secession. The *Knittelvers* establishes the basic unity of the play and the fundamental earthiness of the soldier. The subtle stylistic shifts demonstrate that adherence and betrayal are merely separated by a word. In the gradations of tone are displayed the range from the extreme of coarseness, quarrel-someness, and narrow egotism of the individual in camp and quarters to the opposite of courage and devotion in the moments when the army is conscious of its mission and its unity. And, by finishing with the rousing choral song, Schiller shows the tide set fair for Wallenstein at the moment when the first phase of the drama proper is about to open.

## II. *DIE PICCOLOMINI* AND *WALLENSTEINS TOD*

### 1. FLEXIBILITY

The performance of *Wallensteins Lager* in October 1798 seemed at least to settle one matter. It was hardly imaginable that this 'prologue', being in verse, could be followed by a tragedy in prose. The kind of verse could still be a matter for speculation, but verse of some kind it must be. At this point a simple chrono-logical sequence began to be apparent. With *Don Carlos* the poetic form was established, and it was to be maintained right to the last of Schiller's dramatic works, the unfinished *Demetrius*.

In reality the process was less simple, and the issue not easily

---

[1] Prolog, 1. 118.

determined. Schiller had firmly decided in the summer of 1784[1] to write *Don Carlos* in verse and he stood by his intention. But a letter written two years later (i.e. still a year before the publication of *Carlos*) to his publisher friend Göschen, announcing a new play in prose, *Der Menschenfeind*,[2] proves that he was not yet definitively wedded to verse. No doubt Schiller's reluctance to abandon prose was partly governed by practical considerations. He had little confidence in the capacity of the German actors of his day to speak verse. In October 1786 he had written to Göschen, 'Den Karlos gebe ich ohnehin nicht in Versen auf das Theater',[3] and, though his mind was not as firmly made up as this remark would suggest, he went more fully into his misgivings two months later in a letter to the Hamburg actor-manager F. L. Schröder.[4] Schröder, notwithstanding Schiller's hesitations, gave the play successfully in verse, but in some other German theatres a prose version, prepared by Schiller, was preferred.

Schiller was an acute man of business, but he would not have allowed such fortuitous considerations to determine the ideal form of his drama as it would appear in print. And yet *Wallenstein* was begun in prose, and verse, after serious thought, was rejected, as we see from a letter written to Goethe on 16 December 1796: 'Ich bin, nach reifer Überlegung, bey der lieben Prosa geblieben, die diesem Stoff auch viel mehr zusagt.'[5] Clearly he felt at this stage no overriding impulse toward metrical speech and he justifies his choice of prose with an aesthetic reason. Behind it there lies another equally aesthetic, but more oblique, ground. During his years in Weimar and Jena, Schiller's whole outlook on poetic writing had changed. He had grown tired of broad effects and had come to value a precise adaptation of language to subject. He was filled with a new poetic integrity, and this was accompanied by a revulsion against the extravagance of

---

[1] Letter to Heribert von Dalberg, 14 August 1784 (Jonas, 1. 208).
[2] 5 November 1786 (Jonas, 1. 315).
[3] 9 October 1786 (Jonas, 1. 310).
[4] 18 December 1786 (Jonas, 1. 321).
[5] Jonas, 5. 134.

his early work. Notwithstanding his own former flamboyant use of prose, he could feel that this flexible vehicle offered possibilities of sobriety which were not so easily realized in verse. As late as July 1797 we find him referring disparagingly to 'meine alten Unarten'.[1]

*Wallensteins Lager* was the means of solving his problem. The impulse to poetic writing remained active, and in the *Lager* he hit on a verse which was not a temptation to extravagance. And the feat of writing it determined the future texture of the play. After the verse opening, the rest could no longer be in prose; and Schiller had anyway proved to himself that he could write sober verse. The inward debate continued through the summer and early autumn of 1797. He did not give in readily, but at last in November the decision was taken. Early in the month he notes, 'Angefangen, den Wallenstein in Jamben zu schreiben',[2] and the resolution is confirmed, with a new aesthetic reason, in a letter to Cotta on 14 November: 'Ich habe mich doch entschlossen ihn in Jamben zu bearbeiten, um auch die letzte Foderung zu erfüllen, die an eine vollkommene Tragödie gemacht wird.'[3] Hardly had he made the decision than it seemed the only right and possible one. To Körner he writes on 20 November: 'Es ist nun entschieden, daß ich ihn in Jamben mache; ich begreife kaum, wie ich es je anders habe wollen können, es ist unmöglich, ein Gedicht in Prosa zu schreiben.'[4] This is the moment of decision, the turning-point which determined the manner of all Schiller's later plays.

At a moment when the issue of prose or verse was still undecided, Schiller made, in a letter to Goethe, an interesting comment on the tone and style of *Wallenstein*. He refers to a certain dryness of manner in the scenes already completed (in prose):

Sie [sc. die Trockenheit] entstand aus einer gewissen Furcht, in meine ehemalige Manier zu fallen, und aus einem zu ängstlichen Bestreben, dem Objekte recht nahe zu bleiben. Nun ist aber das

---

[1] Letter to Körner, 10 July 1797 (Jonas, 5. 219).
[2] *Kalendar*, 4 November 1797, quoted in *NA* 8. 402.
[3] Jonas, 5. 286.
[4] Jonas, 5. 287.

Objekt schon an sich selber etwas trocken, und bedarf mehr als irgend eines der poetischen Liberalität; es ist daher hier nöthiger als irgendwo, wenn beide Abwege, das *Prosaische* und das *Rhetorische*, gleich sorgfältig vermieden werden sollen, eine recht reine poetische Stimmung zu erwarten.[1]

In this passage Schiller himself distinguishes the three essential elements of his mature style: the prosaic, the rhetorical, and the poetic. It is true that he here speaks of avoiding the prosaic and the rhetorical. But he has not done it in *Wallenstein* any more than in *Don Carlos*. In *Wallenstein* he converts the prosaic into the colloquial, he controls rhetoric and applies it to specific dramatic purposes, and he holds the play together with a pervasive 'poetic' tone. He had already attempted this solution in *Don Carlos*, but there the rhetoric had not been fully functional and the colloquial elements had been relatively unimportant. In *Wallenstein* he achieves a new and perfect balance.

The characteristics of Schiller's 'poetic' style in this play are: a direct syntax with only moderate variations from normal order, a smooth conformity with the pentametric rhythm of the blank verse, and a sparing use of images. It frequently lies close to the colloquial, which it eases and, so to speak, lubricates. The couplet with which *Die Piccolomini* begins, runs:

Spät kommt Ihr — Doch Ihr kommt! Der weite Weg,
Graf Isolan, entschuldigt Euer Säumen.                    (*P.*, ll. 1–2)

The general structure of these two lines, with their simple vocabulary and syntax and the change of thought indicated by the dash, is colloquial; yet the word 'Säumen' and the careful framing in two regular lines of verse show it to be 'poetic'. Isolani, in his reply, continues the same tone, until at line 7 he drops an unmistakable colloquialism into the flow of speech:

Den griffen die Kroaten mir noch auf.                     (*P.*, l. 7)

Illo's rejoinder—'Er kommt uns grad zu paß'—is equally colloquial, but he adds in the following line an unmistakably poetic epithet:

Die stattliche Versammlung hier zu speisen.              (*P.*, l. 9)

---

[1] 2 October 1797 (Jonas, 5. 270).

In this way the gentle fluctuations and adaptations of the poetic mode temper the vigour and abruptness of realism.

One of the principal elements in the creation of this unobtrusive poetic style is simple anastrophe. So the bald statement 'Die Obersten von dreißig Regimentern haben sich schon zusammengefunden' becomes in poetic speech

> Von dreißig Regimentern haben sich
> Die Obersten zusammen schon gefunden. (*P.*, ll. 15–16)

This simple kind of rhythmic rearrangement permeates the tragedy, and there is not a page on which examples cannot be found.

Schiller engenders in this way a 'low-temperature verse' which gives *Wallenstein* its special texture. Sometimes it is indistinguishable from prose, affirming its poetic quality only by neat rhythm and perfect acquiescence in the single line; such are the words of the Herzogin:

> Ihr Wille, wissen Sie, war stets der meine. (*P.*, l. 647)

Again, the poetic touch may be no more than an omitted inflection—

> Ein schlecht Gemälde wars, doch wars der Freund (*P.*, l. 1465)

—or an entirely normal first clause followed by an anastrophic parallel:

> Er ist heftig,
> Es hat der Hof empfindlich ihn beleidigt. (*P.*, ll. 2421–2)

This smooth rhythmic style, which corresponds to what in *Don Carlos* I have called the medial tone, derives its strength from its affinity with common speech, and its savour from the slight tautening process to which that speech has been subjected. It provides the play with an element of flow, infinitely variable in tempo, but always continuous. And not least important is its function as a tonality, from which Schiller modulates easily and rapidly into everyday speech on the one hand, or exalted rhetorical language on the other. Thus we find Isolani, in the first scene

of *Die Piccolomini*, greeting the impending arrival of Wallenstein's wife and daughter in Schiller's poetic mode, transferring
the infinitive and, surprisingly, introducing a rhetorical 'Lo
behold!':

> Desto besser.
> Erwartet ich doch schon von nichts als Märschen
> Und Batterien zu hören und Attacken;
> Und siehe da!                                    (*P.*, ll. 35–8)

But the solemnity of the 'siehe da!' proves ironical, and Isolani
concludes with a naturalistic line which conveys a wink and nudge
as clearly as any stage direction:

> Der Herzog sorgt dafür,
> Daß auch was Holdes uns das Aug ergötze.         (*P.*, ll. 38–9)

The shift from the poetic to the elevated is equally easy.
Isolani begins a speech to Illo with the colloquial 'Hab ichs schon
erzählt?', passes gradually to the poetic with

> Der Fürst
> Will meine Kreditoren kontentieren,
> Will selber mein Kassier sein künftighin          (*P.*, ll. 60–2)

and then glides smoothly into the elevated and majestic by the
insertion of exalted words into the normal grammatical pattern:

> Und das ist nun das dritte Mal, bedenk Er!
> Daß mich der Königlichgesinnte vom
> Verderben rettet und zu Ehren bringt.             (*P.*, ll. 64–6)

In these brief examples we discern hints of some of the functions
which Schiller entrusts to his verse in *Wallenstein*. The smoking
room wink displays a facet of Isolani's character, and the word
of splendour at the mention of Wallenstein's name helps, by
sounding the note of magnificence, to build up in advance an
image of the man's stature. These touches suggest the progress
Schiller has made. In *Don Carlos* he had demonstrated his
mastery of blank verse. In *Wallenstein* he does something more:
he shows himself to be a master in the application of blank verse
to dramatic ends. The style of the later play is less lyrical and

less obtrusive; instead it has increased its range and become functional to an extraordinary degree. But the free and expert handling of large groups remains. Indeed, in his skilful distribution of syntactic units of divergent length and his suppression of final-line pauses, he shows himself to be even bolder. So in these three lines of the first scene the five-beat unit is twice deliberately disrupted:

Auch auf dem Rathaus, seh ich, habt ihr euch
Schon ziemlich eingerichtet — Nun! nun! der Soldat
Behilft und schickt sich, wie er kann! (*P*., ll. 12-14)

In such a group Schiller allows the line structure to disintegrate, whilst retaining the faint beat of iambic rhythm. This is one of the almost countless variations of structure and grouping, rhythm and pattern, by which a flowing, yet never monotonous, poetic or medial style is maintained, ready to modulate smoothly into colloquial or rhetorical variation. The range of tone which Schiller thus attains fits the poetic presentation of coarse and blunt soldiers engaged in events of high significance. And the whole is harmonious, because the colloquialism is confined within decorous limits and the rhetoric restrained and muted.

## 2. THE FUNCTION OF ELEVATED SPEECH

With the entry of Octavio and Questenberg (Scene Two) a new note is heard. Octavio's first speech takes a decided step into the elevated and rhetorical, with three anastrophic genitives and two conventional epithets in the space of four lines:

Wie? Noch der Gäste mehr? Gestehn Sie, Freund!
Es brauchte diesen tränenvollen Krieg,
So vieler Helden ruhmgekrönter Häupter
In *eines* Lagers Umkreis zu versammeln. (*P*., ll. 82-5)

There is a hollowness about this language which is entirely appropriate to the character of Octavio and the role which he has assumed. It is perceptibly forced, keyed up a tone higher than the circumstances seem to warrant. He continues with

> Und siehe da! ein tapfres Paar, das würdig
> Den Heldenreihen schließt. (*P.*, ll. 92–3)

The repeated lofty formula *Held* is intended blandly to flatter those rough soldiers Isolani and Buttler. And the neatness with which the dialogue of Octavio and Questenberg is dovetailed betrays how closely they are hand in glove:

> OCTAVIO. (*Buttlern und Isolani präsentierend*) Es ist die Stärke,
> Freund, und Schnelligkeit.
> QUESTENBERG. (*zu Octavio*)
> Und zwischen beiden der erfahrne Rat. (*P.*, ll. 96–7)

Elaborate and well-thought-out periods flow from Octavio:

> Dem Kammerherrn und Kriegsrat Questenberg,
> Den Überbringer kaiserlicher Befehle,
> Der Soldaten großen Gönner und Patron
> Verehren wir in diesem würdigen Gaste. (*P.*, ll. 98–101)

How truly these empty formulas correspond to the false façade which he so carefully maintains is brought out by his immediate relapse into colloquial speech after the departure of the angry, almost mutinous, generals:

> Drei Viertel der Armee vernahmen Sie (*P.*, l. 279)

and

> Empfindlichkeit — gereizter Stolz — nichts weiter! —
> Diesen Buttler geb ich noch nicht auf.... (*P.*, ll. 284–5)

The 'Heldenreihen' has now declined into 'der Armee', the rounded period into fragmentary interjections. The first moment of relaxation past (and the point clearly made by Schiller), Octavio glides into the poetic mode; but, when the conversation swings round to his hypocrisy and double-dealing, Schiller at

once has him revert to the artificial and stilted manner which
is used to symbolize his insincerity:

> Denken Sie nicht etwa,
> Daß ich durch Lügenkünste, gleisnerische
> Gefälligkeit in seine Gunst mich stahl,
> Durch Heuchelworte sein Vertrauen nähre. (*P.*, ll. 346-9)

Two parallelisms hint at the duplicity of Octavio's conduct, a
carefully constructed period indicates the calculating and circum-
spect politician. And though Octavio, speaking to his son in
Questenberg's presence, later relaxes into a conversational
couplet—

> Er kommt vom Hofe, wo man mit dem Herzog
> Nicht ganz so wohl zufrieden ist als hier (*P.*, ll. 403-4)

—he shows even here the diplomat at work, for the lines are a
masterpiece of discreet understatement.

In general he maintains even to Max the oratorical tone which
serves as a screen to conceal his thoughts:

> Die großen, schnellen Taten der Gewalt,
> Des Augenblicks erstaunenswerte Wunder,
> Die sind es nicht, die das Beglückende,
> Das ruhig, mächtig Daurende erzeugen. (*P.*, ll. 486-9)

Even on so relaxed an occasion as the uninhibited banquet in
Act Four, we find him testing Buttler obliquely with a cautious
question which includes a classical allusion—

> Ihr liebt die Bacchusfeste auch nicht sehr (*P.*, l. 2168)

—and after Illo's drunken disclosure he speaks to his son, in
intimate tête-à-tête in the small hours of the morning, in the
formal terms of public address:

> Danks deinem Engel, Piccolomini!
> Unwissend zog er dich zurück vom Abgrund. (*P.*, ll. 2289-90)

And, when immediately after the assassination of Wallenstein
he appears for the last time, he again uses formal rhetoric, though
he thereby seeks a different kind of concealment. He no longer

has to screen political plans—he seeks now to maintain a façade which the stirrings of conscience threaten to undermine:

> Nichts von Mißhandlung! Nichts von Rache, Gräfin!
> Die schwere Schuld ist schwer gebüßt, der Kaiser
> Versöhnt, nichts geht vom Vater auf die Tochter
> Hinüber, als sein Ruhm und sein Verdienst.          (*W.T.*, ll. 3834–7)

How sharply Octavio's public manner contrasts with the direct address of the commander is made particularly clear at two points in the play. In the fifth act of *Die Piccolomini* his interchange with the Kornett who brings news of Sesina's capture is swift and brutal, with such laconic sentences and fragments of speech as, 'Was ists?', 'Mein Sohn weiß alles', 'Wen meint Ihr?', 'Habt ihr?', 'Und die Depeschen —', 'Keins von des Fürsten Hand?', 'Und der Sesina?'. Even more remarkable is the terse and imperious bluntness of his words to Isolani in Act II. v of *Wallensteins Tod*:

> OCTAVIO. Ihr unterwerft Euch dem Befehl?
> ISOLANI.                                            Ich — aber
> Ihr überrascht mich auch so schnell — Man wird
> Mir doch Bedenkzeit, hoff ich —
> OCTAVIO.                                  Zwei Minuten.
> ISOLANI. Mein Gott, der Fall ist aber —
> OCTAVIO.                                  Klar und einfach.
> Ihr sollt erklären, ob Ihr Euren Herrn
> Verraten wollet, oder treu ihm dienen.          (*W.T.*, ll. 1009–14)

This is language of the utmost directness. It corresponds to Octavio's tactics with Isolani—the surprise attack with blunt truth. When, however, he has to sway Buttler, he knows that a more subtle and tortuous policy is necessary. Immediately the pattern of rhetoric reasserts itself:

> Losreißen wollte er Euch von Eurem Kaiser—
> Von Eurer Rache hofft' er zu erlangen,
> Was Eure wohlbewährte Treu ihn nimmer
> Erwarten ließ, bei ruhiger Besinnung.
> Zum blinden Werkzeug wollt er Euch, zum Mittel
> Verworfner Zwecke Euch verächtlich brauchen....
>
>                                            (*W.T.*, ll. 1147–52)

The use of rhetorical touches to convey insincerity is not confined to Octavio Piccolomini. The protagonist of the play is at least as much concerned in concealment, duplicity, and 'seeming' as his antagonist, and Schiller has made this perceptible, not only in the substance of what Wallenstein says, but in his way of speaking also. He is the most mobile character in the play, far more chameleon-like than the uninspired Octavio. Schiller has given him moments of sincerity, moments in which he affects sincerity, moments of simulation, and moments of dissimulation. The clue to the swift mutations of Wallenstein's manner occurs in a well-known passage, in the lines which he addresses to Terzky, his confidant if anyone is, in Act II. v of *Die Piccolomini*:

Und woher weißt du, daß ich ihn nicht wirklich
Zum besten habe? Daß ich nicht euch alle
Zum besten habe? Kennst du mich so gut?
Ich wußte nicht, daß ich mein Innerstes
Dir aufgetan — Der Kaiser, es ist wahr,
Hat übel mich behandelt! — *Wenn* ich wollte,
Ich könnt ihm recht viel Böses dafür tun.
Es macht mir Freude, meine Macht zu kennen;
Ob ich sie wirklich brauchen werde, *davon* denk ich,
Weißt *du* nicht mehr zu sagen als ein andrer. (*P.*, ll. 861–70)

After this calculated indiscretion, revealing an impulse of play, it is no surprise to find that Wallenstein speaks with more than one voice. The insincerity, which is associated with a total self-centredness,[1] expresses itself in exaggeration, or in pathos, which is, indeed, a mode of exaggeration.

When Wallenstein, the unprincipled opportunist, makes a parade before Terzky of high-souled patriotism, he overdoes it, and his fivefold 'fort!' is a sign that his protestations do not ring true:

Sie müssen fort,
Fort, fort! Wir brauchen keine solche Nachbarn.
. . . . . . . .
Fort, fort mit ihnen — das verstehst du nicht. (*P.*, ll. 826–31)

---

[1] Cf. Max's judgement on Wallenstein, *W.T.*, ll. 2088–101.

To the Pappenheim Cuirassiers, too, he overstates his case, speaking of his new allies, the Swedes, with a violence which is palpably uncalled for and a deliberate distortion:

> Was geht der Schwed mich an? Ich haß ihn, wie
> Den Pfuhl der Hölle, und mit Gott gedenk ich ihn
> Bald über seine Ostsee heimzujagen.             (*W.T.*, ll. 1973-5)

So deeply ingrained is this impulse to exaggerate and inflate, as he attempts to cast a smoke-screen across his real thoughts and aims, that the technique is invoked even in moments of emotion such as the denunciation of Octavio's treachery. Here the insincerity is contained in the attempt to conceal from himself and others the guilt of his own treachery:

> O mich hat Höllenkunst getäuscht. Mir sandte
> Der Abgrund den verstecktesten der Geister,
> Den Lügekundigsten herauf, und stellt' ihn
> Als Freund an meine Seite. Wer vermag
> Der Hölle Macht zu widerstehen! Ich zog
> Den Basilisken auf an meinem Busen,
> Mit meinem Herzblut nährt ich ihn, er sog
> Sich schwelgend voll an meiner Liebe Brüsten....
>                                          (*W.T.*, ll. 2105-12)

Here the extravagance of the images is a sign of emotional disturbance, but it is also the symbol of a fundamental insincerity, of Wallenstein's awareness of discrepancy between the reality within and the image he seeks to maintain without.

Wallenstein's range of masks extends also to bluff heartiness and a show of affection. These, too, are expressed by touches of exaggeration, as in his rhetorical address to the Pappenheim delegation:

> Mich, mich verrät man! Aufgeopfert hat mich
> Der Kaiser meinen Feinden, fallen muß ich
> Wenn meine braven Truppen mich nicht retten,
> Euch will ich mich vertrauen — Euer Herz
> Sei meine Festung! Seht, auf diese Brust
> Zielt man! Nach diesem greisen Haupte!     (*W.T.*, ll. 1913-18)

The parallelisms proliferate, the clauses accumulate, in a way which would occasion no surprise in the turbulent language of Schiller's youth; but set amidst the controlled flow of his mature verse the note is felt to be overdone, the tone forced. Even when Wallenstein comes close to sincerity, established habit and the pressure of self-interest slant his speech; and the tell-tale rhetorical touches reveal to the spectator his duplicity, barely conscious though this is in, say, his appeal to Max Piccolomini in Act III. xviii of *Wallensteins Tod*. Here the opening might seem to ring true, though the repeated 'Max!' may arouse a faint suspicion:

Max! Bleibe bei mir. — Geh nicht von mir, Max!

(*W.T.*, l. 2142)

And the suspicion may grow more substantial when it is realized that the heartfelt appeal takes the rhetorical form of a chiasmus. As Wallenstein goes on, the direct and moving plea is dotted with phrases of unmistakably deliberate and elevated character, such as 'erstarrt an der gewichtigen Fahne', 'nicht schämt ich / Der kleinen Dienste mich', or 'Mit weiblich sorgender Geschäftigkeit'. Schiller uses these slight touches to reveal the impurity of motive; the emotion may pass as genuine, but the hope of furthering an aim lives beside it, intertwining with it. In the final appeal Wallenstein heightens the urgency by the use of the third person; and automatically he reveals his hand as a schemer, standing back and watching the effect of his move:

Max! du kannst mich nicht verlassen!
Es kann nicht sein, ich mags und wills nicht glauben,
Daß mich der Max verlassen kann.     (*W.T.*, ll. 2160-2)

Wallenstein, however, does not always speak in the presence of others. Three times he stands alone upon the stage and speaks a monologue. If he is honest anywhere, surely it must be in these passages in which there is no stage audience to be impressed, no interlocutor to be persuaded.

The first soliloquy (*Piccolomini*, II. v) is short, a mere ten lines. Schiller emphasizes the intimacy of the situation, the communing of the man with himself, by his stage direction—*in tiefem Nachdenken, zu sich selbst*. After a beginning in the poetic mode, in verse with fluent motion and steady unobtrusive rhythm, the tone rises to express bitterness in terms of rhetorical irony:

> Der Ungarn König ists, der Ferdinand,
> Des Kaisers Söhnlein, der ist jetzt ihr Heiland,
> Das neu aufgehende Gestirn! Mit uns
> Gedenkt man fertig schon zu sein, und wie
> Ein Abgeschiedner sind wir schon beerbet.          (*P.*, ll. 800–4)

Here the anastrophes, the exclamation, and the images are the instruments of an ironic structure.

The second monologue is the longest, extending to eighty lines, and, like the first, it begins in Schiller's quasi-prosaic manner:

> Wärs möglich? Könnt ich nicht mehr, wie ich wollte?
> Nicht mehr zurück, wie mirs beliebt?          (*W.T.*, ll. 139–40)

Artless though this beginning seems, it establishes a structural pattern. A triad of questions includes as its second and third components two parallel sentences which point in opposite directions, probing the situation. They are followed by other sets of parallels, double, treble, even quadruple:

> Nicht die Versuchung von mir wies — das Herz
> Genährt mit diesem Traum, auf ungewisse
> Erfüllung hin die Mittel mir gespart,
> Die Wege bloß mir offen hab gehalten?          (*W.T.*, ll. 142–5)

The images are terse, compressed; they do not dazzle or captivate, they represent a series of rapid illuminations of a state of mind. Far from concealing, they reveal; they are instruments of truth, not of deception. Therefore the style, though rhetorical in structure, is transparently simple, abstaining from the florid, distracting adornment in which Wallenstein indulges in the presence of others, whether friends or enemies. The expression is compact in the grammatical concision of the image of the poisoned spring—

Und — selbst der frommen Quelle reine Tat
Wird der Verdacht, schlimmdeutend, mir vergiften;

(*W.T.*, ll. 162–3)

and it is even more compressed in aphorisms or *sententiae*, such as

Kühn war das Wort, weil es die Tat nicht war        (*W.T.*, l. 170)

or

In meiner Brust war meine Tat noch mein.        (*W.T.*, l. 186)

This soliloquy is in four movements, each of which has as a coda a metaphor of some complexity. The first section is brought to an end by the image of the barred return:

Bahnlos liegts hinter mir, und eine Mauer
Aus meinen eignen Werken baut sich auf,
Die mir die Umkehr türmend hemmt!        (*W.T.*, ll. 156–8)

The second section ends with the image of the net, woven for Wallenstein's downfall by his enemies out of material which he himself has incautiously provided (*W.T.*, ll. 171–9). The third phase deploys the powers of fate, first in the figure of the drawing of lots and then in that of the child exposed to the forces of life. And the last elaborates with a wealth of figurative detail the 'invisible enemy' which is habit, custom, tradition.

These passages recall the rhetorical elements of *Don Carlos*, yet on examination they prove to be restrained and taut. There is no touch of extravagance, the language is economical, even functional. Indeed, compactness, enforced by a potent use of adverbs, is a feature which these extended images share with the rest of the speech, which is stylistically as well as psychologically a unity.

The coda to the whole soliloquy, an extended passage on custom and its powerful inertia, employs the following images or imagistic words—'thronend', 'festgegründet', 'mit tausend zähen Wurzeln', 'entflammt', 'Amme', 'würdig alten Hausrat', and 'das teure Erbstück seiner Ahnen'. It seems a medley of unrelated expressions; but they are all harnessed to the central theme, all illustrate it from various angles, and in the overlapping of their associations they reproduce the parallel procedure with which Schiller has opened the speech.

Such devices have affinities with the principle of repetition which is so conspicuous a feature of Schiller's style from *Die Räuber* onwards. The extravagance, ruthlessness, and vehemence have gone out of it. With the decline of emphasis the need for doubly and trebly underlining has faded. The experienced dramatist has applied recurrence, synonymy, and parallelism to another purpose. Firstly it supplies a supplement to understanding. The attention of the spectator at a verse play is subjected to considerable strain; all too easily his listening becomes a series of perceptions separated by brief intermissions. If comprehension of a sentence is delayed for a second, the following one is lost. Schiller's repetitive technique, with its series of related yet distinct images, succeeds in communicating coherently even with those whose attention is intermittent.[1] No doubt practical experience in the theatre provided a basis for a mode of writing to which Schiller was in any case temperamentally inclined. The method, however, is not solely or even primarily for the absent-minded. For the reader or spectator who grasps the integral text, Schiller's technique offers a rich and rewarding pattern and a remarkable subtlety of variation.

In Wallenstein's self-communing there is no flamboyance. The diversity centres upon a focus, the tone is firmly controlled. Though the temper is elevated, there is no magnification. The words by which Schiller increases scale and evokes splendour— *groß, erhaben, ewig, nimmer* —are absent. The mood is realistic in the sense that the words are spoken by Wallenstein for Wallenstein, without apparent consciousness of the audience. And the basis of the language is the ebb and flow of private speech. Even the multiplicity of image, which has some analogy with musical

[1] Cf. M. L. Gansberg, 'Zur Sprache in Hebbels Dramen', in *Hebbel in neuer Sicht*, ed. H. Kreuzer, 1963, p. 69 f.

variations, may be interpreted as a succession of explorations by the probing mind.

Wallenstein's third soliloquy shows an elevation of tone corresponding to an altered mood. It begins with a formula of address ('Du hasts erreicht, Octavio'), thereby establishing a relationship outside the self and so escaping from the self-enclosure of the monologue of Act One. The note, once sounded, is repeated with 'habt ihr schon erfahren', 'galt ich euch', 'eure Heere', 'euer letzter Hort'. The language throughout is that of one addressing an audience, and the reference to himself in the third person as 'Friedland' is a certain sign that Wallenstein is here striking a public attitude. The heightened language of the speech tells us why. It betrays his inner uncertainty, the need to set forth a case in order to convince himself. Once more the adoption of the rhetorical mode in *Wallenstein* suggests a form of insincerity, a discrepancy between feelings and the words used to express them.

An important variation of this function of rhetoric is seen in Questenberg's speech in Act Two of *Die Piccolomini*. The emissary from Vienna addresses Wallenstein in the presence of an audience and the style of his speech is therefore elevated, as befits the agent of an exalted principal. He speaks in set periods with an abundance of conventional epithets:

> Als seine Majestät
> Der Kaiser ihren mutigen Armeen
> Ein ruhmgekröntes, kriegserfahrnes Haupt
> Geschenkt in der Person des Herzogs Friedland,
> Geschahs in froher Zuversicht, das Glück
> Des Krieges schnell und günstig umzuwenden. (*P.*, ll. 1021-6)

This is the opening of a carefully contrived speech, and its formality contrasts glaringly with the plainness of the ironical interjections with which Wallenstein punctuates it. Thus Questenberg in three rounded lines directs a shaft of irony at Wallenstein—

> Doch in großmütge Hand war er gefallen,
> Statt Strafe fand er Lohn, und reich beschenkt
> Entließ der Fürst den Erzfeind seines Kaisers (*P.*, ll. 1120-2)

—which is immediately countered in relaxed and easy manner by Wallenstein:

> Ich weiß, ich weiß — Sie hatten schon in Wien
> Die Fenster, die Balkons voraus gemietet,
> Ihn auf dem Armensünderkarrn zu sehn —
> Die Schlacht hätt ich mit Schimpf verlieren mögen,
> Doch das vergeben mir die Wiener nicht,
> Daß ich um ein Spektakel sie betrog.　　　　(*P.*, ll. 1123–8)

It is irony in contrasting modes, formal and informal.

The distinction between the deliberate, almost stilted, declamation of Questenberg and Wallenstein's easy, flexible commentary is a key to the interpretation of the scene. Questenberg's formalism is a symbol of his role. He is a mouthpiece, expressing the views and conforming to the instructions of the Imperial Government, which has sent him to Pilsen. Wallenstein's relaxed manner indicates his first-hand knowledge and the security he feels in his own camp in the presence of his own supporters. Before Wallenstein's effortless certainty, Questenberg's confidence falters, and his style slides away from formal rhetoric to colourless near-prose:

> Wenns *so* steht, hab ich hier nichts mehr zu sagen.　　(*P.*, l. 1213)

Or he falls back on a lame defensive:

> Es ist nichts dahinter
> Zu sehn. Die Klugheit räts, die Not gebeuts.　　(*P.*, ll. 1237–8)

There are two figures in *Wallenstein* who often (though by no means always) speak in the rhetorical mode, and yet are characters of integrity, quite foreign to the scheming, the duplicity, and the deceit which the rhetorical mode so frequently and so subtly suggests. Nevertheless the function of the rhetoric is fundamentally similar. It expresses a dissonance; the disharmony, however, is no longer within the divided character, but between the integral personality and the world around him.

Together, in their rare moments of relaxation and intimacy, Max and Thekla speak a language of simplicity and directness.

But for the most part they are conscious of a harsh and unsympathetic world around them, or they are actually in conflict with the forces of intrigue and deceit, with the politics of opportunism and power; confronted with this hostile environment their language swings into the assertiveness of a heightened rhetoric. So Thekla expresses their sense of harmony and intimate alliance in plain, almost homely, language:

> Wir wollen diesen Terzkys dankbar sein
> Für jede Gunst, doch ihnen auch nicht mehr
> Vertrauen, als sie würdig sind, und uns
> Im übrigen — auf unser Herz verlassen.  (*P.*, ll. 1717–20)

But the world around them cannot be so easily dismissed. The moment of happy insensibility dissolves, and at once Thekla's style becomes forced and heightened as the awareness of conflict returns:

> Wir haben uns gefunden, halten uns
> Umschlungen, fest und ewig. Glaube mir!
> Das ist um vieles mehr, als sie gewollt.
> Drum laß es uns wie einen heilgen Raub
> In unsers Herzens Innerstem bewahren.
> Aus Himmels Höhen fiel es uns herab,
> Und nur dem Himmel wollen wirs verdanken.  (*P.*, ll. 1729–35)

The sense of strain can extract from Max Piccolomini, too, the rhetorical note. Indeed, the exalted and elevated comes more readily to his lips than to Thekla's. This is a sign of the more intricate stresses to which he is subjected, but it also reveals an element of insecurity in his more complex personality. It is an awareness of the gulf between his vision of peace and his grim and warlike environment that impels him to the splendour of his imagined description of the army's homecoming:

> O schöner Tag! wenn endlich der Soldat
> Ins Leben heimkehrt, in die Menschlichkeit,
> Zum frohen Zug die Fahnen sich entfalten,
> Und heimwärts schlägt der sanfte Friedensmarsch.  (*P.*, ll. 534–7)

Selection in vocabulary, anastrophe, and ellipsis characterize the

measured rhetoric of this speech. It corresponds to an exaltation
arising from a tension between ideal and reality.

But when the opposition between Max and his environment
touches his emotional life, as it does in the scene of disillusion-
ment in Act Two of *Wallensteins Tod*, then the rhetorical language takes on more complex, exclamatory, forms:

> O Gott des Himmels! was ist das für eine
> Veränderung! Ziemt solche Sprache mir
> Mit dir, der wie der feste Stern des Pols
> Mir als die Lebensregel vorgeschienen!
> O! welchen Riß erregst du mir im Herzen!        (*W.T.*, ll. 732–6)

Max's mind is here in a state of division, and for such a situation
of strain, in which the integrity of the soul is threatened, Schiller's
linguistic equivalent is the flight of rhetoric, which symbolizes
the effort to escape from the grasp of reality. The same note
prevails in Max's speech in his parting from Thekla in the
hostile presence of Wallenstein; and it reaches a climax in the
desperate and anguished tirade which he addresses to the rescuing
cuirassiers who crowd the hall at the end of the act (*Wallensteins Tod*, III).

In addition to this passionate and distracted utterance, there
are a number of tracts of elevated style which may properly be
termed tirades. They all stand out sharply with some measure of
contrast to the preceding or following speeches. They fulfil a
special role in the economy of the drama, and may be divided
into contingent and absolute tirades. Contingent tirades are
closely related to the circumstances of the scene and the character of the speaker. They represent in stylized form the response
to the critical phase of a situation. The absolute tirades are
independent of character; they stand out as excrescences upon
the general texture, and have their justification, not in the development of action or character, but in some overriding necessity
which the author feels bound, in pursuance of his general aim, to
impose upon the play.

An untypical contingent tirade occurs when Buttler, intervening in the altercation between Questenberg and the colonels

(*Piccolomini*, I. ii), makes a speech which has little in common with the character he is to bear throughout the play. He sets forth in poetic terms the heterogeneous composition of Wallenstein's forces and their focal unity in the figure of the generalissimo; and his splendid rhetoric echoes in exalted terms the message of *Wallensteins Lager* —

> Doch alle führt an gleich gewaltgem Zügel
> Ein Einziger, durch gleiche Lieb und Furcht
> Zu *einem* Volke sie zusammenbindend.
> Und wie des Blitzes Funke sicher, schnell,
> Geleitet an der Wetterstange, läuft,
> Herrscht sein Befehl vom letzten fernen Posten,
> Der an die Dünen branden hört den Belt,
> Der in der Etsch fruchtbare Täler sieht,
> Bis zu der Wache, die ihr Schilderhaus
> Hat aufgerichtet an der Kaiserburg.      (*P*., ll. 231–40)

This speech threatens to slip out of the stylistic frame of the play, but before its intrusive tone can become established the whole thing is cut down to size by Questenberg's acid irony:

> Was ist der langen Rede kurzer Sinn?

Thus, by a stroke of derision, Schiller secures at the last moment the contingency of Buttler's tirade.

Gräfin Terzky's tirades in *Wallensteins Tod* (I. vii) are entirely related to character and situation. The countess lets herself go because her ambition and her impetuosity drive her to a tone which (her instinct tells her) is also the certain means of goading Wallenstein from depressive inertia into decision and action. Similarly Max Piccolomini's eloquent outburst in Act II. vii ('O wärst du wahr gewesen und gerade', etc.) is an expression of a highly-strung youthful character subjected to abnormal stress. This is equally true of his tirades in the third act, notably the one beginning 'Sieh! Alles — alles wollt ich dir verdanken' (ll. 2085 ff.), and of the uncontrolled paroxysm which ends the act: 'Blast! Blast — O wären es die schwedschen Hörner . . .' (ll. 2413 ff).

A more difficult problem confronts us in the absolute tirades.

In Illo's speech in Act II. vi of *Die Piccolomini* an extended tract of exalted rhetorical speech occurs, which has admittedly some relevance to Illo's aims and desires, but possesses no affinity at all with his natural mode of expression:

> O! nimm die Stunde wahr, eh sie entschlüpft.
> So selten kommt der Augenblick im Leben,
> Der wahrhaftig wichtig ist und groß....          (*P.*, ll. 928–30)

When Illo begins thus, it is apparent that the language is appropriate to a critical situation in a matter of great importance, but not that it fits a character whose most obvious features are coarseness, brutality, and self-interest. And the discrepancy becomes more obvious as the speech continues with anastrophic genitives ('des Glückes Fäden'), disjoined epithets ('Die Häupter / Des Heeres, die besten, trefflichsten'), and poetic images ('Die hohe Flut ists, die das schwere Schiff / Vom Strande hebt'). What is here attributed to Illo is a sententious passage of elevated rhetoric, generalized in character and providing a perceptive commentary on Wallenstein's affairs; and at the same time it seeks by its exalted tone to persuade him into a far-reaching decision. Schiller has momentarily abandoned the verisimilitude and consistency of *Wallenstein* and taken a short cut, in order to achieve an effect by concentrated and quick-acting means.

The speech with which Thekla concludes the third act of *Die Piccolomini* is equally remarkable. With two conspicuous exceptions (of which this is one) Thekla's utterances are more notable for homely simplicity than for elevation. In this tirade of twenty-six lines, however, she rises to a pitch of rhetoric which seems inconsistent with her normal mode. After a brief constatation (ll. 1887–91) she speaks an invocation in the manner of French classical tragedy:

> Du, Liebe, gib uns Kraft, du göttliche!

There follows a commentary on the situation couched in the loftiest language:

> Das ist kein Schauplatz, wo die Hoffnung wohnt,
> Nur dumpfes Kriegsgetöse rasselt hier.          (*P.*, ll. 1895–6)

Love, the private concern of Thekla herself and Max, thereupon enters personified, as Thekla summarizes the position in allegorical terms:

> Und selbst die Liebe, wie in Stahl gerüstet,
> Zum Todeskampf gegürtet, tritt sie auf. *(P.*, ll. 1897–8)

This is no longer the expression of a suffering, sentient human being: it is poetic comment from outside and above; and this is even more apparent when Thekla goes on to assume the role of prophetess:

> Es geht ein finstrer Geist durch unser Haus,
> Und schleunig will das Schicksal mit uns enden.
>
> . . . . . . . .
>
> Es zieht mich fort, mit göttlicher Gewalt,
> Dem Abgrund zu, ich kann nicht widerstreben. *(P.*, ll. 1899–1906)

The climax of this speech is an extended image of the destruction of a house by lightning. The symbolism is plain enough, but the real function of this coda is to establish this tirade on a plane above the personal impulses and stresses, desires and sufferings, which beset the characters:

> O! wenn ein Haus im Feuer soll vergehn,
> Dann treibt der Himmel sein Gewölk zusammen,
> Es schießt der Blitz herab aus heitern Höhn,
> Aus unterirdschen Schlünden fahren Flammen,
> Blindwütend schleudert selbst der Gott der Freude
> Den Pechkranz in das brennende Gebäude! *(P.*, ll. 1907–12)

The anastrophes, the select vocabulary, the invocation, and the elaborate concluding image all give this passage a special tone and single it out as something distinct from the rest of the act. The repeated exclamatory 'O' emphasizes it, and the final seal of the consciously sublime is set by the modulation into rhyme which occurs, in interlocking form, in the second half of the tirade, until a full close is achieved by a final couplet.

Clearly this passage of high tragic style is intrusive. Schiller has admittedly provided a transition of a sort to it in the tone of the preceding altercation between Thekla and the Gräfin Terzky, which even includes two short sections of stichomythic speech;

but the language to that point remains attuned to situation and character; the Gräfin's rhetoric is designed to impose her will and Thekla's crisp and lapidary retorts reflect her courageous and high-spirited temper. The final tirade has no such psychological basis.

It may be assumed that this excursion into the sublime gave pleasure to Schiller himself; yet it would be naïve to see self-indulgence as the principal motive. The key is in the position of the lovers as the representatives in the play of truth and integrity, as the only characters who refuse to compromise with expediency. Their wider significance could not be fully expressed in the ebb and flow of personal feelings; they could not be allowed to be completely overrun and outplayed (as they are in the action) by the egotism of the opportunists surrounding them. It was necessary to give them a platform, a point of vantage, from which they could speak with authority of a higher truth than that acknowledged by the contending parties of the play.

In similar fashion Max Piccolomini, in *Wallensteins Tod* (III. xviii), rises above the turmoil of his own personal anguish and despair to express the poet's verdict on Wallenstein's character. He begins with a judgement almost factually phrased—'Gleich-gültig / Trittst du das Glück der Deinen in den Staub' (ll. 2088–2089). The assessment is then generalized and elevated: 'Der Gott, dem *du* dienst, ist kein Gott der Gnade.' Thereupon Max passes to a denunciation in the form of an elaborate, rhetorically phrased, image:

> Wie das gemütlos blinde Element,
> Das furchtbare, mit dem kein Bund zu schließen,
> Folgst du des Herzens wildem Trieb allein.
> Weh denen, die auf dich vertraun, an dich
> Die sichre Hütte ihres Glückes lehnen,
> Gelockt von deiner gastlichen Gestalt!
> Schnell, unverhofft, bei nächtlich stiller Weile
> Gärts in dem tückschen Feuerschlunde, ladet
> Sich aus mit tobender Gewalt, und weg
> Treibt über alle Pflanzungen der Menschen
> Der wilde Strom in grausender Zerstörung.　　(*W.T.*, ll. 2091–101)

Thekla's extended speech in the fourth act is also a commentary from above, but it turns from a denunciation of the evil powers of the real world to a transfiguration of the moral and spiritual values of which she and Max are the representatives and guardians. The speech begins as an elegy for Max and his companions in death, and reaches its climax in the rejection of a life deprived of spiritual content:

Was ist das Leben ohne Liebesglanz?
Ich werf es hin, da sein Gehalt verschwunden. (*W.T.*, ll. 3163–4)

After this *sententia*, thinly disguised as a rhetorical question, the elegy continues, but now Thekla laments, not so much her lost lover, as her own love. Schiller's characteristic exalted simple epithets and nouns accumulate. 'Glänzend', 'der neue goldne Tag', 'zwei himmelschöne Stunden', 'von tausend Sonnen aufgehellt', 'ein guter Engel'. Suddenly the nostalgic simplicity is torn by a flash of reality—

Da kommt das Schicksal — Roh und kalt
Faßt es des Freundes zärtliche Gestalt...

—whereupon the link with a harsh and violent actuality is brilliantly and tersely established by a rhythmic reference to the plunging hooves beneath which Max has met his end:

Und wirft ihn unter den Hufschlag seiner Pferde.[1]

The speech is then concluded (and the couplet completed) by an epigrammatic summarizing sentence of so bald and blatant a character that it requires all the skill and sensitiveness of a fine actress if bathos is to be avoided and the spectators' sympathies retained for Thekla:

Das ist das Los des Schönen auf der Erde! (*W.T.*, l. 3180)

Here the dangers of Schiller's predilection for a bold treatment of the obvious become all too evident. No doubt the adoption of rhyme in these tirades made the undertaking more perilous.

[1] Kurt May first detected in the metrical irregularity of this line a brief reference to the dactylic rhythm of the galloping horses: K. May, *Friedrich Schiller: Idee und Wirklichkeit im Drama*, 1948, p. 153.

Certainly the firm two-syllabled rhyme *Pferde — Erde* emphasizes triteness. But the chief reason for the failure of this climax is Schiller's attempt to provide a summary in too narrow and set a compass. Thekla has already fully made her point, and the final rounding off is merely a superfluous and inadequate generalization.

The absolute tirade with which Buttler opens the fourth act of *Wallensteins Tod* is an altogether different matter. Illo's powerful pleading and Max Piccolomini's denunciation can, in spite of stylistic divergence, still function as elements in the dialogue. Even Thekla's eloquent declamation can, at a pinch, be regarded as the communing of the character with herself. But Buttler's seventeen lines are addressed to the spectators, and in this they occupy a unique position in this vast trilogy.

Buttler begins, not with a rhetorical and apostrophic *du*, but with an informative *er*—'Er ist herein'—to which he at once adds a metaphysical gloss with 'Ihn führte sein Verhängnis' (*W.T.*, l. 2428). The laconic statement is then graphically amplified and symbolically pointed:

Der Rechen ist gefallen hinter ihm,
Und wie die Brücke, die ihn trug, beweglich
Sich niederließ und schwebend wieder hob,
Ist jeder Rettungsweg ihm abgeschnitten.     (*W.T.*, ll. 2429–32)

Buttler goes on to summarize Wallenstein's career, crystallizing it in the image of the meteor. This section of the speech is formally addressed to the absent Wallenstein and so constitutes an apostrophe. Its opening words, following on the drawbridge metaphor, are the clue to the special function of the passage. Buttler begins his apostrophe with

Bis hieher, Friedland, und nicht weiter! sagt
Die Schicksalsgöttin.     (*W.T.*, ll. 2433–4)

The apostrophe, therefore, is spoken, not by Buttler, but by the 'Schicksalsgöttin', by Nemesis. Buttler acts purely as a medium, transmitting to the audience the message of another. As the speech proceeds, it becomes more and more evident that what is said is not spoken by Nemesis either, but is the author's own commentary. The shift from Buttler as an individual is demonstrated in the style. The terse opening of the speech is characteristic of the fierce, tough man of action. But the splendid rhetoric which follows, with its symbolism, its elaborate image, the personification of fate, and the classical allusion ('Den heiligen Herd der Laren umzustürzen'), all this has nothing more to do with Buttler, but is the voice of the chorus to a tragedy. What the tirades of Illo, Max, and Thekla attempted almost surreptitiously is here done openly and directly. The problem of fate touches the periphery of classical tragedy, and at once Schiller responds by adopting a device of the classical mode. And, since he has here no chorus, this choral introduction is put into the mouth of the one character who can best be seen as the instrument of fate.

It is well known that Schiller had for some years been fascinated by Greek tragedy. He had read a scene from Euripides with Caroline von Beulwitz in September 1788, and in the winter of 1788–9 he had given much of his spare time to translating a group of Euripidean tragedies. His interest was not antiquarian, but sharply focused on his own aesthetic needs.

Die Hauptsache [he wrote of his study of Greek tragedy] ist die Manier, die im Schlechten herrscht wie im Besten, und in jenem fast noch leichter bemerkt wird. Mein Stil hat dieser Reinigung sehr nötig. Ich hoffe, ehe ein Jahr um ist, sollst du an diesem Studium der Griechen — Studium kann ich es aber für jetzt noch kaum nennen — schöne Früchte bei mir sehen.[1]

Precisely because he was so convinced of the value for him of Greek tragedy, his enthusiasm persisted, and in October 1791 he writes to Körner, 'Überhaupt und vorzüglich strebe ich durch diese Übersetzungen der tragischen Dichter nach dem griechischen Stil...'.[2] Nor did his work at *Wallenstein* diminish his preoccupation with ancient drama; particularly in 1797 he devoted considerable time to it.

[1] Letter to Körner, 12 December 1788 (Jonas, 2. 180).
[2] 24 October 1791 (Jonas, 3. 163).

The rhetorical tirades and Buttler's entry as a pseudo-chorus are doubtless linked with Schiller's classical studies. Equally attributable to them is the use made in this play of stichomythia. In *Die Piccolomini* it is relatively sparse. Two short passages occur in Act One in the altercation between the generals and Questenberg.[1] More than once in the third act a single-line retort by Thekla seems about to initiate a stichomythic passage, which then fails to develop.[2] The sharp confrontation between father and son Piccolomini in Act Five crystallizes in stichomythic writing, but it is all over in four lines:

OCTAVIO. Ich drängte mich nicht selbst in sein Geheimnis.
MAX. Aufrichtigkeit verdiente sein Vertraun.
OCTAVIO. Nicht würdig war er meiner Wahrheit mehr.
MAX. Noch minder würdig deiner war Betrug.     (*P.*, ll. 2443–6)

Since opportunities for such writing were abundant in *Die Piccolomini*, either Schiller was not sufficiently interested in the form, or he was holding his hand. And this latter seems the more probable, since the quite extensive stichomythia of *Wallensteins Tod* occurs exclusively in the fourth and fifth acts, the climax of the whole great trilogy.

The scene in which Buttler announces his intention to assassinate Wallenstein and is weakly opposed by Gordon (IV. vi) begins with an introductory passage of broken verse which, despite the breaking up of single lines, is essentially of stichomythic character:

BUTTLER. Er darf nicht leben.
GORDON.                         Ihr vermöchtets?
BUTTLER. Ihr oder ich. Er sah den letzten Morgen.
GORDON. Ermorden wollt Ihr ihn?
BUTTLER.                         Das ist mein Vorsatz.
GORDON. Der Eurer Treu vertraut!
BUTTLER.                         Sein böses Schicksal!
                                 (*W.T.*, ll. 2698–701)

---

[1] ll. 136–9 and 200–9.     [2] ll. 1840 and 1861.

Four lines later stichomythia proper sets in, with couplet answering couplet:

GORDON. Das wäre Mord und nicht Gerechtigkeit,
Denn hören muß sie auch den Schuldigsten.
BUTTLER. Klar ist die Schuld, der Kaiser hat gerichtet,
Und seinen Willen nur vollstrecken wir.     (*W.T.*, ll. 2705–8)

The tempo quickens as the thrust and counter-thrust shorten to the single line:

BUTTLER. Der hurtge Dienst gefällt den Königen.
GORDON. Zu Henkers Dienst drängt sich kein edler Mann.
                                        (*W.T.*, ll. 2711–12)

The alternation between single-line groups and couplet groups, which persists in the continuation of this passage, is characteristic of Schiller's flexible handling of stichomythia. Indeed, from time to time Schiller carries it to the point of answering a couplet with a single line, as here:

GORDON. Auf diesen Wällen wär ich ritterlich,
Des Kaisers Schloß verteidigend, gesunken.
BUTTLER. Und tausend brave Männer kamen um!
GORDON. In ihrer Pflicht — das schmückt und ehrt den Mann;
Doch schwarzen Mord verfluchte die Natur.
                                        (*W.T.*, ll. 2723–7)

In such a variation Schiller demonstrates his capacity to adapt an established form to the expression of character, for the self-pitying volubility of Gordon is set against Buttler's stark and resolute laconicism.

The attack and counter-attack of stichomythia seems particularly in place when the participants are soldiers. It comes as a surprise, however, to find Thekla, a young and inexperienced girl, arguing with her lady-in-waiting in similar terms:

NEUBRUNN. Bedachten Sie auch Ihres Vaters Zorn?
THEKLA. Ich fürchte keines Menschen Zürnen mehr....
                                        (*W.T.*, ll. 3100–1)

Doubtless the stichomythia here reflects the steeling effect which the news of Max's death has had upon Thekla, and symbolizes her transformation in a few short hours into a woman of tragic resolution; and so it shows again the harnessing of a formal device to the expression of character and situation.

However flexibly Schiller succeeded in handling stichomythia, the fundamentally formal nature of this mode of writing cannot be overlooked. It is so distinctive a mode that its onset and cessation are instantly recognizable.

Both in its ritualistic, antiphonal manner and in its historical association with Greek tragedy, stichomythia elevates the tone and stylizes the drama; and it is significant that its principal incidence in *Wallenstein* is precisely at the point where the quasi-choric tirade also makes its entry. Clearly its employment is deliberate and does not represent a subconscious drift towards the Greek manner, since the fifth act of *Wallensteins Tod* lacks both the tirades and the stichomythia. In the ritualistic tone of the fourth act an unexpected parallelism is discovered between Buttler and Thekla. Each speaks a significant tirade and no similar passage is allocated to any other character; and each participates in an extended tract of stichomythia, which likewise is used at no other point. The similarity of style suggests an affinity of role. The formalism of presentation stresses the symbolical function of these two figures, neither of whom appears at first sight to be central. Buttler, not Wallenstein, is the representative of the dark and earth-bound, to whom Thekla opposes her integral character and her devotion to spiritual values. The stylization of speech before the catastrophe of the fifth act is a means of setting in relief the symbolic stature of these two characters, and so of firmly establishing the metaphysical background before the final crunch.

### 3. THE COLLOQUIAL TONE

Though the fourth act of *Wallensteins Tod* is set in an elevated key, it is not inconsistent in style nor unrelated to the tone of the remainder of the work. Thekla's exalted speech and its prelude of stichomythia are enclosed within tracts of the simplest and most direct language. When, in the numbness of her pain and grief, she addresses the Swedish officer, she does so in a series of plain, straightforward questions—'Wo ist sein Grab?', 'Wie heißt das Kloster?', 'Ists weit bis dahin?', 'Wie geht der Weg?', and even (soldier's daughter that she is) 'Wer kommandiert sie?' And the climax of her magniloquent speech is followed, not by a curtain, but by a continuation of the scene in monosyllabic terseness, returning us from the thrilling splendour of powerful declamation to the desolation of Thekla's real life:

THEKLA. Willst du uns Pferde schaffen, Rosenberg?
STALLMEISTER. Ich will sie schaffen.
THEKLA. Willst du uns begleiten?
STALLMEISTER. Mein Fräulein, bis ans End der Welt.

(*W.T.*, ll. 3182–4)

It is all muted and flat, and the poignancy is conveyed obliquely by Rosenberg's reticent devotion and by Thekla's inability to pronounce the name Neustadt, where Max lies buried:

Nach — sags ihm, Neubrunn!

Though this language is valid on the realistic plane, it is strictly disciplined in its sobriety. No momentary irrelevance, no twist or turn of slovenly colloquial speech, mars its highly selective directness.

Nevertheless even in this fourth act the rhythm of ordinary speech is audible, tingeing the language of Wallenstein's baser associates. Terzky joins Buttler and Gordon with a jovial shoulder-clapping speech:

Nun solls bald anders werden! Morgen ziehn
Die Schweden ein, zwölftausend tapfre Krieger.
Dann grad auf Wien. He! Lustig, Alter! Kein
So herb Gesicht zu solcher Freudenbotschaft. (*W.T.*, ll. 2755–8)

And Illo chimes in a moment later with his old grievance in his familiar tone:

Hört, alter Freund! Das ist es, was mir nie
Am Herrn gefiel, es war mein ewger Zank,
Er hat die Welschen immer vorgezogen.

Auch jetzo noch, ich schwörs bei meiner Seele,
Säh er uns alle lieber zehnmal tot,
Könnt er den Freund damit ins Leben rufen. (*W.T.*, ll. 2770–5)

The coarseness of the man is perfectly caught and the nagging rancour of his mind is touched in with a reminiscence of his violent outburst in Act Two:

Weil er ein Welscher ist, drum taugt er dir. (*W.T.*, l. 873)

If the colloquial tone is perceptible in this, the most classical and astringent of the five acts, it is even more evident in the remainder. Wallenstein expresses in Act One his hesitation in a complete line of 'unconscious' blank verse, such as any man may unwittingly speak:

Ich will es lieber doch nicht tun. (*W.T.*, l. 414)

The flatness of this prosaic line represents no failure on Schiller's part; the feebleness of the rhythm corresponds to the momentary feebleness of the man. Again, when the duchess breaks in upon Wallenstein at a moment of catastrophe, she expresses her lamentation in completely colloquial form:

O Albrecht! Was hast du getan!

And Wallenstein's irritation is put in equally familiar terms:

Nun das noch! (*W.T.*, l. 2010)

Schiller does not flinch from risking this touch of domestic comedy; and yet the two short speeches together make up an entirely regular line, so that the rhythmic impulse is not lost.

Schiller displays a singular mastery in the distribution of verse between two characters, catching the interchange as well as the vocabulary and syntax of everyday speech, as in this example, in which the duchess is pressed by Wallenstein to admit the change of climate at court:

HERZOGIN. . . . . . . .
Man spreche, sagt er — ach! ich kanns nicht sagen.
WALLENSTEIN. (*gespannt*) Nun?
HERZOGIN. Von einer zweiten — (*Sie stockt*)

WALLENSTEIN.         Zweiten —
HERZOGIN.                 Schimpflichern
  — Absetzung.               (*P.*, ll. 699–701)

Even more remarkable is the extended rapid dialogue which occurs when Buttler reveals the interception of Wallenstein's dispatch-rider:

BUTTLER (*hält ihn zurück*). Mein Feldherr, wen erwartet Ihr?
WALLENSTEIN. Den Eilenden, der mir die Nachricht bringt,
  Wie es mit Prag gelungen.
BUTTLER.            Hum!
WALLENSTEIN.         Was ist Euch?
BUTTLER. So wißt Ihrs nicht?
WALLENSTEIN.         Was denn?
BUTTLER.                Wie dieser Lärmen
  Ins Lager kam? —
WALLENSTEIN.    Wie?
BUTTLER.          Jener Bote —
WALLENSTEIN.           Nun?
BUTTLER. Er ist herein.
TERZKY und ILLO.    Er ist herein?
WALLENSTEIN.         Mein Bote?
BUTTLER. Seit mehrern Stunden.
WALLENSTEIN.         Und ich weiß es nicht?
                      (*W.T.*, ll. 1722–8)

Of these seven lines, one is divided into four speeches and three others each into three. The whole thing has a breathless impulsion, yet the beat is maintained in snatches such as 'So wißt Ihrs nicht?' or 'Er ist herein'.

    This application of colloquial language, in quick, sharp interchange, to the urgent revelation of vital news, is so suitable to its purpose, combining speed, the sense of vivid reality, and the throb of the verse, that Schiller uses it on four other occasions in this critical third act: when Terzky reports the defection of the Croat squadrons, when Illo brings news that Tiefenbach's troops have refused to obey orders, when Wallenstein's temper blazes up at the shooting down of Neumann, and finally when Wallenstein's personal intervention fails to quell the revolt. And of similar character is the hushed and hurried converse between Octavio and the Kornett in the last act of *Die Piccolomini*.

The colloquial mode, moreover, is distributed among the characters without regard to their stature. The minor figures repeatedly speak the language of everyday, as they might be expected to do. We see it clearly in the servants' talk in Act Two of *Die Piccolomini*, or with the deputation of Pappenheimer Cuirassiers in Act Three of *Wallensteins Tod*, where the corporal puts his point in these simple homely words: 'Braucht nicht viel Worte. Sprich / Ja oder Nein, so sind wir schon zufrieden' (*W.T.*, ll. 1889–90).

Secondary figures, too, such as Illo and Terzky, Wrangel and Isolani, speak in plain and straightforward tones, still recognizable after a century and a half as real speech; but these are rough soldiers and their blunt language might be reckoned a form of characterization. It is much more remarkable that Max and Thekla, the two characters who, though in, are not of this world of opportunism, intrigue, and deceit, also frequently speak in the colloquial mode. Max expresses his contempt of the Viennese court in plain terms with conversational ellipses:

Ja! so sind sie! Schreckt
Sie alles gleich, was eine Tiefe hat;
Ist ihnen nirgends wohl, als wos recht flach ist.    (*P.*, ll. 446–8)

To his father's stilted and tendentious questions he replies with disjointed simple sentences:

Es war ein ernst Geschäft — ich war zerstreut —
Die Sache selbst erschien mir nicht so dringend.    (*P.*, ll. 2285–6)

Or he uses detached phrases, not bothering to form complete sentences:

Worüber Argwohn? Nicht den mindesten.    (*P.*, l. 2288)

Max's famous line with the three repeated sentences with shifting emphasis employs the bare materials of ordinary speech:

Es kann nicht sein! kann *nicht* sein! *kann* nicht sein!

(*P.*, l. 2430)

He expresses a resolute decision with brisk straightforwardness—

Ich will auf kürzerm Weg mir Licht verschaffen          (*P.*, l. 2599)

—and his anguish (*W.T.*, III. xvii) tails off in the inarticulateness of real life:

O Gott! Wie kann ich anders? Muß ich nicht?
Mein Eid — die Pflicht —                              (*W.T.*, ll. 2176–7)

Thekla is even more addicted to plain, unvarnished, speech. Her first entry, in its straightforwardness, tears apart the Gräfin's web of intrigue—

Spart Euch die Mühe, Tante!
Das hört er besser von mir selbst.                     (*P.*, ll. 1518–19)

And in her conversations with aunt and mother she preserves the same unaffected colloquial tone.

In an astonishing passage in the third act of *Die Piccolomini*, Thekla asserts the tone of simplicity and directness, sweeping Max along with her. As long as the Gräfin is present an air of unreality and affectation prevails. No sooner has she left the room than Thekla turns to Max with the sudden words

Trau ihnen nicht. Sie meinens falsch,                  (*P.*, l. 1684)

initiating an interchange of pure (though persistently rhythmic) realism:

MAX.                    Sie könnten —
THEKLA. Trau niemand hier als mir. Ich sah es gleich,
Sie haben einen Zweck.
MAX.                    Zweck! Aber welchen?
Was hätten sie, uns Hoffnungen —
THEKLA. Das weiß ich nicht. Doch glaub mir, es ist nicht
Ihr Ernst, uns zu beglücken, zu verbinden.             (*P.*, ll. 1684–9)

In this swift and direct language Thekla demonstrates the unerring accuracy of her instinctive mind. She reaches the highest point of this mode in her impulsive and deeply felt response to Max's praise of Wallenstein—

MAX.       .       .       .       .       .       .       .       .
   Er ist so gut, so edel —
THEKLA.                    Das bist du!                    (*P.*, l. 1702)

The straightforwardness of the girl chooses the most straightforward of words.

The act in which colloquial speech is most consistently used is the fourth of *Die Piccolomini*, in which Schiller portrays a banquet attended by hard-drinking soldiers, and culminating in a drunken brawl. Down-to-earth language was in place here, if anywhere; and Schiller grasps the opportunity with both hands. This is the only point at which he frankly uses prose—for the document, prepared by Illo and Terzky as a snare and read aloud by Max. And the verse speech which frames it is plentifully studded with short and simple colloquial phrases, such as Isolani's half-tipsy toast to Max—'Herr Bruder, was wir lieben!'— or Illo's self-gratulatory words—'Sie sind / Ganz kordial. Ich denk, wir haben sie.'

Though in Buttler's speeches a slightly more formal tone interposes (it is significant that, apart from Max, Buttler is the only one to drink little and remain sober, and so this tone serves to contrast him with the rest), the conversational presently returns, as the attention is focused upon the Kellermeister. Here Schiller achieves a relief to the broken and coarse tone of the rest by attributing to the pompous steward a speech which corresponds realistically to the portentous manner of the man. The description of the gilded loving-cup constitutes a poetic interlude which still remains consistent because it fits the character of the speaker. It is a central point of rest, throwing into relief the brash and coarse colloquialism of the verse which, broken up and thrown from one speaker to another, occupies the rest of the act.

The final section begins in an atmosphere of alcoholic bonhomie:

ISOLANI. Gut Nacht! — Gut Nacht, Colalto — Generalleutnant,
   Gut Nacht! Ich sagte besser, guten Morgen.

GÖTZ. Herr Bruder! Prosit Mahlzeit!
TIEFENBACH. Das war ein königliches Mahl!
GÖTZ.                                        Ja, die Frau Gräfin
   Verstehts. Sie lernt' es ihrer Schwieger ab,
   Gott hab sie selig! Das war eine Hausfrau!       (*P.*, ll. 2143–8)

With the entry of Illo and the discovery that Max Piccolomini
has not signed the crucial document, the lax verse suddenly
becomes taut and staccato as the scene blazes up into a brawl.
Yet the realism of stylistic mode remains unchanged. The verse
continues without irregularity, yet the conversational phrases
pass easily from man to man in couplets, single lines, or fragments
of a line. Only Illo's revealing outburst—'Schreib — Judas!'—
breaks the metrical scheme, and the stage direction shows why,
with its indication *vor Wut stammelnd*. The whole is a brilliant
and extended application of the colloquial mode to the blank-
verse form, achieving realism, irony, and humour, and yet
imparting to it all the cachet and the memorable shape of
conscious art. The most realistic act of all continues to move
within the frame of poetic drama.


### 4. VOCABULARY AND IMAGE

Since so much of *Wallenstein* is set in colloquial terms it comes
as no surprise to find that much of the vocabulary tends to be both
broader and simpler than in the earlier plays. The images of this
everyday speech are inclined to be stereotyped, mostly homely or
proverbial phrases, such as Wallenstein's 'ließ / Durch eine
Hintertür euch stets entwischen' (*W.T.*, ll. 250–1) or Illo's 'Das
Eisen muß / Geschmiedet werden, weil es glüht' (*P.*, ll. 1377–8).
   The pattern of imagistic speech has changed, too, in the more
elevated tracts of the work. Fire, which was once so conspicuous
an element in Schiller's language, has now burned low. The
incendiary words are few and are chiefly allocated to secondary
characters such as the Herzogin, Octavio, and Questenberg; and
they are employed in contexts and connotations altogether more
mild than their forerunners of the earlier plays. The passionate

intensity of the repeated *brennend* gives way to 'ein mild erwär-
mend Feuer' (*W.T.*, l. 1398), to Wallenstein's 'im leichten Feuer
mit dem Salamander' (*W.T.*, l. 795), or even to 'Im schlechten
Winkel still verlöschen lassen' (*W.T.*, l. 3554). For the rest fire
operates as a purely conventional turn of speech, such as 'die
fluchbeladne Fackel dieses Kriegs' (*P.*, l. 1118), or quite simply
'die Kriegesfackel' (*W.T.*, l. 1981) or 'des Krieges Flamme' (*W.T.*,
l. 2715). Such a diminution partly reflects the requirements of
the subject and corresponds also to a slackening of youthful
impetuous ardour.

It is more surprising that the words of disguise and of playing
a part are relatively inconspicuous in *Wallenstein*; for the three
most important characters, Wallenstein, Octavio, and Buttler, in
their different ways, maintain a façade which conceals their true
intentions. For the most part *Maske* and *Larve* are used as
commonplaces without symbolical overtones. Only once does
this group provide an image which illuminates the play, when
Wallenstein unconsciously discloses the dualism of his life by
referring to it as 'die große Lebensrolle' (*W.T.*, l. 1519). This is a
meagre harvest of a crop of words which are obviously closely
related to the content of *Wallenstein*, and it contrasts strikingly
with the abundance of words of this kind in *Fiesco*. It is a sign both
of subtlety and of economy. Words which are obviously related to
the subject are not squandered, but are held in reserve until the
most effective moment for their deployment. Thus *Abgrund*,
which could well have been used repeatedly in connection with
Wallenstein's situation, occurs only three times in the trilogy and
each time in some relation to Max. It is only on the third occasion
that this so obvious word, unblunted here by frequent use, is
linked also with Wallenstein himself. Similarly the commonplace
image of the bridge appears only twice, and so can operate with
tremendous power when Buttler, in his chorus speech in Act Four
of *Wallensteins Tod*, uses the drop of the portcullis and the lift of
the drawbridge as a symbol for the close of Wallenstein's career.

Cosmic images, which greatly fascinated Schiller and are
especially evident in his poems, are employed in *Wallenstein*, not

to express an exaltation, a kind of vast and limitless euphoria, but for specific and limited purposes. The foremost of these is the astrological background, which makes the stars an almost inevitable feature of the play. Through the astrological passages runs the familiar stellar vocabulary, with its suggestion of a world of order and harmony, superior to and immune from the confusion of the Earth:

> Es ist ein holder, freundlicher Gedanke,
> Daß über uns, in unermeßnen Höhn,
> Der Liebe Kranz aus funkelnden Gestirnen,
> Da wir erst wurden, schon geflochten ward. (*P.*, ll. 1646–9)

But the cosmic vocabulary has an accompaniment. Interwoven with the repetitions of *Sterne*, with their evocation of immensity and splendour, are the all-too-human figures of the ancient gods. This intimate association of the two separate planes symbolizes Wallenstein's real guilt—his readiness to prostitute the highest in the interest of mere advantage. So we find the stars degraded into political agents:

> Glückseliger Aspekt! So stellt sich endlich
> Die große Drei verhängnisvoll zusammen,
> Und beide Segenssterne, *Jupiter*
> Und *Venus*, nehmen den verderblichen,
> Den tückschen *Mars* in ihre Mitte, zwingen
> Den alten Schadenstifter mir zu dienen.
> Denn lange war er feindlich mir gesinnt
> Und schoß mit senkrecht- oder schräger Strahlung,
> Bald im *Gevierten*, bald im *Doppelschein*,
> Die roten Blitze meinen Sternen zu,
> Und störte ihre segenvollen Kräfte.
> Jetzt haben sie den alten Feind besiegt
> Und bringen ihn am Himmel mir gefangen. (*W.T.*, ll. 9–21)

And so the cosmic vocabulary of *Wallenstein* is suspect and the occasions on which the grand and splendid stellar or solar image is used provoke an insidious doubt. When the Gräfin Terzky likens Wallenstein's gaze to 'dem Feuerblick der Sonne' (*P.*,

l. 1876), the response of the listener is less than whole-hearted. The general's apparently resolute words—

> *Die* Sonnen scheinen uns nicht mehr,
> Fortan muß eignes Feuer uns erleuchten       (*P.*, ll. 685–6)

—fail to assure us either of the power of the 'suns' or of the strength of the inherent 'fire'. And the brave words, in which Wallenstein likens himself to the soldiers' sun, no longer match reality:

> Laß sehn, ob sie das Antlitz nicht mehr kennen,
> Die ihre Sonne war in dunkler Schlacht.       (*W.T.*, ll. 2264–5)

This defiant gesture is already belied by the image of the lesser stars shining in the sun's absence, an image which implies that Wallenstein certainly does not now dominate the scene as the sun dominates the day:

> Nacht muß es sein, wo Friedlands Sterne strahlen.
> (*W.T.*, l. 1743)

So Schiller has used this favourite symbolism, not only to make splendid rhetoric, but also subtly to suggest the hollowness of this great and imposing figure, who knows deep within him that his inward strength, on which others rely, has forsaken him.

Another source of potent images is the world of plants, and especially their seed, growth, and bloom. In *Don Carlos* they had formed a group new to Schiller's work, a recognition of tranquil development in rivalry with violent change. And, since they are a symptom of maturity, their recurrence in *Wallenstein* is not surprising. Quantitatively they are unimportant, perhaps a dozen instances in six thousand lines. Their weight, however, is considerable. And the need to focus on a few images of low incidence is a reminder that Schiller has advanced far beyond the limitations of his subjective early style, in which obsessive words appeared with compulsive abundance.

As we might expect, *blühen* and *Blume* are mostly associated with Thekla and Max. Wallenstein himself only uses 'Blume' once, in the decline of his fortunes:

> Die Blume ist hinweg aus meinem Leben.            (*W.T.*, l. 3443)

The line is ambiguous; it appears to refer to the death of Max, but simultaneously it is turned in upon Wallenstein himself. It picks up a motif touched earlier by Thekla when she had praised her father's vigour and vitality—

> So steht er blühend jetzt vor meinen Augen            (*P.*, l. 741)

—signifying in visual terms the change which has taken place within.

When Wallenstein speaks of growth, the image serves to underline the element of mystic fatalism in his character, for it is a growth which is unamenable to control. So in his long rebuke to Illo and Terzky in Act One of *Die Piccolomini* he says:

> Auch des Menschen Tun
> Ist eine Aussaat von Verhängnissen,
> Gestreuet in der Zukunft dunkles Land.            (*P.*, ll. 989-91)

And he counters the facile and premature triumph of the Gräfin Terzky with a warning image:

> Frohlocke nicht!
> Denn eifersüchtig sind des Schicksals Mächte.
> Voreilig Jauchzen greift in ihre Rechte.
> Den Samen legen wir in ihre Hände,
> Ob Glück, ob Unglück aufgeht, lehrt das Ende.
> (*W.T.*, ll. 659-63)

In the third act of *Wallensteins Tod* a plant image is put to a different and striking use. Deserted by his trusted friend and abandoned by most of his troops, Wallenstein speaks in soliloquy:

> Den Schmuck der Zweige habt ihr abgehauen,
> Da steh ich, ein entlaubter Stamm! Doch innen
> Im Marke lebt die schaffende Gewalt,
> Die sprossend eine Welt aus sich geboren.            (*W.T.*, ll. 1791-4)

The crux of this image is in the last line with its past tense. The tree was once lopped, it had put out shoots more vigorously than before and grown into an even greater, more majestic, tree. Wallenstein assumes a repetition. But the image, if properly understood, suggests the contrary. Such severe surgery will probably prevent the tree from re-establishing itself, despite its vigour. The new shoots may wilt and die. And so this memorable formulation (perhaps derived from Schiller's perusal of his father's treatise)[1] throws into relief at one and the same time Wallenstein's self-confidence and the thought, not—at least overtly—entertained by him, that such confidence may be unfounded. A stroke of dramatic irony is economically achieved by a single image.

The illustrative comparisons in *Wallenstein* are not all of this terse and strictly metaphorical kind. A new feature is the elaborate simile, expanded into a formal rhetorical device. It is not always accompanied by *wie*, but it works in parallel comparison, not by identification. Such extended images, if apposite, illuminate character or situation with great vividness and simultaneously widen the scope and deepen the perspective of the play. They are frankly deliberate. They do not flow with the speech; they are interpolated as autonomous sections of conscious illustrative intention. Their subjects are varied: the pirates who know only the unfriendly coasts, not the fertile interior, the lightning flash destroying a house by fire, the exploding ship, reckless building on insecure foundations, cosmic cataclysm, or the calculator who overreaches himself. Violent images preponderate and a piquant contrast arises between these subjects and the rhetorical formalism in their presentation, as for instance in the simile with which Max prefigures Wallenstein's impending fall:

Denn dieser Königliche, wenn er fällt,
Wird eine Welt im Sturze mit sich reißen,
Und wie ein Schiff, das mitten auf dem Weltmeer
In Brand gerät mit einem Mal, und berstend

---

[1] *Die Baumzucht im Großen aus zwanzigjähriger Erfahrung im Kleinen*, Neustrelitz 1795.

Auffliegt, und alle Mannschaft, die es trug,
Ausschüttet plötzlich zwischen Meer und Himmel,
Wird er uns alle, die wir an sein Glück
Befestigt sind, in seinen Fall hinabziehn. (*P.*, ll. 2639–46)

Whether any of the more violent similes represent a controlled residue of the earlier impulses of violence must remain a matter for speculation; they certainly provide in concentrated form a poetic element, which may well have compensated Schiller in some degree for the prosaic sobriety of which he was so conscious in *Wallenstein*.

He had from the first found the subject in some respects an uncongenial one. When it was finished he expressed himself with impatience: 'Soldaten, Helden und Herrscher habe ich vor jetzt herzlich satt'.[1] But, as long as he was at work on it, the streak of distaste served only as a spur. In the same breath in which he speaks of his disinclination ('kaum eine Neigung') he mentions his enthusiasm—'doch bin ich für die Arbeit begeistert'. It was a combination which was not to recur in Schiller's artistic life. His best work was generated in adversity. At first it had been personal straits and duress, and the results, though impressive, were impure. In *Wallenstein* for the first time he wrestled with artistic adversity. He called in aid Shakespeare and Sophocles, both of whom he studied while at work on *Wallenstein*,[2] using them to achieve a new discipline of writing. The outcome is a play the language of which is more closely wrought than that of any of his earlier works. The essence of the style in *Wallenstein* is its functional quality. The down-to-earth, subtly stylized, colloquialism, the exploitation of rhetoric, now as a deceiving, now as a protecting screen, the austere tension of the points at which classical technique is applied, combine into a strong, resilient linguistic presentation. *Wallenstein* is not stylistically Schiller's most harmonious work. But it is the one in which style most closely corresponds to purpose.

[1] Letter to Goethe, 19 March 1799 (Jonas, 6. 20).
[2] '... der Lectüre des Shakespeare und Sophokles, die mich seit mehrern Wochen beschäftigt.' Letter to Körner, 7 April 1797 (Jonas, 5. 171).

# VI · *MARIA STUART*

## I. LINKS WITH THE PAST

THE world of *Wallenstein* is centred on hard facts and grasping ambition. Schiller had had enough of it and sought, for his next play, something more personal and more human. On 19 March 1799, with the first performance of *Wallensteins Tod* still a month away,[1] he wrote to Goethe: 'Neigung und Bedürfniß ziehen mich zu einem frei phantasierten, nicht historischen, und zu einem bloß leidenschaftlichen und menschlichen Stoff.'[2] It is then not surprising that the new play, even though it is historical, seems to revert to an earlier theme. *Maria Stuart*, like *Don Carlos*, is a play of individual passion. But that which was formerly enacted before our eyes is in the new play finished and done with before the curtain rises. The destructiveness of a love magnified and out of control belongs to both plays. In *Don Carlos* passionate love is finally subdued. *Maria Stuart* begins at a point when chastening experience has already brought Maria to the condition which Carlos attains at the end of the play.

The comparison with *Don Carlos* is not fortuitous. Schiller's interest in Carlos, first aroused in May 1782,[3] began to germinate in December,[4] and did not rise to a pitch of enthusiasm until the end of March 1783.[5] In these winter months he had in his mind a rival subject, and it was only on 27 March that he settled in favour of *Don Carlos*. This alternative was the story of Mary Stuart, which he mentions three times in his letters between late

[1] 20 April 1799.
[2] Jonas, 6. 20.
[3] Letter to Dalberg, 15 July 1782 (Jonas, 1. 64).
[4] Letter to Reinwald, 9 December 1782 (Jonas, 1. 85)
[5] Letters to Reinwald, 27 March and 14 April 1783 (Jonas, 1. 107 f. and 115).

February and late March 1783.[1] In the end he shelved it, and it remained in abeyance for exactly sixteen years. It was in April 1799 that he began *Maria Stuart*, completing it on 9 June 1800. There is therefore a genetic affinity between the two plays, and the desire to treat passion in his new play directed his mind back to his old self of sixteen years before. Between then and now, however, lay the friendship with Goethe, the new-found admiration for Greek tragedy, and the achievement of *Wallenstein*. He could not, and doubtless did not wish to, recapture the structure, style, and outlook of *Don Carlos*. Outwardly, in its harmoniousness, the verse might seem to revert to the earlier type. The sources of its harmony, as we shall see, are quite different. Traces of the manner of *Don Carlos* are, however, detectable. Here and there a turn of phrase or a touch of semi-colloquial dialogue brings the earlier play to mind. And once when Elisabeth speaks of the sultry political atmosphere—

Schwarz hängt der Himmel über diesem Land     (*M.S.*, l. 1148)

—we hear an unmistakable reminiscence, in rhythm as well as vocabulary, of Carlos's confession:

Schwer liegt der Himmel zu Madrid auf mir.     (*D.C.*, l. 1225)

It is even possible that this line survives from a draft[2] and that it preceded the line from *Carlos*. But we cannot know, since the sketches, if they existed, are lost.

A substantial point of difference between the verse of *Maria Stuart* and its two predecessors is in the role of colloquial speech. *Wallenstein* had greatly augmented the important role which common speech had already played in *Don Carlos*. *Maria Stuart* reverses the trend, so that the colloquial becomes rare. It is still employed occasionally for characterization, chiefly in the speech of Ritter Paulet, whose bluff, forthright temper invites the use of simple, plain dialogue. He uses a quasi-proverbial formulation—

---

[1] Letters to Reinwald, 24(?) February, ? March, 27 March 1783 (Jonas, 100 f., 102, 107).

[2] According to Christophine Reinwald (Schiller's sister), Schiller wrote a few scenes in 1783. The information is given in a letter to Gottfried Körner dated 28 May 1811, and so 28 years later. Cf. *NA* 23. 294,

'Wo das gesteckt hat, liegt noch mehr!' (l. 8)—or throws in a meaningless interjection from ordinary conversation:

Es sind Unziemlichkeiten vorgegangen
In diesem Rechtstreit, wenn ichs sagen darf.          (ll. 985-6)

Or Leicester abandons for a moment his stilted elevation and reveals in nervous directness his moral bankruptcy:

LEICESTER. Es ist nichts mit Gewalt. Das Wagestück
  Ist zu gefährlich.
MORTIMER.          Auch das Säumen ists!
LEICESTER. Ich sag Euch, Ritter, es ist nicht zu wagen.
                                                      (ll. 1863-5)

Now and then Schiller has recourse to the colloquial to express sudden brutal disclosure or great urgency. So Mortimer, startled and angered by Maria's obstinate reliance on Leicester, blurts out:

Wer? Er? Das ist ein Feiger, Elender!          (l. 2481)

And Shrewsbury anxiously implores Maria to moderate her tone and expectations with the pressing yet homely entreaty:

                      trotzt nicht, jetzt nicht
Auf Euer Recht, jetzo ist nicht die Stunde.          (ll. 2196-7)

In this example, however, is manifested the fundamental stylistic unity of the play. Common speech though it is, it constitutes a rhetorical triad. And even Paulet, the chief exemplar of ordinary language, is discovered on examination to intertwine his simple vocabulary with parallelisms, triads, and anastrophes.

## 2. THE ROLE OF RHETORIC

The decline in ordinary speech is, indeed, complemented with a considerable expansion of rhetorical language. A shift was taking place in Schiller's view of tragedy, involving a conscious rejection of realism. A revealing comment is made by Schiller in

writing to Körner about the performance of the actress Friede-
rike Unzelmann in the part of Maria:

Die Unzelmann spielt diese Rolle mit Zartheit und großem Verstand;
ihre Declamation ist schön und sinnvoll, aber man möchte ihr noch
etwas mehr Schwung und einen mehr tragischen Stil wünschen. Das
Vorurteil des beliebten Naturlichen beherrscht sie noch zu sehr, und
alles wurde mir zu *wirklich* in ihrem Mund.[1]

This swing away from realism and towards a deliberate stylization certainly owes something both to Goethe's classical style of
theatrical presentation[2] and to Schiller's own study of the Greek
dramatists. It also stems from a renewal in Schiller of his earlier
impulse towards rhetorical expression, not this time as the
vehicle of passionate commitment, but as a conscious and
organized policy of persuasion.

Schiller did not, with *Maria Stuart*, deliver something at once
new and masterly, as he had done in *Don Carlos* and *Wallenstein*.
All the devices on which he drew were already familiar in his
work. The novelty is in the abandonment of the poetic (or medial)
mode in favour of the rhetorical. The characteristic form of
dialogue in *Maria Stuart* is the argument, conducted with fluent
exalted rhetoric manifested in long set speeches. The characters
take it in turn to deliver rival pleas; they set them out to full
advantage, urging their acceptance in persuasive, yet dignified
terms. Each speech is delivered complete; the next speaker
awaits his turn and then, as it were, rises to address the jury. For
that is what the audience is. And this conferment on the public of
a juridical function is the real novelty which Schiller introduces
in *Maria Stuart*. To this end the style is in essence forensic, and
the decorum of its declamation is that of behaviour on a public
occasion. It is true that Schiller, by implication, elsewhere
expects from the audience an act of judgement. But in the
earlier plays it judges on the bare evidence of action and character;
in *Maria Stuart* it is subjected, so to speak, to the skilled advocacy of counsel. In scene after scene the similitude of judicial

[1] 23 September 1801 (Jonas, 6. 300)
[2] Cf. H. Knudsen, *Goethes Welt des Theaters*, 1949, pp. 47 ff.

argument is preserved, even to the central episode, the meeting of the queens. Here decorum finally succumbs under strain, as it sometimes does in courts of law. The naked dispute not only provides a relief from tension; it draws attention to the degree of dignity and restraint in the flanking acts and spotlights the effort which is needed to maintain them. The vehicle which Schiller adopts for his forensic tone is a controlled rhetoric.

It is probably not mere chance that leads a modern treatise on the elements of rhetoric to take 94 per cent of its German examples from Schiller and 84 per cent of these from *Maria Stuart*,[1] for the consistency of rhetorical speech certainly exceeds that of any earlier play by Schiller, whilst the range of the rhetorical devices probably goes beyond that of the later plays.

The basic element of Schiller's elevated style is repetition. Even antithesis, to which he is so much addicted in his early work, is a disguised form of repetition. But antithesis fades in *Maria Stuart*, occurring on average not more than five times in each act, whereas in the earlier works one or more examples can be found on almost every page. And where it does occur in *Maria Stuart* it is so treated as to mitigate its starkness. So death and marriage are obliquely handled in the lines:

> Und besser ziemte mir der Trauerflor
> Als das Gepränge bräutlicher Gewände.　　　　(ll. 1149–50)

Or the contrast of life and death is softened by three intervening lines of rapture:

> Bei ihr nur ist des Lebens Reiz —
> Um sie, in ewigem Freudenchore, schweben
> Der Anmut Götter und der Jugendlust,
> Das Glück der Himmel ist an ihrer Brust,
> Du hast nur tote Güter zu vergeben.　　　　(ll. 1647–51)

It is clear from the joyous eloquence of the first four lines that Mortimer has very little attention left for the 'tote Güter'. Even in the rare instance of terse antithesis, a pleasurable and piquant note is introduced, as in the following example with its chiasmus:

> Ihr Leben ist dein Tod! Ihr Tod dein Leben!　　　　(l. 1294)

---

[1] H. Lausberg, *Elemente der literarischen Rhetorik*, 2nd edn., 1963.

There is a good reason for the diminution of antithesis in *Maria Stuart*. Antithesis sharpens, and the aim here is to harmonize. Contradiction breaches decorum and threatens dignity. And so it had virtually to be excluded from the court in which Maria's case is heard. Repetition, on the other hand, is a potentially harmonious element and so it is not surprising that the pages of this play are thronged with recurrences. Nor, in view of Schiller's mastery of the medium, is it unexpected that they should serve a functional rather than an ornamental purpose.

Plain repetition expresses Maria's unreasoning, panic-stricken insistence:

> Ich kann sie nicht sehn! Rettet, rettet mich
> Von dem verhaßten Anblick — (ll. 2173–4)

It conveys Leicester's embarrassed anxiety:

> Hinweg, hinweg
> Von diesem unglückselgen Ort! (ll. 2445–6)

And it provides the response for Maria's almost inexpressible relief:

> Endlich, endlich
> Nach Jahren der Erniedrigung, der Leiden,
> Ein Augenblick der Rache, des Triumphs! (ll. 2455–7)

In this example a triple recurrence reinforces the effect, for the simple repetition is followed by a double synonymy.

More remarkable is the ritualistic function of the device in Act One, when Maria, testing and seeking to discourage Mortimer, uses a construction which is itself of repetitive (i.e. anaphorical) type and Mortimer then repeats the vital four and a half lines virtually unchanged:

> Mich schrecken
> Nicht Babingtons, nicht Tichburns blutge Häupter,
> Auf Londons Brücke warnend aufgesteckt,
> Nicht das Verderben der unzählgen andern,
> Die ihren Tod in gleichem Wagstück fanden . . . (ll. 654–8)

The effect is that of a solemn conjuration, the extended repetition converts the words into a significant formula, so that they acquire an incantatory force, which accords well with Mortimer's blind, almost intoxicated, determination.

Synonymy, a variant of repetition which can easily degenerate into mannerism, is functional and purposeful in Schiller's writing. It can express the voluble evasiveness of Hannah Kennedy as she seeks to mitigate and to mislead:

Unbedeutende
Papiere, bloße Übungen der Feder.     (ll. 10–11)

In its simplest form it indicates the naïveté of Leicester's egocentricity:

Ich bin entdeckt, ich bin durchschaut.     (l. 2741)

It reproduces Mortimer's cold, perverted ferocity:

Von meinen Händen stirbt er. Ich ermord ihn.     (l. 2521)

And yet it can also be used, with Maria herself, to show anguish and profound dismay:

und ins Gedächtnis eingeschrieben,
Wie ich sie rühren wollte und bewegen!
Vergessen plötzlich, ausgelöscht ist alles.     (ll. 2179–81)

The first synonymous repetition here produces, with the aid of a hyperbaton, the effect of an agitated afterthought; the second conveys an intensification.

Other forms of recurrence are used with equal skill, subtlety, and diversity. Mortimer's anaphoric reiteration of *du* has all the sudden attack of his frighteningly intense personality:

Du hast gesiegt! Du tratst sie in den Staub,
*Du* warst die Königin, *sie* der Verbrecher.     (ll. 2469–70)

As he so often does, Schiller here combines two repetitive forms, anaphora and augmentation, and each enhances the other. The *du* provides the initial blow, the lengthening predicate adds the crescendo.

The use of a word in two forms (*erfleht/Flehn*)[1] suggests intertwining and, coupled with the lingering alliteration on *fl*, conforms with a wringing of the hands in hopeless lament:

> Ach, mein Verderben hab ich mir erfleht,
> Und mir zum Fluche wird mein Flehn erhört! (ll. 2198–9)

Augmentation, though perhaps a less frequent form of repetition here than in earlier works, is evoked for passionate anguish, and especially for the motif of non-recurrence, the 'never again'. So Maria rises from *nie* through *niemals* to a double *nimmer*, *nimmer*:

> Nie hätten wir uns sehen sollen, niemals!
> Daraus kann nimmer, nimmer Gutes kommen! (ll. 2200–1)

And this is later paralleled by Elisabeth with:

> Ich will ihn nicht sehn. Niemals, niemals wieder! (l. 2861)

Flaring anger is expressed by Maria in a two-stage anaphoric augmentation, which rises with great suddenness to hyperbole:

> Nicht um dies ganze reiche Eiland, nicht
> Um alle Länder, die das Meer umfaßt,
> Möcht ich vor Euch so stehn, wie Ihr vor mir! (ll. 2400–2)

The most frequent of Schiller's repetitive forms is the parallelism, a typical example of which occurs in Maria's confrontation with Elisabeth:

> Jetzt ist kein fremder Mund mehr zwischen uns,
> Wir stehn einander selbst nun gegenüber. (ll. 2319–20)

This is the dual form, which is also the basis of the fourfold parallelisms of *Maria Stuart*, which prove on examination to consist of two adjacent dual examples as in these words of Mortimer to Leicester:

> Weg mit Verstellung! Handelt öffentlich!
> Verteidigt als ein Ritter die Geliebte,
> Kämpft einen edlen Kampf um sie... (ll. 1923–5)

---

[1] The device is really a polyptoton—e.g. 'How many be commanded that command!' *The Merchant of Venice*, II. ix.

Schiller uses triadic as well as dual parallelisms, but the function of the two groups is not the same. The dual forms are compact, their syntax is simple, their role is largely synonymous. So Kennedy deplores the harsh treatment suffered by her mistress with the words

Der Tyrannei, der Härte wird kein Ziel.     (l. 145)

So Shrewsbury pleads for Maria:

Verzeih der Rasenden, der schwer Gereizten.     (l. 2444)

And with a similar parallelism Burleigh questions the means by which Leicester has achieved the confrontation of the queens:

Durch welche Macht, durch welche Zauberkünste...     (l. 2826)

Each time the second component emphasizes and clarifies the first. But it is more than a device for underlining or for aiding the inattentive. The balanced clauses or phrases contribute to the decorously harmonious style. The effect is seen in Hannah Kennedy's lament—

Ihr hattet
Kein Ohr mehr für der Freundin Warnungsstimme,
Kein Aug für das, was wohlanständig war     (ll. 335–7)

and is equally evident in Mortimer's affirmation:

Das letzte Sakrament empfingen wir,
Und fertig sind wir zu der letzten Reise.     (ll. 2508–9)

The triadic parallelisms are more complex, tending to be woven together by more elaborate syntactical means. Like the dual parallelisms, they achieve harmony, but they also produce augmentation. Elisabeth's summary of Maria's misfortunes, with its three relative clauses, governed by the same antecedent, mounts to a climax:

Wie weit ist diese Königin gebracht,
Die mit so stolzen Hoffnungen begann,
Die auf den ältsten Thron der Christenheit
Berufen worden, die in ihrem Sinn
Drei Kronen schon aufs Haupt zu setzen meinte!     (ll. 1529–33)

Schiller also makes use of triads which are not strictly parallel, undergoing a change in the third component. It is possible in such groupings to emphasize the climax, as happens in the first disclosure of Mortimer's passion:

> Wie dich der edle königliche Zorn
> Umglänzte, deine Reize mir verklärte!
> Du bist das schönste Weib auf dieser Erde! (ll. 2476–8)

Such constructions can reach the point of a pseudo-syllogistic triad, when Paulet warns Mortimer:

> Lockend ist die Gunst
> Der Könige, nach Ehre geizt die Jugend.
> — Laß dich den Ehrgeiz nicht verführen! (ll. 1665–7)

Whether it is the simple dual parallelism or the more highly organized triad, the pluralizing trend of this syntactical device smoothes and unifies, so that even the expression of passion is assimilated into the general harmonious texture.

Beside this elaborate pattern of multiplication there occurs one simple yet distinctive figure of speech, which in itself is not repetitive. The anastrophic genitive, in which the genitive case precedes the noun to which it is attached, is more abundant in *Maria Stuart* than in any of Schiller's earlier plays.[1] More perhaps than any other single device the anastrophic genitive establishes elevation of tone. It is foreign to current speech, and so it is an instant signal of lofty and formal style. Its frequent use establishes a key of splendour, artifice, or ritual.

It has, moreover, certain positive advantages beyond its tone-setting capacity. Being a form of ellipsis, it makes for terseness and directness. 'Drum übergab ich ihn des Richters Hand' (l. 2993) gains in strength from the exclusion of an article. Furthermore the anastrophic genitive is climactic in structure. The normal decline from governing noun to attached case is reversed, and the phrase mounts to a firm climax on the grammatically

---

[1] It occurs 172 times, an average of once in every 23 lines. This is about half as often again as in *Don Carlos* or in the two *Wallenstein* plays.

vital word. When, as sometimes happens, the weight of sense
falls on the prefixed genitive (e.g. 'Sie hat der Menschen Urteil
nichts geachtet', l. 1979), the crisp tautness remains as an
advantage.

Schiller's anastrophic genitives cover a wide range. In such a
simple form as 'dieses Zimmers Boden' (l. 128) the device invades
the semi-colloquial speech of Paulet. It appears in effective,
lapidary, formulations, such as 'Mein Schicksal liegt in meiner
Feinde Hand' (l. 215), and in dual parallelism as in 'Der Kirche
Trost, der Sakramente Wohltat' (l. 183). Schiller diversifies it in
bold syntactical combinations, such as the following, with its
ambiguous hyperbaton: 'Des Lebens mich, der Erde Lust zu
freun' (l. 1983). A phrase of Maria's uses it as one component of
a chiasmus: 'nicht / Der Wert des Goldes, nicht der Steine
Pracht' (ll. 3558–9).

Schiller's most impressive use of the anastrophic genitive
occurs when he adds an epithet to the governing noun, so transforming a figure of speech into a phrase of originality. So the
dead Darnley is for Maria 'Des Gatten rachefoderndes Gespenst'
(l. 288). Hannah Kennedy speaks of 'des Menschen unverwahr-
ter Brust' (l. 364), and Mortimer lauds Providence as 'Des
Himmels wundervolle Rettungshand' (l. 539). In argument with
Burleigh Maria adds an epithet to each component to create a
powerful and pregnant phrase—'Der alten Zwietracht unglück-
selge Glut' (l. 834)—and Elisabeth in the confrontation scene
achieves a triad in which the last component has balanced epithets:

Der Priester Zungen und der Völker Schwert,
Des frommen Wahnsinns fürchterliche Waffen.          (ll. 2340–1)

These are the highlights. Many of the anastrophic genitives in
*Maria Stuart*, however, are mere routine. Some, such as 'dieses
Landes Küste' (l. 83), appear strained, because the sense of
possession is weak. Many are commonplaces, familiar stereotyped couplings which were common currency in Schiller's day;
among these are 'des Lebens schönen Tag' (l. 456), 'der Kirche

Schoß' (l. 486), 'der Krone Glanz' (l. 2033), 'meines Geistes Schwingen' (l. 2380), or 'der Gegner Haß' (l. 3225). The facelessness of these drab reproductions is a price Schiller paid for his policy of smoothing the verse texture of this play.

The elevation of tone and the play of rhetorical artifice in *Maria Stuart* are the elements which support the forensic structure. Though the characters address each other and in doing so perform the action, they simultaneously address themselves in overtones to the audience. They do this, not by converting themselves into a chorus as Buttler does in *Wallensteins Tod*, but by a discreet inflation and over-emphasis, which raises the tone above the needs of the action and is felt by reader or onlooker as a note of persuasion.

### 3. MARIA'S SPEECH

As a truly skilled rhetorician, Schiller was well aware that the most effective forensic strokes are achieved when, after a passage of exalted eloquence, there is a pause and the speech is resumed or answered in a lower tone and simpler style. This is a function reserved almost entirely to Maria herself. The Queen of Scots appears only in the first, third, and fifth acts. A central act of passion is flanked by outside acts in which her moral potential is revealed and fulfilled. That the restrained verse, of which she is the chief exponent, is not her special characteristic is made plain enough by the third act, in which all the stops are pulled out and she expresses herself with the full rhetorical skill and resource of which Schiller was capable.

Parallelisms, triads, repetitions, and augmentations follow one another as the verse sails on from one splendid climax to the next. For all her passion, her speech is purposeful. The announcement of Elisabeth's imminent arrival renders her almost speechless, and for a moment her utterances are disjointed and incoherent. But, though she is subject to confusion and anxiety, her speech quickly organizes itself and gathers momentum; and immediately the pattern of insistent repetition, parallelism, and triad becomes apparent:

> Ich habe drauf geharret — jahrelang
> Mich drauf bereitet, alles hab ich mir
> Gesagt und ins Gedächtnis eingeschrieben,
> Wie ich sie rühren wollte und bewegen!
> Vergessen plötzlich, ausgelöscht ist alles,
> Nichts lebt in mir in diesem Augenblick,
> Als meiner Leiden brennendes Gefühl. (ll. 2177–83)

As the scene develops, the tide of eloquence rises higher, each speech becomes a distinguishable rhetorical entity culminating in a *sententia*, a pause of pathos, or an indictment. The images proliferate, and extended simile enters:

> wie
> Die Felsenklippe, die der Strandende
> Vergeblich ringend zu erfassen sucht. (ll. 2269–71)

The vocabulary is 'ennobled' with an abundance of words such as *Himmel*, *Sieg*, and *König*, and expressions such as 'der Völker heilig Recht', 'Um alle Länder, die das Meer umfaßt', or 'das Fluchgeschick der Könige'. The gods of antiquity are barely concealed in the background and the note of Nemesis is recognizably though faintly heard. 'Es leben Götter, die den Hochmut rächen' (l. 2262) is followed by a reference to 'jeder Zwietracht Furien' (l. 2318); and the climax of Maria's passionate (but highly organized) rhetoric is marked by a series of apostrophes, a Homeric epithet, and a classical allusion:

> Fahr hin, lammherzige Gelassenheit,
> Zum Himmel fliehe, leidende Geduld,
> Spreng endlich deine Bande, tritt hervor
> Aus deiner Höhle, langverhaltner Groll —
> Und *du*, der dem gereizten Basilisk
> Den Mordblick gab, leg auf die Zunge mir
> Den giftgen Pfeil. (ll. 2437–43)

The limits prescribed by rhetorical procedure are here stretched to allow an expression of uncontrolled, frothing, fury.

Very different is the restrained style in which Maria speaks
in the first and last acts. Her first words enjoin restraint in the
minimum of words: 'Faß dich! / Sag an, was neu geschehen ist?'
(ll. 147–8). When, after receiving her answer, she resumes, it is in
simple sentences, employing normal grammatical order:

> Diese Flitter machen
> Die Königin nicht aus. Man kann uns niedrig
> Behandeln, nicht erniedrigen. Ich habe
> In England mich an viel gewöhnen lernen,
> Ich kann auch das verschmerzen... (ll. 154–8)

It does not need an acute ear to detect that this is not the easy
speech of relaxation, but a tense and taut style indicating an
immense restraint. As Maria goes on, the occasional anastrophe
or parallelism appears and the syntax sheds its extreme simplicity;
but the measured pace and the sense of *self*-control remain. In
the rhetorically conceived scene reviewing Maria's past, the bulk
of the verse is spoken by Hannah Kennedy, Maria's part being
limited to interventions usually of two lines. Yet Schiller, in
spite of this apparent imbalance in favour of the servant, easily
maintains Maria's superiority by allocating to her ten simple
words to form the culmination of the scene:

> Vollende nur!
> Und reicht ihm meine Hand vor dem Altare! (ll. 354–5)

Thus the Queen, despite her reticence, commands the scene, and
Schiller is able to indulge the rhetorical tone and yet preserve the
hierarchy of his characters.

The following scene between Maria and Mortimer again allots
the larger share of lines to the inferior; and again Maria maintains control by her steady and deliberate tempo, which is twice
reinforced by the stage direction, first with *mit Fassung*, and then
with *nach einer Pause*. Even the frontal clash between Maria and
Burleigh (i. vii) is conducted in the decorous atmosphere of
forensic argument, and its climax is expressed in a succession of

short sentences which are certainly rhetorical, but handle
rhetoric with moderation:

> Ich bin die Schwache, sie die Mächtige — Wohl!
> Sie brauche die Gewalt, sie töte mich,
> Sie bringe ihrer Sicherheit das Opfer.
> Doch sie gestehe dann, daß sie die Macht
> Allein, nicht die Gerechtigkeit geübt...                    (ll. 961–5)

Here the restraint is stressed by the activity of the logical intellect.
After the *allegro furioso* of the third act (and her extravagance
here both spotlights the subterranean fires and heightens the
provocation she suffers) Maria's speech returns in the fifth act to
the tone of control and balance, yet with a difference. The mood
of solemn sadness and subdued suffering invites a freer use of
rhetorical expression. Schiller achieves the blending of elevation
and containment by a ready use of parallelism and a minimal
employment of the anastrophic genitive. Maria begins her farewell with two brief questions, followed by two rich yet restrained
periods, sinking then to shorter, solemn sentences, and in all of
these simple parallelism is evident:

> Was klagt ihr? Warum weint ihr? Freuen solltet
> Ihr euch mit mir, daß meiner Leiden Ziel
> Nun endlich naht, daß meine Bande fallen,
> Mein Kerker aufgeht, und die frohe Seele sich
> Auf Engelsflügeln schwingt zur ewgen Freiheit.
> Da, als ich in die Macht der stolzen Feindin
> Gegeben war, Unwürdiges erduldend,
> Was einer freien großen Königin
> Nicht ziemt, da war es Zeit, um mich zu weinen!
> — Wohltätig, heilend, nahet mir der Tod,
> Der ernste Freund!...                    (ll. 3480–90)

The combination of sobriety and dignity which marks this
passage sets the tone for Maria's speech throughout the fifth act,
and from her it spreads outward to those around her, to Melvil
her confessor, to Amyas Paulet, and even to Burleigh. The

solemnity is augmented by the invocation of the Bible by Maria
in virtual quotation:

> Doch der Erlöser spricht:
> Wo zwei versammelt sind in *meinem* Namen,
> Da bin ich gegenwärtig unter ihnen.     (ll. 3634-6)

This conscious and deliberate simplicity does not represent a
deviation from the rhetorical tone of the play. It is rhetoric in its
most effective key. The opportunity of intimacy is rejected and
the tone of address maintained. The symptom of this public
consciousness is the *sententia* or general statement. In this last
scene of Maria's tragedy the *sententiae* fall thick and fast. Maria
herself makes such a general reflection as

> den Menschen adelt,
> Den tiefstgesunkenen, das letzte Schicksal,     (ll. 3491-2)

so de-personalizing her own fate; or she affirms a commonplace
of morality: 'Betrüglich sind die Güter dieser Erden' (l. 3578).
And Melvil in three lines speaks a sequence of four *sententiae*:

> Tyrannenmacht kann nur die Hände fesseln,
> Des Herzens Andacht hebt sich frei zu Gott,
> Das Wort ist tot, der Glaube macht lebendig.     (ll. 3598-600)

The special style apportioned to Maria is related to her central
role in this forensic tragedy. At the outset of the play she is a
condemned person, and the action is the hearing of her appeal. If
she is to win and retain the spectator's sympathy, she must be
seen to speak the truth and prove her innocence; averting her
fate merely by adroit advocacy would avail her nothing with the
jury-audience. And so the solemnity of style in the communion
scene of the fifth act is only partly related to the solemn rite there
celebrated. This is also the scene of ultimate judgement, in which
Melvil, the priest administering the sacrament in the name of
God, is also God's judicial deputy. Indeed, he explicitly presses
the charge of which the temporal court has convicted Maria. And

Maria's sacramental confession is at once, though at different points, evidence of guilt and proof of innocence; in this dilemma, the style of presentation insists that the finding of innocence concerns a far weightier charge than the verdict of guilt. Maria's oratory is nowhere so impressive as in the noble simplicity of her last words in this, her ultimate, 'trial':

Ich fürchte keinen Rückfall. Meinen Haß
Und meine Liebe hab ich Gott geopfert.　　　　(ll. 3761–2)

One short scene of the third act of *Maria Stuart* forms an exception to the pervading rhetorical eloquence. The newly granted freedom to walk in the park is greeted by Maria in lyrical passages. Their function is clear. Just once in the play the mind must escape from the claustrophobic oppressiveness of the courtroom; it must somehow reassert the values of life and freedom before returning to a more deeply felt constriction. The intensity of that moment of life could best be conveyed by a shift to a remote style.

Through the seventy lines of this scene are interspersed four eight-line stanzas. Structure and rhyme-pattern are familiar; their originality lies in mode of employment and in rhythm. Inserted stanzas to be sung are a traditional element in tragedy, and Schiller had used such songs in *Die Räuber* and in *Wallenstein*. Maria's stanzas, however, are spoken, not sung; and they are not inserted either, but occur as four separate phases, separated from each other by groups of blank-verse lines, and each is a stage in a process of impulsive expression. Each time the change from blank verse to stanza corresponds to a quickening of the pulse. And this effect is enhanced by the dancing dactylic rhythm, which is new to Schiller's plays and, indeed, to German drama. Yet these stanzas are woven into the psychological texture of the play, as we can see from the outburst of rancour tied to dramatic situation, which suddenly splutters up ('Ihr seid nicht dieser Königin untertan') at the end of the most famous stanza of all, the one beginning, 'Eilende Wolken! Segler der Lüfte!' The fusion of the lyrical and the dramatic is evident also in the tracts of intervening blank verse, in which lyrical feeling is clearly related to the progress of the action:

> Die Blicke, frei und fessellos,
> Ergehen sich in ungemeßnen Räumen.
> Dort, wo die grauen Nebelberge ragen,
> Fängt meines Reiches Grenze an,
> Und diese Wolken, die nach Mittag jagen,
> Sie suchen Frankreichs fernen Ozean.           (ll. 2092–7)

The geographical poles of this passage refer to the crime Maria has committed in Scotland and to the French-inspired crime of which she is wrongly convicted.

Yet, though the blank verse of this scene is unmistakably tinged with lyricism, it maintains also, as the sample quoted shows, a note of rhetorical elevation. By this means the over-all harmony is maintained and the style even of this contrasting section has an affinity with the tone of the whole.

### 4. THE DASH OF BLOOD

It is tempting to interpret the heightened style of *Maria Stuart* as an insulation from reality. And it is certainly clear that Schiller has here turned his back on the kind of 'realism' which he had so successfully achieved in *Wallenstein*. Yet nobility of language does not necessarily anaesthetize the sensitivity to suffering. And, lest the controlled exaltation which is used to convey the tragedy of Maria should seem to gloss over the reality of pain, Schiller takes care to provide numerous reminders of the physical realities which lie at the root of the psychological conflict. This is the function of 'blood' in *Maria Stuart*. *Blut* and *blutig* are the commonest emotive words in this play. *Blut-gerüste* makes its appearance in the first scene, the spirit of Maria's dead husband is 'der blutge Schatten König Darnleys', and her guilt rises 'Frischblutend . . . / Aus ihrem leicht bedeckten Grab empor'. A polyptoton sees to it that the image of blood must have our attention and not be dismissed as an empty form:

> Ihr rächtet blutig nur die blutge Tat.           (l. 320)

In a vivid and grisly phrase, repeated by Mortimer so that the visual image of butchery shall not be disregarded, the heads of the conspirators are exposed in their horrifyingly fresh mutilation:

Nicht Babingtons, nicht Tichburns blutge Häupter
Auf Londons Brücke warnend aufgereckt...                    (ll. 644–5)

And Burleigh speaks of Maria thirsting for Elisabeth's blood:

Die nach dem Blut der Königin gedürstet.                    (l. 1517)

Again and again the word recurs—'blutger Frevel' (l. 2522), 'blutge Rechenschaft' (l. 2695), 'die Mörderhand, die blutig schrecklich / ... / Dazwischenkam' (ll. 2755–7), 'einem blutgen Auftrag' (l. 2967), 'die blutge Tat' (l. 3128), and, perhaps most significant of all, Kurl's reference to 'Menschen ..., / ... die, heiße Blutgier in dem Blick, das Opfer / Erwarteten' (ll. 3475–8). Almost equally revelatory are two sentences which have to do with blood, though they do not use the word. Maria in her passionate exultation at her Pyrrhic victory over Elisabeth exclaims:

Das Messer stieß ich in der Feindin Brust.                    (l. 2459)

(The phrase is not used in the heat of the engagement, but in the ensuing pause.) And Mortimer unwittingly discloses a frightening sadism as he makes unwelcome love to Maria:

Sie wollen dich enthaupten, diesen Hals,
Den blendendweißen, mit dem Beil durchschneiden.    (ll. 2555–6)

Clearly, the gold of harmonious eloquence is plentifully bespattered with blood.

The importance of this vocabulary of violence, outrage, and cruelty is even greater than its quite considerable incidence. The whole of Schiller's emotions and responses, as they were implicated in the play, refused to be subsumed in the noble and mostly controlled rhetoric of the courtroom. Even the explosion of the third act was not a sufficient release. Other impulses, properly involved, demanded expression, and, since they could not find it in the imposed stylistic pattern, they forced their way through in the resuscitation of verbal elements which had been on the wane since the completion of *Kabale und Liebe*. The effort at harmonious assimilation had progressed far, but it could not entirely succeed, because the subject contained elements with a strong appeal for Schiller which were recalcitrant to idealizing treatment. In the last resort the harmonious approach in terms of disciplined rhetoric proves inadequate for Schiller's purpose with this subject. The vocabulary of horror confronts the rhetoric with an accusation of inadequacy, if not of falseness.

# VII · DIE JUNGFRAU VON ORLEANS

## I. RHETORICAL VIRTUOSITY AND METRICAL EXPERIMENT

WITH *Die Jungfrau von Orleans* Schiller ventured into a field remote from anything he had hitherto attempted. Though outwardly he continued the historical vein of *Wallenstein* and *Maria Stuart*, he boldly opted with the story of Joan of Arc for a miraculous interpretation. Even in the years of incipient romanticism (and Schiller sub-titled his play 'Eine romantische Tragödie') it could scarcely be expected that a modern public would grant this denial of reason an undivided approval. But, whatever doubts might be felt about the miracles, the style, at least, elicited general praise. Phrases such as 'eine himmlische Diktion',[1] 'schönste Melodie',[2] 'Stanzen... von köstlicher Wirkung für den höheren Kunstsinn'[3] are fair samples of an acceptance as unanimous as it was warm.

The virtuosity of style in *Die Jungfrau von Orleans* is indeed beyond question. The verse has power, movement, splendour. Its momentum sweeps it along, brushing aside, at least temporarily, objections to detail or doubts of justification. It is a feast for the ear. Grandiose accumulations drive on irresistibly, as in the following lines:

> Gnug
> Des Blutes ist geflossen und vergebens!
> Des Himmels schwere Hand ist gegen mich,

[1] Letter from Göschen to Schiller, 6 October 1801, quoted in *NA* 9. 443.

[2] Duke Karl August, in *Literarischer Nachlaß der Caroline von Wolzogen*, quoted in *NA* 9. 442.

[3] Körner's letter of 9 May 1801; *Schillers Briefwechsel mit Körner*, ed. K. Goedeke, 2nd edn., 1874, ii. 370.

Geschlagen wird mein Heer in allen Schlachten,
Mein Parlament verwirft mich, meine Hauptstadt,
Mein Volk nimmt meinen Gegner jauchzend auf,
Die mir die Nächsten sind am Blut, verlassen,
Verraten mich — die eigne Mutter nährt
Die fremde Feindesbrut an ihren Brüsten. (ll. 757–65)

Despondency has rarely been expressed with such complacent pleasure. The same buoyant rhythm, the same rich vocabulary carry the archbishop's hope for the future and mourning for the past:

Des Landes tiefe Wunden werden heilen,
Die Dörfer, die verwüsteten, die Städte
Aus ihrem Schutt sich prangender erheben,
Die Felder decken sich mit neuem Grün —
Doch, die das Opfer eures Zwists gefallen,
Die Toten stehen nicht mehr auf, die Tränen,
Die eurem Streit geflossen, *sind* und *bleiben*
Geweint! Das kommende Geschlecht wird blühen,
Doch das vergangne war des Elends Raub,
Der Enkel Glück erweckt nicht mehr die Väter. (ll. 1995–2004)

It is a triumph of eloquence, but a certain commonplaceness is perhaps detectable. We have already observed that Schiller had an addiction for the obvious, but he also had an astounding gift for endowing the obvious and well worn with something of the gleam and weight it had when it was struck new. In *Die Jungfrau von Orleans*, however, the suspicion arises that the style is somehow out of step with its matter. It may be said perhaps that Karl, when he disposes of the feud with Burgund in a triad with a trite conclusion, is betraying his own superficial character:

Vergeßt es! Alles ist verziehen. Alles
Tilgt dieser einzge Augenblick. Es war
Ein Schicksal, ein unglückliches Gestirn! (ll. 1976–8)

And a similar psychological argument may justify his mixed bag of images (again in triad form):

Doch endlich legt sich jedes Sturmes Wut,
Tag wird es auf die dickste Nacht, und kommt
Die Zeit, so reifen auch die spätsten Früchte! (ll. 1916–18)

But, if the aim is to expose the inadequate character of the king, the means employed are unduly opulent.

Schiller pours out his verse with almost prodigal generosity. Again and again the clauses override the line endings without ever falsifying the basic pentametrical grouping of blank verse. And the impression is given of mastery in a technique of exceptional brilliance. The skill extends beyond blank verse to include rhyming stanzas and Greek trimeters; and Schiller proves himself able to assimilate for his purposes the idiosyncratic tone of another writer. Some of König Karl's speeches faintly suggest the Shakespeare of *Richard II*, and Johanna's 'Gleichmessend gießt der Himmel seinen Tau' (l. 2060) hints at Portia's words on 'the quality of mercy'; but it is the scenes in the English camp which are unmistakably Shakespearian, and of these Talbot's death-scene is the most remarkable. The words and rhythms have a pungent, astringent quality which is in sharp contrast to the soaring speech of the rest of the play:

> Bald ists vorüber und der Erde geb ich,
> Der ewgen Sonne die Atome wieder,
> Die sich zu Schmerz und Lust in mir gefügt —
> Und von dem mächtgen Talbot, der die Welt
> Mit seinem Kriegsruhm füllte, bleibt nichts übrig,
> Als eine Handvoll leichten Staubs. — So geht
> Der Mensch zu Ende — und die einzige
> Ausbeute, die wir aus dem Kampf des Lebens
> Wegtragen, ist die Einsicht in das Nichts,
> Und herzliche Verachtung alles dessen,
> Was uns erhaben schien und wünschenswert.          (ll. 2346–56)

The sense of disciplined self-control is strong, in contrast to the euphoric self-indulgence which is suggested by so much of the verse of *Die Jungfrau*.

*Maria Stuart*, for all its rhetoric, had evinced a tautness and concentration of style, which in *Die Jungfrau* is replaced by a manner which is flexible, now lyrical, now epic, and only at intervals dramatic. The tension is not constant, but is marked by surges. This undulatory mode of writing is perceptible on a small scale in even so small a sample as Thibaut's opening speech of less than forty lines. It begins with four syntactically simple flowing lines with homely vocabulary:

> Ja, liebe Nachbarn! Heute sind wir noch
> Franzosen, freie Bürger noch und Herren
> Des alten Bodens, den die Väter pflügten;
> Wer weiß, wer morgen über uns befiehlt! (ll. 1–4)

Then, with a single line of transition, the style rises; the English invasion is conveyed in two graphic images, balancing victory and destruction:

> Denn aller Orten läßt der Engelländer
> Sein sieghaft Banner fliegen, seine Rosse
> Zerstampfen Frankreichs blühende Gefilde. (ll. 5–7)

But the swelling tone quickly subsides and we sink back into the smooth flow; though not for long. The image of war flares up again:

> Rings brennen Dörfer, Städte. Näher stets
> Und näher wälzt sich der Verheerung Rauch
> An diese Täler, die noch friedlich ruhn. (ll. 16–18)

The vision promptly fades, and the even domestic tenor is resumed:

> Drum, liebe Nachbarn, hab ich mich mit Gott
> Entschlossen, weil ichs heute noch vermag,
> Die Töchter zu versorgen. (ll. 19–21)

The small scale is appropriate to the rural environment and modest circumstances of Thibaut and his daughters, but the rhythm of peak and trough is characteristic for the whole play.

Such surges may be seen to threaten dangers. When Thibaut's flat, steady tone suddenly begins to glow, it rises irresistibly to hyperbole:

> — Ich sehe dich in Jugendfülle prangen,
> Dein Lenz ist da, es ist die Zeit der Hoffnung,
> Entfaltet ist die Blume deines Leibes,
> Doch stets vergebens harr ich, daß die Blume
> Der zarten Lieb aus ihrer Knospe breche,
> Und freudig reife zu der goldnen Frucht! (ll. 55–60)

In the rapid uprising, control is lost and the outcome is a strongly erotic image which goes far beyond what Thibaut and Schiller presumably intend.

The language in *Die Jungfrau von Orleans* varies, not so much according to the character of the person who is speaking, but according to the nature of the subject which is being spoken about. It is a technique familiar in opera and especially cultivated by Wagner, but its legitimacy in spoken drama is at least questionable. The method is particularly clear in Bertrand's account of the siege of Orleans. The simple peasant at once leads off with a Schillerian epithet of immensity:

> Unermeßliches
> Geschütz ist aufgebracht von allen Enden.

Thereupon he plunges into an elaborate double simile:

> Und wie der Bienen dunkelnde Geschwader
> Den Korb umschwärmen in des Sommers Tagen,
> Wie aus geschwärzter Luft die Heuschreckwolke
> Herunterfällt und meilenlang die Felder
> Bedeckt in unabsehbarem Gewimmel,
> So goß sich eine Kriegeswolke aus
> Von Völkern über Orleans Gefilde.                    (ll. 215–21)

It is brilliantly done, with the word 'Geschwader' providing a point of military reference right at the outset, but it is neither truly descriptive nor dramatic. Its widely ranging associative technique opens perspectives and broadens the vision. It diffuses rather than concentrates, and so is essentially non-dramatic. Such speeches tend towards panorama, towards the distant prospect of conflict instead of its vivid presence.

Up to *Die Jungfrau von Orleans* Schiller's dramatic style, with a few rare and brief exceptions, had taken some note of character. Karl Moor's temper, Carlos's passion, and Maria Stuart's hardwon self-control all secured appropriate expression. And *Wallenstein* is built upon correspondence between person and speech. But in *Die Jungfrau von Orleans* such conformity is accidental. Dunois's ringing tones fit the character because the character happens to be an extrovert figure of heroic temper, and these straightforward heroics are at the same time part of the general tone of the work. Yet even Dunois may be thought to take the heroic and military too far in transferring it to his father's love affairs:

> Ich bin so sehr nicht aus der Art geschlagen,
> Daß ich der Liebe Herrschaft sollte schmähn,
> Ich nenne mich nach ihr, ich bin ihr Sohn,
> Und all mein Erbe liegt in ihrem Reich.
> Mein Vater war der Prinz von Orleans,
> Ihm war kein weiblich Herz unüberwindlich,
> Doch auch kein feindlich Schloß war ihm zu fest. (ll. 531–7)

An obvious incongruity occurs when Agnes Sorel, the epitome of femininity, lets herself go in a tirade of supra-heroic tone:

> Komm! Komm! Wir teilen Mangel und Gefahr!
> Das kriegerische Roß laß uns besteigen,
> Den zarten Leib dem glühnden Pfeil der Sonne
> Preisgeben, die Gewölke über uns
> Zur Decke nehmen; und den Stein zum Pfühl. (ll. 643–7)

Such magniloquence on the lips of the sweet and gentle is in danger of sliding into rodomontade. Exalted rhetoric is always poised upon a knife-edge, and a false association can swiftly reduce it, as here, to the level of bathos.

Thibaut, too, the melancholic quietist, gives unheroic counsel in heroic terms:

> Kommt an die Arbeit! Kommt! Und denke jeder
> Nur an das Nächste! Lassen wir die Großen,
> Der Erde Fürsten um die Erde losen,
> Wir können ruhig die Zerstörung schauen,
> Denn sturmfest steht der Boden, den wir bauen.
> Die Flamme brenne unsre Dörfer nieder,
> Die Saat zerstampfe ihrer Rosse Tritt,
> Der neue Lenz bringt neue Saaten mit,
> Und schnell erstehn die leichten Hütten wieder! (ll. 374–82)

A similar incongruity is visible in a speech by König Karl in Act One. In a moment of deep despondency the king expresses his total impotence to raise either military forces or financial support; yet the splendid words in which he phrases his weakness are, in contrast to his speech elsewhere, vigorous and powerful:

> Kann ich Armeen aus der Erde stampfen?
> Wächst mir ein Kornfeld in der flachen Hand?
> Reißt mich in Stücken, reißt das Herz mir aus,
> Und münzet es statt Goldes! Blut hab ich
> Für euch, nicht Silber hab ich, noch Soldaten!    (ll. 596–600)

These would seem to be the words of a strong man in extremity, not the expression of the dilatory and effete weakling which Karl otherwise shows himself to be.

Nor does the sublimity of his praise of poetry (Act I. ii) consort well with the tone, now peevish, now affected, of his preceding and following speeches. Schiller is clearly out to laud poetic art, and puts that aim before relevance to the speaker of the words. The passage drops all pretence of being dramatic poetry and would be more at home in any of Schiller's aesthetic poems, the more so in that it makes use of rhyme.

A most interesting scene from the point of view of congruity— or the lack of it—is the opening of the fifth act. Schiller's aim was to set the scene, suggesting an environment of storm and tempest and adding to this meteorological disturbance the proximity of the warring armies. Up to a point he performs this task in two brief sentences of stage direction: *Ein wilder Wald, in der Ferne Köhlerhütten. Es ist ganz dunkel, heftiges Donnern und Blitzen, dazwischen Schießen.* These simple and effective indications do not, however, satisfy him. The task of amplifying them is handed over to the charcoal-burner:

> Das ist ein grausam, mördrisch Ungewitter,
> Der Himmel droht in Feuerbächen sich
> Herabzugießen, und am hellen Tag
> Ists Nacht, daß man die Sterne könnte sehn.
> Wie eine losgelaßne Hölle tobt
> Der Sturm, die Erde bebt und krachend beugen
> Die alt verjährten Eschen ihre Krone.    (ll. 3050–6)

The first question is why it was necessary at all for Schiller, with the technical resources of the theatre of his day at his disposition, to write a storm passage of this Shakespearean character. His justification lies in the need to convey firstly the nature of this particular darkness and secondly the symbolism of the gloom. The lines make it clear that, intense though it is, it is a darkness of the day and not of the night; for the rapid shift from preternatural gloom to the serenity of sunlight is more apt to Schiller's purpose than the natural yielding of night to day. Furthermore, by the use of moral epithets ('grausam', 'mördrisch'), he attributes to the storm a sense of malevolence and therefore of human association, which provides a link with the coming reference to the warring armies. And finally he is able to remind us, by his unexpected allusion to the invisible stars, of an ordered and serene universe unaffected by human confusion:

> und am hellen Tag
> Ists Nacht, daß man die Sterne könnte sehn.

In the lines that follow the storm is seen to parallel the fury of battle, augmenting human ferocity by showing the beasts quelled into concord, whilst man's hostility to man remains unabated:

> Und dieser fürchterliche Krieg dort oben,
> Der auch die wilden Tiere Sanftmut lehrt,
> Daß sie sich zahm in ihre Gruben bergen,
> Kann unter Menschen keinen Frieden stiften.     (ll. 3057–60)

The whole passage is a quasi-choric introduction to the last act. And, if such a scene could be tolerated in *Wallensteins Tod* (IV. i), how much more so here, where the characteristic is abandoned for an all-pervading glow. Buttler, as the instrument of fate, had some right and authority to speak with its voice. The charcoal-burner represents the patient, inarticulate, long-suffering, good-natured peasantry of France ('Ihr seht, es sind nicht alle Menschen grausam, / Auch in der Wildnis wohnen sanfte Herzen'); and his attributes of quietness, humility, and unobtrusiveness render him singularly inept for the role of magniloquent chorus. It is one further sign that Schiller has adopted in *Die Jungfrau* a style which ignores character as a basis of drama.

A special feature of the play is the variety of its poetic forms, which is in itself a part of the self-conscious effort to write a poetic, rather than a verse, play. The quantity is relatively modest —there are 233 lines of various forms other than blank verse in a play which amounts to 3,544 lines. But these variants are conspicuous out of proportion to their statistical frequency. There are three substantial tracts of unfamiliar verse, placed at widely separated points. The Prolog ends in a set of rhyming stanzas; the second act contains the well-known Montgomery scene cast in an imitation of Greek trimeters; and the fourth act begins with a complicated pattern in which poems of three different forms occur, as well as a passage of blank verse.

The final stanzas of the Prolog, with the exception of the first (which has nine lines), are in *ottava rima*. They begin with a stanza and a half of farewells to Johanna's home and pass on to a statement of her mission and destiny. Accumulation, augmentation, and repetition give the poem its basic pattern. The repeated valedictions, covering ten objects, are consciously ceremonial, and the account of the mission reinforces its solemnity with a double biblical allusion. It has been said that the passage is an imitation of Philoctetes' farewell to Lemnos. If so, it is a free one, for the proportions of the speeches spoken respectively by Johanna and Philoctetes are quite different. Schiller's work here may stand alone without reference to a Greek original. For all its brilliance, the relationship of tone to form and of form to genre in Johanna's speech remains questionable. Schiller had an admitted partiality for *ottava rima*, which he used in the poems *An Goethe* and *Die Begegnung*, and especially in his translation of Book IV of the *Aeneid*. He even contemplated writing an epic on Frederick the Great in this measure. In short, he had hitherto used it for lyrical and epic purposes. Its use in drama was a bold experiment and was perhaps one of its 'romantic' features. As a highly developed strophic form *ottava rima* lends itself to sophisticated narrative or to a balanced, even lyricism. In Johanna's monologue, however, it is used to convey a mounting enthusiasm, expressed in rhetorical terms. To such a crescendo its steady repetitive pattern seems unsuited. The divergence between static form and dynamic tone, noticeable throughout, becomes especially acute at the climactic close—

> Ein Zeichen hat der Himmel mir verheißen,
> Er sendet mir den Helm, er kommt von *ihm*,
> Mit Götterkraft berühret mich sein Eisen,
> Und mich durchflammt der Mut der Cherubim,
> Ins Kriegsgewühl hinein will es mich reißen,
> Es treibt mich fort mit Sturmes Ungestüm,
> Den Feldruf hör ich mächtig zu mir dringen,
> Das Schlachtroß steigt und die Trompeten klingen.     (ll. 425–32)

The curtain descends as Johanna, at the height of her triumphant jubilation, strikes an attitude of heroic ecstasy; but the stanza, instead of seconding the climax, declines in the final line, dying away in the unemphatic slur of a muted feminine rhyme. The pre-determined pattern will not allow it to finish, as it should, on a strongly accented syllable. The form proves unsuitable for the dramatic use to which Schiller puts it.

A more complicated movement is involved in the first scene of Act Four, seventy-eight lines of which are in rhyming stanzas and eighteen in blank verse. It opens with three stanzas of *ottava rima*, displaying Johanna's tormented solitude amidst the general rejoicing and forming a balanced poem in triadic form. Its formal pattern, however, insists on its decorative quality, inhibiting immediacy and poignancy.

There follow nine shorter lines with irregular rhymes, which give way to a poem of three stanzas, two of four lines, one of five, which are trochaic in metre and so impose a new rhythm on the scene. A passage of blank verse next traces a more cerebral phase in Johanna's mental process, as she inwardly debates with question and reply. Finally a trochaic poem in eight-line stanzas expresses in throbbing rhythm her submissive grief.

The whole scene (the stage directions tell us) is accompanied by music—first *hinter der Szene Flöten und Hoboen*, then *Die Musik hinter der Szene geht in eine weiche schmelzende Melodie über*, and finally *Die Flöten wiederholen*. The essence of this scene is the interplay of metre and music, the metrical variations supplying the equivalent of change of tempo. It is a recitative in four sections with dynamic markings in the form of stage directions (*Nach einer Pause lebhafter* and *sie versinkt in eine stille Wehmut*). Schiller here uses lyrical forms in an experiment with a quasi-musical pattern. But the actual music is no more than an unspecified background; the musical effect is demanded from the words, which are powerless to supply it. Appreciative as Schiller was of environmental music,[1] his imagination functioned in terms of words, gestures, and groupings. And the musical effect he intended was not attainable in such terms.

The third important variation from the predominant blank verse is the Montgomery scene (II. vi, vii, viii). This is modelled on the slaying of Lykaon by Achilles in the twenty-first book of the *Iliad*. Its stylistic interest lies primarily in the metre. For the Homeric hexameter Schiller has substituted the trimeters of Greek tragedy. The abandonment of the epic metre was inevitable. Bold as Schiller was, even he could not contemplate the use of the dactylic hexameter in drama; on the other hand encouragement to try his hand at trimeters came from Goethe's successful handling of the metre in the Helena episode of *Faust*, II.[2]

Trimeters lend themselves to a slow, measured, relentless tread, which accords well with the heroic aspects of the scene; their aptness to express Montgomery's panic fear is more questionable. As long as the young man's vision is riveted on the

---

[1] Cf. Streicher, *Schillers Flucht von Stuttgart*, p. 147: 'Denn schon in Stuttgart ließ sich immer wahrnehmen, daß er durch Anhören trauriger oder lebhafter Musik außer sich selbst versetzt wurde, und daß es nichts weniger als viele Kunst erforderte, durch passendes Spiel auf dem Klavier alle Affekte in ihm aufzureizen. . . .
'Er machte daher meistens schon bei dem Mittagstische mit der bescheidensten Zutraulichkeit die Frage an S.: „Werden Sie nicht heute Abend Klavier spielen?"— Wenn nun die Dämmerung eintrat, wurde sein Wunsch erfüllt, während dem er im Zimmer, das oft bloß durch das Mondlicht beleuchtet war, mehrere Stunden auf und ab ging und nicht selten in unvernehmliche, begeisterte Laute ausbrach.'
[2] Goethe was at work on this act in 1800 and Schiller wrote to him on 26 September, 'Ihre neuliche Vorlesung hat mich auf die Trimeter sehr aufmerksam gemacht und ich wünschte in die Sache mehr einzudringen' (Jonas, 6. 205).

fearful sights of war, the march of the trimeters rings out with conviction:

> Wo soll ich hinfliehn? Feinde ringsumher und Tod!
> Hier der ergrimmte Feldherr, der mit drohndem Schwert
> Die Flucht versperrend uns dem Tod entgegentreibt.
> Dort die Fürchterliche, die verderblich um sich her
> Wie die Brunst des Feuers raset. (ll. 1552–6)

But, when his tone turns to imploration, words and form are no longer in accord—

> O so erbarme meiner jammervollen Eltern dich,
> Die ich zu Haus verlassen. Ja gewiß auch du
> Verließest Eltern, die die Sorge quält um dich. (ll. 1625–7)

Though the second sentence deftly and ironically prefigures Johanna's suffering through her father's 'care', the syntactical feebleness of the two relative clauses betrays the flagging of the inner tension.

How strong that tension can be at its best is seen when Schiller seems to wrestle with the form, when the words are wrung from his characters in short, weighty, rough-hewn phrases, as in Johanna's climactic speech:

> Doch weggerissen von der heimatlichen Flur,
> Vom Vaters Busen, von der Schwestern liebe Brust
> Muß ich *hier*, ich *muß* — mich treibt die Götterstimme, nicht
> Eignes Gelüsten, *euch* zu bitterm Harm, *mir* nicht
> Zur Freude, ein Gespenst des Schreckens würgend gehn,
> Den Tod verbreiten und sein Opfer sein zuletzt.
> (ll. 1658–63)

It is clear from these lines that Schiller can handle trimeters with tremendous power and with as much freedom as the form allows. If we detect in the Montgomery scene a certain rigidity, that is inherent in the verse form, at any rate when it is transplanted into German. A dramatist uses it at his peril. By the addition of a mere two syllables to the blank-verse line, the tone is shifted into a remote and inaccessible region. The hard outline of the verse is incapable of expressing the flux of human emotion. Its inflexibility corresponds to the inhuman or the superhuman. In this scene it conveys a barbarity and cruelty which is inaccessible to pity and immune from compassion. Johanna's remorseless enmity finds appropriate expression; but Montgomery's tears appear no more than a formal exercise. To have made Johanna speak in trimeters and Montgomery in blank verse might have been psychologically apt, but it was aesthetically impossible. For trimeters will not mix. They stand out hard and insoluble in the flow of the drama. In a play in which over-all unity of style is an important element, the failure to integrate these exotic measures seems to be a serious defect.

## 2. VOCABULARY

Integration in exaltation appears to be the principle which has governed the choice of words in *Die Jungfrau von Orleans*. *Held* and *edel* are conspicuous tone-setters. So Johanna speaks of 'Frankreichs Heldensöhnen' (l. 423), König Karl of 'Der Ritter große Heldenherzen' (l. 519), Saintrailles is termed 'der edle Held' (so comprehending both words in one expression, l. 584), the kings of France are 'geborne Helden' (l. 856), Dunois enjoys 'Heldenruhm' (l. 1837), and so on. These unliteral, stylized applications, employed without a trace of irony, 'peg' the tone at an exalted level. And *edel*, applied conventionally to *Held*, *Dauphin*, and *Herzog*, and to *Leib*, *Angesicht*, and, unexpectedly, to 'Bürgerblut', performs a similar function. These words are intended to affirm the nobility of the plane on which *Die Jungfrau* operates. And they are supported in their ennobling function by elaborate rhetorical patterns, as in Agnes Sorel's address to Johanna:

> Sein edles Herz,
> Dem Ruhm nur offen und der Heldentugend,
> Es glüht für dich in heiligem Gefühl.
> O es ist schön, von einem Helden sich geliebt
> Zu sehn — es ist noch schöner, ihn zu lieben!           (ll. 2648–52)

It is one of many passages in *Die Jungfrau von Orleans* which seem to push conventional elevation to the point of affectation and insincerity. Other words of intrinsically 'noble' character plentifully reinforce *Held* and *edel*; they include *sieghaft*, *Stahl*, *Erz*, and *Rittertat*, *Glanz* and *Sonne*, *Glück* and *Freude*, *tapfer*, *strahlend*, *kühn* and *stolz*. All of them function, not as individual words, but as notes in a musical texture of exaltation.

We are accustomed to find in Schiller's work that the words of elevation are balanced by a dark and even savage vocabulary. In *Die Jungfrau von Orleans*, too, the ethereal element is paralleled by an element of violence. Images of fire are both metaphorical ('Des Bürgerkrieges Flammen' or 'Der Verheerung Rauch') and factual ('Der Bürger zündet seine Stadt, der Landmann / Mit eignen Händen seine Saaten an', ll. 833–4). Similarly images of storm serve to lift the events of war on to an impressive but generalized plane, with such expressions as 'des Krieges Stürme', 'sturmfest', 'sturmbewegt', and 'Kriegeswolke'. The element of convention is less obvious in the uses of *mordbegierig*, a compound which serves, not to soothe, but to shock. So Salisbury peers from the look-out 'mit mordbegiergem Blick' (l. 257); and even more startling are Johanna's words spoken to Burgund on the threshold of reconciliation:

> Wer ist der Feind,
> Den deine Blicke mordbegierig suchen?     (ll. 1730–1)

Boldly coined phrases of blood occur, such as 'Kein Unrecht sei so blutig' (l. 2047), 'blutig fürchterlich' (l. 3065), or 'grimmig blutge Rache' (l. 3118). Yet these examples are a mere handful compared with the abundance of conventional uses such as 'mit mörderischem Schwert' or 'Strömen Feindesbluts'. The horror is for the most part lightly veiled in convention, and only rarely does it break through to reveal its full potency. Even the Montgomery scenes, which in their action constitute the most brutal episode of the play, are screened not only by conventions of language current in Schiller's day, but by the stylization of classical treatment. And, when Johanna's ruthless violence becomes too fierce to be screened, it is neutralized by a swift change to the other extreme, to a hyperbole so extravagant that belief is withheld:

> Wenn dich das Unglück in des Krokodils Gewalt
> Gegeben oder des gefleckten Tigers Klaun,
> Wenn du der Löwenmutter junge Brut geraubt,
> Du könntest Mitleid finden und Barmherzigkeit,
> Doch tödlich ists, der Jungfrau zu begegnen.          (ll. 1594–8)

These are not images of frightening reality, they are the stereotyped metaphors of public address, and one is almost tempted to believe that Schiller gave his tiger spots, not from ignorance, but in order to deprive him of all immediacy.

It was in the nature of the subject that God and the Devil, Heaven and Hell, should be prominent elements in the vocabulary of this play, in which holiness and sinfulness confront each other and are for a time confused. *Heilig*, *Himmel*, and *Gott* on the one side face *Hölle* and *Teufel* on the other. *Zauber* and *irdisch* are opposed by *wunderbar*. And *Sonne* and *Tag* repeatedly face *Nacht* and *Finsternis* as symbols of this theomachy.

The religious background is strongly supported by a number of isolated Biblical allusions. So Thibaut refers to the temptation in the wilderness—

> in der Wüste trat
> Der Satansengel selbst zum Herrn des Himmels          (ll. 155–6)

—prefiguring in this allusive paradoxical compound Johanna's role in Acts Four and Five as the sinful saint. Johanna herself confirms her mission by the analogy of Moses and the burning bush (Exodus 3) and of David the son of Jesse (I Samuel 16). Karl supports his pacifism in Act I. v with a reference to the false and true mothers in the judgement of Solomon. And at the reconciliation of the warring factions the archbishop crowns his speech of thanksgiving with an allusion to Simeon (Luke 2: 29–30)—

> ich kann fröhlich scheiden,
> Da meine Augen diesen Tag gesehn!          (ll. 1954–5)

But all these Biblical links are surpassed in weight, vigour, and vehemence by Johanna's denunciation:

Ihr blinden Herzen! Ihr Kleingläubigen!          (l. 2251)

—reproducing exactly the apostrophe of Matthew 8: 26. This is immediately reinforced by a line which, granted the alteration of person, quotes literally Matthew 24: 26:

Mir wäre besser, ich wär nie geboren!          (l. 2260)

The example of Samson is invoked by Johanna when she prays for strength to burst her bonds (v. ii); and the last line of the play is an allusion to the rainbow of Genesis 9, with its divine promise:

Seht ihr den Regenbogen in der Luft?          (l. 3536)

These religious co-ordinates, suggested by the subject and favoured by the new Romanticism, are opposed by a set of contrasting references to classical antiquity. The pagan fierceness of the Montgomery scenes with their Greek metre is the most obvious instance. But an antique yeast is spread through the play by other stylistic features, notably by stichomythia and by Homeric epithets and subjoined adjectives, as in

diesen Talbot,<br>Den himmelstürmend hunderthändigen          (ll. 319–20)

or

Doch nimm das Schwert, das tödliche, nicht selbst.          (l. 1513)

And epithets as nouns increase the ferment (e.g. *die Fürchter-liche*). The focal concentration of the words of antiquity is on fate. Though some of these are merely conventional, others clearly pertain to the world of pagan theology. 'Das verderbliche Geschick' not only expresses what befalls, but hints at that which causes it to befall. Lurking behind this use of *Schicksal* and *Geschick*, this sense of impending misfortune willed by the gods, is Schiller's ever-present awareness of the judge, of the bringer of retribution. It is in this sense that Johanna's outburst of submission, at once dynamic and passive, is to be understood:

> Befiehl, daß man die Kriegstrommete blase!
> Mich preßt und ängstigt diese Waffenstille,
> Es jagt mich auf aus dieser müßgen Ruh,
> Und treibt mich fort, daß ich mein Werk erfülle,
> Gebietrisch mahnend meinem Schicksal zu.        (ll. 2266–70)

When Johanna speaks these words, her sin, though imminent, is uncommitted. The suggestive ambiguity of the fate that befalls and the fate that wills is Schiller's symbol for the seed of evil within, the ripening of which will be guilt. This presence of fate is then powerfully developed in Acts Four and Five in Johanna's references to fate, both forward- ('Mein Schicksal führt mich', l. 3115) and backward-looking ('Ich unterwarf mich schweigend dem Geschick', l. 3147).

This does not exhaust the pagan element in *Die Jungfrau*. The gods (whom we may take to be the gods of Greece) play an appreciable part in the verbal texture. In the monologue with which the innocent and obstinate Johanna concludes the Prolog, she takes the first step into polytheism with 'Götterkraft' (l. 427). Raoul has seen her 'wie eine Kriegesgöttin' (l. 956), and to Montgomery she speaks of 'die Götterstimme' (l. 1660) which impels her. Dunois opts for a franker paganism and suggests an alternative interpretation when he calls her 'ein Götterkind der heiligen Natur' (l. 1844) and sees a 'Götterschein' surrounding her. The angry Talbot exclaims in his death agony, 'Mit der Dummheit kämpfen Götter selbst vergebens' (l. 2319) and Johanna transposes a Biblical aphorism into a polytheistic context with 'ohne Götter fällt kein Haar / Vom Haupt des Menschen' (ll. 3192–3). By such classicizing motifs an element of the statuesque is injected into the veins of the figures of this play; it is a quality which accords with the rhetorical handling of the language which is also ultimately classical in its derivation.

How then, in a play which seems to aim at stylistic harmony, are we to reconcile sources of language so divergent as the God-Devil relationship of Christianity and the divine plurality of the ancient world? And the answer must be that the disparity cannot be removed, it can only be played down. And that is precisely what Schiller does. A major factor in this mitigation of stresses is the overriding unity of rhetorically organized syntax and the accompanying tropes. An important reinforcement is found in the use of *Herz*, which occurs in *Die Jungfrau* with exceptional frequency.[1] Some of its uses are merely conventional, yet even when it has no special significance its associations vibrate and make their slight contribution to the total effect. It is for Schiller an evocative word, spreading a warmth and glow. It is distributed among all the principal characters and is not denied to Johanna's adversaries. It permeates the play and sets up sympathetic vibrations. And its pervasive warmth harmonizes and dispels dissonances.

*Herz* was clearly an important word for Schiller in connection with this play; for it occurs not only in it, but with reference to it. In a letter to Körner, written on 5 January 1801, Schiller contrasts his approach to *Die Jungfrau* with his relationship to his earlier plays in the following terms: 'Schon der Stoff erhält mich warm; ich bin mit dem ganzen Herzen dabei, und es fließt auch mehr aus dem Herzen, als die vorigen Stücke, wo der Verstand mit dem Stoffe kämpfen mußte.'[2] So prominent is the word *Herz* in his mind here that he uses it twice in the one sentence. A few months after completing the play, he confirms the persistent association with *Herz* in another dual utterance, contained in a letter to his friend and former publisher Göschen: 'Dieses Stück floß *aus dem Herzen* und *zu dem Herzen* sollte es auch sprechen.'[3] To these significant personal confessions must be added a public declaration in Schiller's poetic apologia, *Das Mädchen von Orleans*, published in 1802. Here the word *Herz* occurs three times, most expressively in the second stanza:

Dich schuf das Herz, du wirst unsterblich leben.

And yet one may wonder how deep all this goes. *Herz* gets further prominence in *Die Jungfrau* by the threefold occurrence

---

[1] It occurs 78 times.          [2] Jonas, 6. 234.
[3] 10 February 1802 (Jonas, 6. 349).

of one phrase, which at first sight seems thereby to become something of a leitmotiv. It is 'Mir sagts das Herz'. After all Schiller's remarks about the role of the heart in writing the play, surely this phrase must be the assertion of the ultimate authority. By whom, however, are the words spoken? Twice by Agnes Sorel, and once by Burgund. That is to say by characters of secondary rank in the structure of the play. And the expressive phrase is not used to any great purpose either. When first spoken by Agnes (l. 794) it conveys her confidence that Karl, despite the apparently hopeless situation, will be successful in reuniting France. But the words are not significant. This is no prophecy (only Johanna can prophesy in this play), it is no more than a well-meant encouragement. And when Agnes repeats the words in l. 2291 Johanna has made success so certain that the assertion is valueless. In between comes Burgund's utterance (l. 1804), expressing his newly-won conviction of the divinity of Johanna's mission. But, since by this time Karl and Agnes, Dunois and La Hire, not to speak of the archbishop, are all believers in her inspiration, the voice of Burgund's 'heart', though politically important, is spiritually negligible. The occurrence of the phrase at three points of no special significance suggests that it had a particular personal appeal for Schiller. It is probably no coincidence that it is already found in Goethe's *Iphigenie*, where Orest speaks the words

Es löset sich der Fluch, mir sagt's das Herz.        (l. 1358)

Schiller had read *Iphigenie* a few months before he went to work upon *Die Jungfrau von Orleans* and it seems more than plausible that the phrase delighted him and that it anchored itself in his mind, emerging three times in the writing of his play. And so what had at first sight seemed significant has every appearance of being a mere unimportant act of self-indulgence. And the word *Herz*, which by its associations and its frequency generates a warmth throughout the play, turns out in a number of its individual uses to be merely trivial.

The use of *Herz* is impressionistic and not intended for close examination. And this is true also of another means which Schiller has adopted in order to harmonize the disparate elements in *Die Jungfrau*. Alliteration occurs on what, for Schiller, is an unprecedented scale. It appears in manifold repetition of a single consonant, as in

> Ein finster furchtbares Verhängnis waltet
> Durch Valois' Geschlecht, es ist verworfen
> Von Gott, der Mutter Lastertaten führten
> Die Furien herein in dieses Haus          (ll. 777–80)

with its sevenfold *f/v* and the closely related *w*. It occurs in linked pairs, as when Talbot speaks:

> Kann ich der Feinde Flut entgegenstellen,
> Die wachsend, wogend in das Lager dringt!          (ll. 1536–7)

Or it comes in a triple group:

> Denn der zu Moses auf des Horebs Höhen
> Im feurgen Busch sich flammend niederließ.          (ll. 401–2)

Schiller shows a predilection for coining strikingly compressed alliterative phrases, for example, 'Nicht eine Welt in Waffen fürchten wir' (l. 1132), 'Doch in den Falten wohnt die Finsternis' (l. 2064), or 'Mir soll der Mut nicht weichen und nicht wanken' (l. 2453). He does not recoil from well-worn and even trite couplings, using 'aus tiefem Tal', 'unter dünner Decke', 'Herz und Handschlag', 'Hohe Himmelskönigin', or 'der Himmel Herrlichkeit'. He uses alliteration without regard to person; Isabeau is as alliterative as Johanna, Talbot as König Karl. It spreads through all the forms of verse, blank verse, stanzas, and trimeters, and it is as abundant in the last act as in the Prolog. If the alliteration helps to make the verse memorable, it also gives more than a hint of the facile.

The poetic speech of *Die Jungfrau von Orleans* is more than ordinarily rich. Schiller's enthusiasm for his subject pours out in flowing and generous tone. Intricate structures of rhetoric are handled with ease. The rhyme in the stanzas and the universal alliteration give an impression of word music. And the varied pattern of Schiller's experiments in metre and tone appealed to a generation attuned to the kaleidoscopic glitter of the new Romanticism. It is not surprising that the contemporaries were mostly enthusiastic.

This style, however, has not worn well. In spite of Schiller's virtuosity, the verse is often perceptibly inappropriate to its purpose. Indeed, Schiller's dazzling facility with rhetoric is itself a cause of failure. On the heights along which this verse moves, it is easy to make a false step and to slide into bathos. The ever-present danger becomes reality in *Die Jungfrau*. Johanna's bombast overreaches itself when she addresses the mysterious 'Schwarzer Ritter' with

> Dich weg zu tilgen von dem Licht des Tags
> Treibt mich die unbezwingliche Begier.          (ll. 2412–13)

And Dunois, justifying his love for Johanna, unintentionally achieves the comic:

> Denn nur die Starke kann die Freundin sein
> Des starken Mannes, und dies glühnde Herz
> Sehnt sich an einer gleichen Brust zu ruhn . . .          (ll. 1832–4)

And even more unfortunate is Johanna's line:

> Und einen Donnerkeil führ ich im Munde.          (l. 1798)

The repeated self-application of conventional epithets of nobility also puts a strain upon the style, as in Dunois's lines

> Mir blutet in der Brust
> Das tapfre Herz;          (ll. 435–6)

or in Johanna's

> Mein edles Herz im Busen zu erschüttern.          (l. 2449)

The insistent stilted forms of address overshoot their mark, especially in the forms of reprehension—'schwache Seelen!', 'armselge Gleisner!', 'Betrogner Tor! Verlorner!', 'Verfluchte!', 'Verworfne', 'Elende', and so on. In all Schiller's plays there are patches or tracts in which he has let himself go or sacrificed full unity of style to some special effect. But nowhere else in Schiller's work is the sense of discipline so completely lost as here. This relaxation of the strict hold which Schiller normally maintained upon himself in the writing of verse is almost certainly connected with his self-confessed partiality for his subject. In *Don Carlos* a hint of self-indulgence had been redeemed by spontaneity, freshness, and vitality. In *Maria Stuart* it had been held in check by the decorum of public behaviour. But in *Die Jungfrau von Orleans* the 'heart' has its way and the tendencies to exaggeration and the breaches of tact, to which Schiller was by nature prone, have got out of hand, since the *saeva indignatio* of the early plays was past and the discipline of the middle years temporarily in abeyance. It is perhaps significant that this play is the one which makes the least use of colloquial speech, the only traces of which are perceptible in the petulance of König Karl in the first act.

### 3. MUSIC

It seems more than likely that an element of personal involvement prompted Schiller's eclecticism. Though the introduction of the stanzas and the trimeters had a serious purpose in the play, they were also the outcome of an interest in the epic which Schiller had not had an opportunity to work out elsewhere, and little attempt has been made to integrate them.

The most interesting of Schiller's experiments is probably the musical treatment of the opening scene of the fourth act. The stanzas with which Johanna rounds off the Prolog have already some resemblance to a bravura aria. Church bells accompany the news of her first, miraculous, victory. Drums and trumpets are heard in the night attack (Act Two) and drums beat a prelude to the Montgomery scene. Trumpets sound for the reconciliation of Karl and Burgund (Act Three), and martial music symbolizes the battle in which Talbot is mortally wounded. The processional scene of Act Four is accompanied by appropriately solemn march music and the moment of coronation is signalled by trumpets and kettle-drums heard from within the cathedral. More trumpets sound when the King appears, and they are heard again for the final battle. The word 'operatic' has often been used in connection with these effects, and it is true that Schiller became interested in opera and contemplated writing the libretto for one. Nevertheless the operatic quality of *Die Jungfrau von Orleans* can be exaggerated. The only scenes which might in any degree be so called are the battle interlude in Act Three, the first scene of Act Four with its stanzas, oboes, and flutes, and the procession scene later in the same act. And in the latter two Schiller, though he exploits some possibilities of music, retains the chief emphasis unquestionably on the spoken word. The church bells and the martial music of the other scenes are not musical ideas but merely aural support for the action, parallel with the visual support which Schiller seeks from the stage carpenter and scene painter, e.g. *Man sieht die Türme von Rheims in der Ferne, von der Sonne beleuchtet* (III. ix). One must not confuse Schiller's use of supporting music with his adoption of verse procedures which have an analogy with music. In *Die Jungfrau* he makes lavish use of the former, but the musical movement of his verse was still at a rudimentary stage.

And so the play, for all its lavish brilliance, remains stylistically unsatisfactory, a web of unsolved problems. And this is true to the very last line. In every one of Schiller's earlier tragedies the curtain falls on a significant and reticent utterance which suggests a perspective, yet refrains from defining it. We see these restrained and pregnant conclusions in Karl Moor's 'Dem Mann kann geholfen werden', in Verrina's 'Ich gehe zum Andreas', in the Präsident's 'Jetzt euer Gefangener', in Philipp's 'Ich habe / Das Meinige getan, Tun Sie das Ihre', in Gordon's 'Dem Fürsten Piccolomini,' or in Kent's 'Der Lord läßt sich / Entschuldigen, er ist zu Schiff nach Frankreich!' *Die Jungfrau von Orleans* alone seeks to break new ground—and can manage nothing better for its end than a platitudinous *sententia*:

Kurz ist der Schmerz und ewig ist die Freude!

# VIII · *DIE BRAUT VON MESSINA*

## 1. THE CHORUS

THE distinguishing feature of *Die Braut von Messina* is its chorus. The truism is unavoidable; for the Chorus is a key to style as well as structure. That Schiller himself saw this is apparent from his prefatory essay, 'Über den Gebrauch des Chors in der Tragödie', in which he maintains that the chorus should attract to itself all the lyrical elements which might otherwise clog the movement of the tragedy. Compared with *Die Jungfrau von Orleans*, which the lyrical had invaded at many points, *Die Braut von Messina* represents a disciplined reorganization. The lyrical has in the Chorus its own domain, in which rhetoric takes a subordinate place.

Having decided on a chorus, Schiller gave it a substantial share of the text. It speaks one quarter of the lines, and of the single characters only Isabella has a (very slightly) longer part. It is given four extended sections in the first two-thirds of the play and three shorter interventions in the remainder. It offered Schiller an immense enrichment of rhythm, enabling him to use flexible metrical patterns similar to those in Greek tragedy. The lines vary in length from the three syllables of 'Scheidend reicht' (l. 1203) to the twelve of 'Den begünstigten Sohn der Götter beneid ich' (l. 1230). The staple iambic foot is reinforced by copious dactyls and trochees and occasional anapaests. This flexibility permits a remarkable sense of controlled surge and ebb.

After Isabella's haughty address to the Elders and her brief dialogue with Diego, the Chorus takes the stage and speaks its longest continuous passage, embracing 162 lines. So assured an opening establishes its place in the drama. The Chorus begins with a choric ode, followed by two refrains enclosing a short antiphonal section; there follows a long tract of reflection, and the whole is concluded by a second choric ode. The odes, being shared between the two sections of the chorus, also have a partially antiphonal character.

The choric odes use predominantly short lines of five syllables; these are punctuated at intervals by longer lines of ten, eleven, or even twelve syllables, occurring singly or in small groups. The shorter lines express soaring euphoric emotion; the longer lines convey dark or turbid feeling. Flexibility comes from the unaccented syllables of dactyls and anapaests. The type of the short line is composed of a dactyl followed by a trochee:

Prangende Halle. (l. 133)

The longer lines with initial dactyl or anapaest are exemplified by

Zürnend ergrimmt mir das Herz im Busen,
Zu dem Kampf ist die Faust geballt. (ll. 145–6)

The first strophe of the opening choric ode begins with an exalted salutation, set in short lines. Allusions to the lurking presence of evil are accompanied by a slight lengthening of the lines and so by a retardation. The rhythm sweeps the strophe along in a dance-like movement of planned irregularity. The dance expresses strength, not grace. It is Schiller's special gift to devise rhythmic structures displaying power. Power, too, underlies the vocabulary. Words of majesty and splendour ('Ehrfurcht', 'prangend','Herrscher','fürstlich','herrlich') are set against others of sinister or terrible import ('Schwert', 'schlangenhaarigt', 'Scheusal','Erinnyen', 'der Furchtbarste','Hölle'). The strophe is borne on a weighty sequence of nouns, supplemented by a few polysyllabic adjectives ('unverletzlich', 'schlangenhaarigt', 'säulengetragen'). The verbs are negligible. The static, making for strength and weight, predominates over the mobile.

The second strophe stresses dissension and violence. Longer lines are used with a vocabulary of anger ('zürnend', 'ergrimmt',

'Faust geballt', 'verhaßte Gestalt', 'ko chendem Blute'). In inverse movement to the first strophe, this one starts in ferocity and declines into submission. The third strophe unites the motifs of ecstatic exaltation and threatening dissension. Grandeur and strife are firmly established as climatic elements in a poem which, like so much in Schiller, is plainly triadic.

The poetic quality of this ode is heightened by another, and entirely non-classical, feature by which Schiller proved, if this were necessary, that he was not slavishly fashioning a pastiche of Greek tragedy. At the end of the first strophe there occurs a hint of rhyme ('Schwelle'—'Hölle'). The second strophe rhymes throughout in an irregular pattern; and the third rhymes occasionally. By this modern innovation Schiller both enriches and tautens the aural pattern.

In the first choric ode the motif of dissension is stressed by the distribution of the strophes between the two halves of the Chorus with a corresponding differentiation between the outside strophes and the middle one. The second choric ode emphasizes unity by allotting a similar pattern and tone to both parts of the Chorus. This is a hymn of praise, an exaltation of unity, provoked by the sight of Isabella grouped in harmony with her two sons. The lilting lines express serenity and splendour. Words of light and brightness ('mildere Klarheit', 'der Sterne blitzendem Glanz', 'Glänzen erhellt', and 'Aurora berührt sie / Mit den ewigen Strahlen') are linked with a series of magnificence and grandeur ('Der Söhne feuriger Kraft', 'Hoch auf des Lebens / Gipfel gestellt', 'Krönt sich die herrlich vollendete Welt'). The cosmic images of moon and sun combine in themselves illumination and strength, and the fusion of serenity and grandeur is caught in the phrase 'Liebliche Hoheit'.

These two odes begin and end the first long choric passage. Between them, marking the familiar triadic structure, is an extended passage of reflection, quite distinct in pattern, rhythm, and tone. Its basic unit is a line of nine or ten syllables:

Hört, was ich bei mir selbst erwogen,
Als ich müßig daher gezogen. (ll. 190–1)

Though the lines vary in length, the limits of variation are narrower than in the odes. The metre is predominantly trochaic and the risk of monotony is countered by an admixture of dactyls. The consequent rhythmic impulse is strong, smooth, and swift, with slight accelerations or retardations—a discreet *rubato*. An elegiac tone is at first maintained by the confrontation of the words of nature (associated with tranquillity) and the words of present strife. 'Des Korns hochwallende Gassen' and 'Diese Ulmen, mit Reben umsponnen' are set against 'das brausende Blut' and 'mit rasendem Beginnen'. The opposition of peace and conflict shifts into other formulations and gravitates, in accordance with Schiller's fixed tendency, towards moral reflection and *sententia*, expressed in antithetical form:

> Aber hinter den großen Höhen
> Folgt auch der tiefe, der donnernde Fall.                (ll. 238–9)

The whole passage develops in three sections which could be denoted musically as statement, counter-statement, and reprise.

The basic conception of the Chorus seems to be musical. It is true that Schiller showed himself ready to accept performances without music, if we are to judge from a letter to Iffland, in which he wrote 'da die Reden des Chors nicht mit Musik begleitet werden'.[1] Yet, on the other hand, he sent (only a few days later) a letter to Zelter suggesting musical declamation: 'wir hielten es nicht für unmöglich, die lyrischen Intermezzos des Chors, deren fünf oder sechs sind, nach Gesangsweise recitieren zu lassen und mit einem Instrument zu begleiten.[2] And the prefatory essay on the use of the chorus explicitly refers to the support of music: 'er [der Chor] tut es, von der ganzen sinnlichen Macht des Rhythmus und der Musik in Tönen und Bewegungen begleitet'.[3] Even when the music is absent, the basic musical structure, the binary form A–B–A, persists. Moreover, the use of the double refrain in the bridge passage connecting the first ode with the middle section takes a step towards musical effect, transforming statement into incantation.

---

[1] 24 February 1803. Jonas 7, 17.          [2] 28 Febrary 1803. Jonas 7, 18.
[3] *Sämtliche Werke*, (Fricke and Göpferdt), ii, p. 821.

The use of techniques with affinity to music becomes more obvious in the second choric interlude, which concludes the first phase of the tragedy. The Chorus discourses on the pursuits of peace and speculates on the precarious duration of the newly won harmony between the brothers. It is, however, not a continuous passage of choric speech. It is an interlude for solo voices and chorus. The section comprises 120 lines. It begins with ten lines spoken by the whole chorus and ends with a similar passage of twelve lines. The ninety-eight lines between are divided into six speeches allocated to three individual members of the chorus, each of whom speaks twice. Thus six solo passages are framed symmetrically by two relatively short choric sections. This juxtaposition of single and collective voices prepares us for an even more striking contrast when the chorus makes its third important contribution. Here it first speaks a nuptial ode addressed to Beatrice and shortly after delivers one of its characteristic reflective sections in a remarkable mixture of anapaests, dactyls, and trochees:

> Den begünstigten Sohn der Götter beneid ich,
> Den beglückten Besitzer der Macht!
> Immer das Köstlichste ist sein Anteil,
> Und von allem, was hoch und herrlich
> Von den Sterblichen wird gepriesen,
> Bricht er die Blume sich ab. (ll. 1230–5)

The most interesting feature of this interlude is the passage of nineteen lines which links the two poems of the Chorus. It is spoken by Beatrice. Schiller, adhering to his favoured triadic structure, here employs a solo voice of contrasting timbre and pitch. This alternation between the single female voice of quality and the massed rough voices of men is a development of musical character, heard in many musical compositions.[1] Beatrice's 'aria' is also notable for its trochaic metre, soon to become popular in Romantic drama.[2] This metre, which is borrowed from Spanish

---

[1] Verdi's *La forza del destino* and Brahms's *Alto Rhapsody* yield obvious examples.
[2] The first volume of A. W. Schlegel's translation of Calderón appeared in 1803, when *Die Braut von Messina* was finished. Schiller may have discussed the metre with Schlegel or others.

drama and especially from Calderón, can quickly become irritatingly monotonous, but in the short section occurring here it is wholly apt, for its pronounced insistent rhythm parallels the pulsation of Beatrice's anxious heart.

The fourth and last truly choric intervention in the play incorporates a funeral ode. Don Cesar's murder of Don Manuel evokes an instantaneous response from the two parties of the Chorus—the one expresses exultation, the other the impulse to vengeance. These reactions are disposed of, however, in six lines, and in the last two of these there is a hint at a ritual significance which is to be developed later—

> ERSTER CHOR. Mord! Mord! Herbei! Greift zu den Waffen alle!
> Mit Blut gerächet sei die blutge Tat!
> ZWEITER CHOR. Heil uns! Der lange Zwiespalt ist geendigt.
> Nur *einem* Herrscher jetzt gehorcht Messina.
> ERSTER CHOR. Rache! Rache! Der Mörder falle! falle!
> Ein sühnend Opfer dem Gemordeten!               (ll. 1905–10)

Thereupon Don Cesar's half-Chorus departs with its master, and immediately the remaining Chorus intones the lament. A strophe of reflection ushers in the funeral ode, in which two solo voices precede a short passage spoken by the whole group with the effect of a refrain; for the last line of the second speaker is picked up by the Chorus and repeated with slight variation ('Denn der Schlummer der Toten ist schwer. / Schwer und tief ist der Schlummer der Toten', ll. 1956–7), and the *Nimmer* of the line before is twice echoed by the Chorus thus:

> Nimmer erweckt ihn die Stimme der Braut,
> Nimmer des Hifthorns fröhlicher Laut.          (ll. 1958–9)

After this the Chorus, with single voices of its members, enters on a passage of reflection, which achieves a new kind of musical effect by repetition:

> Aber wehe dem Mörder, wehe,
> Der dahingeht in törichtem Mut!
> Hinab, hinab in der Erde Ritzen
> Rinnet, rinnet, rinnet dein Blut.                (ll. 1984–7)

This is no longer the reiteration with which Schiller so often expresses passionate urgency; it is incantation. Throughout the rest of the play the characteristic utterance of the Chorus is a double, treble, or quadruple 'Wehe!' These syllables of lamentation occur five times at significant points. They refer back to the sixfold use of 'Wehe!' following immediately upon the murder:

> Weh dir Messina! Wehe! Wehe! Wehe!
> Das gräßlich Ungeheure ist geschehn
> In deinen Mauren — Wehe deinen Müttern
> Und Kindern, deinen Jünglingen und Greisen,
> Und wehe der noch ungebornen Frucht!     (ll. 1917–21)

The effect is of a chord first heard at a moment of intense suffering, and subsequently evoking, on each repetition, the horror of the moment of the murder.

The quasi-musical techniques are not yet exhausted. When the Chorus leaves the scene of the murder, bearing with it the body of the dead Manuel, it has concluded its last long interlude in the play; but it still has three important short interventions to make. The first is a threnody, the first two strophes of which are processional. Though with its short lines the appearance on the page is similar to that of the earlier odes, this *marcia funebre* advances with solemn, stately step, the slow dactyls recalling the dotted rhythm of its musical equivalent:

> Durch die Straßen der Städte,
> Vom Jammer gefolget,
> Schreitet das Unglück —
>
> .    .    .    .
>
> Heute an dieser
> Pforte pocht es,
> Morgen an jener,
> Aber noch keinen hat es verschont.     (ll. 2267–75)

The strophes diminish in length as the procession prepares to halt. The fourth and final strophe is static, longer in line, and devoted entirely to reflection. It develops the symbol of the sudden, unexpected lightning stroke and the rolling thunder, the long re-echoing of which is strikingly conveyed by the bold device of a line composed solely of three anapaests:

> In des furchtbaren Schicksals Gewalt.          (l. 2300)

The most original piece of choric poetry is the short passage which serves as a prelude to the appearance of Don Cesar by the bier of the brother he has murdered. It takes the form of a short ode expressing, in stylized ritual form, reactions of agitation and horror. The short, impulsive lines, the urgent imperatives, the incantatory repetitions, and the abandonment of a coherent thread of thought all point to its quasi-musical character. It is akin to the short musical prelude which in opera announces an important entry.

Schiller's suggestion in the preface that a chorus attracts to itself all the lyrical elements in a tragedy is not entirely in accord with the practice of *Die Braut von Messina*. Not only does Beatrice, as we have seen, join in a choric passage; at her first entry she speaks a long poem (of 129 lines) which is almost wholly lyrical. It is in four main sections. The first and third are stanzas of *ottava rima*, the second, urgent and agitated, is composed of short lines, each of two amphibrachs or an amphibrach and an iamb:

> Ergriff mich betörend
> Ein rasender Wahn?          (ll. 1007–8)

The fourth is a long lyrical passage of flexible rhythm and intermittent rhyme, which might justifiably be called an aria. Indeed, the whole speech is akin to a *scena* comprising two arias, each preceded by a recitative.

If on the one hand the lyrical brims over from the choric into the speech of the characters, it is also true that the Chorus is not exclusively given over to lyrical expression. At three points it takes a hand momentarily in the action, and it twice, at rather more length, functions as the confidant of French classical tragedy, once with Don Manuel (ll. 592–738) and once with Don Cesar (ll. 2606–47). The latter passage is remarkable, for the

Chorus speaks in trimeters and conducts stichomythia in four-line groups.

In so deliberately classical a play stichomythia was bound to occur. It does so on a considerable scale, making up more than one-tenth of the text, and the Chorus participates in a substantial proportion of this.[1] This involvement of the Chorus is in one respect surprising, for stichomythia is usually remote from lyricism. Indeed, it suggests conflict, the sharp thrust and riposte. Two factors, which were far from contention, operated in Schiller's use of stichomythia in this play. His deeply implanted love of parallel constructions inclined him to answering speeches of equal length; and he showed clearly in *Die Braut von Messina* an inclination for the complete line as a unit. Furthermore parallelisms need not be oppositional, they can be complementary. Schiller's choric stichomythia has precisely this complementary and, since it verges on music, antiphonal character.

It is clear that Schiller himself attached great importance to the lyrico-musical tone of the Chorus. Critics, however, have been far from unanimous about the quality of the choric writing. Some[2] have rated it among his best lyric work; to others[3] it has seemed generalized and pretentious. It may well be that the two groups of views are not focused upon the same thing. The extent of choric writing is considerable, and some parts may move with a genuine poetic impulse whilst others ring hollow.

Many of the choric passages are reflective. They provide a poetic accompaniment which generalizes the fate of the persons in the play. As such they offer a seedbed for platitude. And platitude was an ever-present danger for the reflecting Schiller, whose poetic imagination dealt in the obvious and usually transmuted it into something glowing. He loved well-worn words, which were also the common currency of uninspired orators and would-be poets; and he delighted in a crisp sententious formulation. An illustration of the danger and its avoidance by the

---

[1] About two-fifths.

[2] e.g. E. L. Stahl, *Schiller's Drama. Theory and Practice*, 1954, p. 136; and G. Storz, *Der Dichter Friedrich Schiller*, 1959, p. 385.

[3] Typical of this view is B. von Wiese in *Schiller*, 1959, p. 762.

narrowest of margins is the five-line choric epilogue to *Die Braut von Messina*:

> Erschüttert steh ich, weiß nicht ob ich ihn,
> Beweinen oder preisen soll sein Los.
> Dies *eine* fühl ich und erkenn es klar,
> Das Leben ist der Güter höchstes *nicht*,
> Der Übel aber größtes ist die *Schuld*.          (ll. 2835–9)

What saves these lines from bathos is first the note of uncertainty in the opening which removes the cock-sureness from the final pronouncement, and secondly the abstention from rhyme. How great a contribution this self-discipline makes is apparent in the choric poem which fills the gap between Don Cesar's departure from the stage and his reappearance (ll. 2560–88). The Chorus deplores the precariousness of prominence, praising idyllic rural existence, monastic seclusion, and mountain solitude; suddenly the alternating rhymes are dropped and the passage concludes with two couplets, of which the second must comprise one of the tritest formulations Schiller ever coined:

> Auf den Bergen ist die Freiheit! Der Hauch der Grüfte
> Steigt nicht hinauf in die reinen Lüfte,
> Die Welt ist vollkommen überall,
> Wo der Mensch nicht hinkommt mit seiner Qual.

Fortunately these lines stand alone in their banality. There are other couplets, but the vocabulary is more vivid, the syntax tauter, or the rhythm more compelling. Usually they are not pure reflection but refer to the action, as in

> Zeit ists, die Unfälle zu beweinen,
> Wenn sie nahen und wirklich erscheinen.          (ll. 979–80)

Or they function effectively as hard statements of fact:

> Und jetzt sehen wir uns als Knechte
> Untertan diesem fremden Geschlechte!          (ll. 210–11)

Where reflective couplets occur, Schiller avoids the danger by bringing his thought to a halt on the *first* line, using the second to initiate a new movement—distributing, for instance, the couplet

of ll. 227–8 between two separate speakers. Or the dead finality of
the couplet is avoided by enclosing it with another rhyme:

> Aber nichts ist verloren und verschwunden,
> Was die geheimnisvoll waltenden Stunden
> In den dunkel schaffenden Schoß aufnahmen —
> Die Zeit ist eine blühende Flur,
> Ein großes Lebendiges ist die Natur,
> Und alles ist Frucht und alles ist Samen. (ll. 1997–2002)

Generally speaking the Chorus transforms its abstractions by
personal reference and concrete image. So the strife in Messina is
put in individual terms:

> Wir haben uns in des Kampfes Wut
> Nicht besonnen und nicht beraten,
> Denn uns betörte das brausende Blut. (ll. 194–6)

And the contrast between war and peace is graphically symbolized by 'Korn', 'Ulmen', and 'Reben' set against 'Schwert', and
'Korsaren' The sinister violent character of the ruling house is
embodied in a discreet allusion to blood and catastrophe:

> Auf dem Meerschiff ist es gekommen,
> Von der Sonne rötlichtem Untergang. (ll. 206–7)

The evocative words of landscape, of sunrise and sunset, of
Arcadian piping, of hunting horns, continually open fresh
perspectives of wide-ranging scenic imagination. Modulations,
achieved by change of rhythm, accompany the shift from general
reflection to particular apprehension, as in this speech, in which
the focus switches from the images of sea and earth to the
sensitive threatening spot of the brothers' hostility:

> Aber nicht bloß im Wellenreiche,
> Auf der wogenden Meeresflut,
> Auch auf der Erde, so fest sie ruht
> Auf den ewigen, alten Säulen,
> Wanket das Glück und will nicht weilen.
> — Sorge gibt mir dieser neue Frieden,
> Und nicht fröhlich mag ich ihm vertrauen . . . . (ll. 939–45)

Moreover, the reflective passages do not stand alone. They are set among choric poetry expressing quivering emotion, ranging from exultation to lamentation. The musical effects of modulation from major to minor and back again, of dynamic contrast and pronounced rhythmic variation, trace a pattern of poetry which justifies the claim that the utterance of the Chorus in *Die Braut von Messina* is Schiller's supreme lyric achievement.

## 2. THE DRAMATIC SPEECH

The poetry of the Chorus, however, is not intended to be isolated. Not only has it a movement and a light and shade of its own; it contributes to a pattern of contrasting texture, manifested in the alternation of dramatic and choric speech. The syphoning off of the lyrical elements into the Chorus enables the dramatic tracts to act with remarkable force, concentration, and intensity.

The basis of the dramatic dialogue of *Die Braut von Messina* is the unit of the complete line. This tendency is in strong contrast to the verse-writing in Schiller's previous plays. Isabella's opening speech of 100 lines contains twenty-five sentences, of which twenty-one end firmly on the line closure. And, if the play is compared with *Don Carlos*, line and sense terminate together twice as often in the later play. And, whether it is a cause or a result, the pattern of stichomythia conforms with the general design, and by its emphasis produces an enhancement.

The linear organization of the periods gives to the language a sense of balance, which is emphasized by symmetrical syntax, as in Isabella's three-line period with its triple parallelism:

> Ich seh auch, daß sie zärtlicher Gefühle,
> Der schönen Neigung fähig sind, mit Wonne
> Entdeck ich, daß sie ehren, was sie lieben.    (ll. 2048–50)

Tremendous power is lent by the shift (to which the German language lends itself) of the emphatic word to the end of the sentence and simultaneously to the end of the line:

> Seid edel, und großherzig schenkt einander
> Die unabtragbar ungeheure Schuld.    (ll. 426–7)

By overrunning the line-endings in the longer periods Schiller forestalls the danger that the full close might conduce to monotony. The shorter sentences commonly occupy two lines, coupling two clauses of equal length. Typical examples are:

Wann endlich wird der alte Fluch sich lösen,
Der über diesem Hause lastend ruht?　　　　　　(ll. 1695–6)

and

Wohl läßt der Pfeil sich aus dem Herzen ziehn,
Doch nie wird das verletzte mehr gesunden.　　　(ll. 2719–20)

But in the longer periods the pattern becomes more complex. So Isabella, in a sentence of four complete lines, has a pause at the end of the first, but pauses *within* the second and third lines:

O ihr seid undurchdringlich harte Herzen,
Vom ehrnen Harnisch eurer Brust, gleichwie
Von einem schroffen Meeresfelsen, schlägt
Die Freude meines Herzens mir zurück!　　　　(ll. 2197–200)

Linear and interlinear pauses are mixed, whilst the structure continues to be dominated by the full close.

The importance of the measured tread of the verse, achieved by frequent use of the full-line unit, becomes most apparent at the moment at which it is abandoned. As grief and horror overtake the characters, the steady rhythmic step is deranged. When Isabella, whose iron nature translates suffering into anger, learns the terrible truth of the murder, she modulates into more flexible rhythms, speaking in six lines four sentences, only one of which closes a line:

Was kümmerts *mich* noch, ob die Götter sich
Als Lügner zeigen, oder sich als wahr
Bestätigen? *Mir* haben sie das Ärgste
Getan — Trotz biet ich ihnen, mich noch härter
Zu treffen, als sie trafen — Wer für nichts mehr
Zu zittern hat, der fürchtet sie nicht mehr.　　(ll. 2490–5)

It is still recognizably the tense speech of Isabella, but the distortion of its characteristics betrays the effects of overpowering emotion.

So Schiller capitalizes the processional rhythm of the play at the moment of its disintegration. If Isabella gives the most complete examples of this rhythmic break, lesser instances occur also in the adjacent speeches of Don Cesar and Beatrice. Yet such is the self-control of Isabella and her son that the linear structure can reassert itself in the midst of turmoil, as in the period of three linear clauses in which Don Cesar sums up his terrible situation:

> Ist sie wahrhaftig seine, meine Schwester,
> So bin ich schuldig einer Greueltat,
> Die keine Reu und Büßung kann versöhnen! (ll. 2481–3)

Blank verse makes up all but a small fraction of the dramatic speech of *Die Braut von Messina*. But the importance of this fraction is out of all proportion to its brevity. It consists of sixty-four lines (2589–652) of trimeters. Schiller had already employed this metre in the Montgomery scene of *Die Jungfrau von Orleans*. It had there self-consciously isolated and emphasized an episode of Homeric origin. The shorter passage in *Die Braut* is more completely integrated into the tragedy. It consists of a passage of stichomythia between Don Cesar and the Chorus, framed within two speeches by Cesar. The stichomythia is composed of eight four-line groups, followed by five two-line units; their use in preference to the more usual single lines stresses the formal character of the interchange.

The metrical change is a brilliant piece of dramatic economy. Don Cesar has left the scene in anger and in anguish. An indefinite interval is filled by a choric passage of general reflection. When at its close he reappears he has undergone a remarkable change. The warring impulses are reconciled, the confusion resolved into a fixed and constant purpose. Schiller has no need to explain the change, though he offers to the actor a gentle, though redundant, hint with the stage direction *gefaßter*. The transformation is fully and effectively notified to the listener by the steely temper of the measured trimeters:

> Das Recht des Herrschers üb ich aus zum letztenmal,
> Dem Grab zu übergeben diesen teuren Leib,

Denn dieses ist des Toten letzte Herrlichkeit.
Vernehmt denn meines Willens ernstlichen Beschluß,
Und wie ichs euch gebiete, also übt es aus
Genau.                                              (ll. 2589–94)

The stern, calm power of this speech determines the texture of
the scene. The Chorus answers Don Cesar in the same metre in
proof of its submission to the dominant force of his will. And Don
Cesar's concluding trimeters reveal, even at this moment, the
colossal force of character and the latent ferocity which have been
so powerful an element in the tragedy:

Du selbst bedenke schweigend deine Dienerpflicht,
Mich laß dem Geist gehorchen, der mich furchtbar treibt,
Denn in das Innre kann kein Glücklicher mir schaun.
Und ehrst du fürchtend auch den Herrscher nicht in mir,
Den Verbrecher fürchte, den der Flüche schwerster drückt.
                                                    (ll. 2648–52)

Thus a change of metre has enabled Schiller to dispense with a
retarding passage of explanation. At the same time the powerful
measure of the trimeters reaffirms the strength and violence of
Don Cesar's character at a moment when the action (through his
change of mind) suggests vacillation. The impression of strength
is further reinforced by the linear pattern of the verse; for, of the
twenty-four sentences making up the passage, only three fail to
close with the line.

The tendency towards forming groups in complete lines,
which is so much a feature of *Die Braut von Messina*, goes hand
in hand in this play with an exceptionally taut, ringing formulation, to which Schiller's rhetorical resourcefulness, the result of
much experience, powerfully contributes. Antithetic phrasings
have a terseness and a snap which leave the lines rounded and
complete:

In diesem einzgen Triebe sind sie eins,
In allem andern trennt sie blutger Streit.          (ll. 32–33)

The many *sententiae* take on a crisp, laconic form of extreme
economy as in the antithetic coupling

Wo kein Gewinn zu hoffen, droht Verlust             (l. 770) or the proverb-like

> Dem Erstbesitzenden gehört die Welt. (l. 1715)

Such lines have a sense of finality, and something of this summary air infuses the whole of the dramatic poetry of the play. It is united, especially in the utterances of the two brothers, with a dynamic balance, a sense of violence poised and restrained by superb willpower. The steely tone is perhaps clearest in the confident assertion, which each brother makes in turn, of his supreme power and strength. Both address themselves to Beatrice, Don Cesar with

> Ich bin Don Cesar und in dieser Stadt
> Messina ist kein Größrer über mir, (ll. 1160–1)

whilst Don Manuel parallels this speech some 600 lines later with

> Don Manuel heiß ich — doch ich bin der Höchste,
> Der diesen Namen führt in dieser Stadt,
> Ich bin Don Manuel, Fürst von Messina. (ll. 1821–3)

The similarity of these two emphatic statements, which in one decisive gesture contain all the pride, the *superbia*, of these two violent and powerful characters, is, of course, not accidental. It is a stylistic device which affirms the inevitability of a conflict with tragic outcome and simultaneously draws attention to the family likeness between the hostile brothers.

The speech of the characters and the songs of the Chorus represent Schiller's style at its furthest point from everyday language. Even when a phrase could be interpreted as a reproduction of current speech, the impression is belied by the rhythm, or the relationship to neighbouring sentences. So Isabella's terse and potentially colloquial 'Jetzt weiß ich nichts mehr' is immediately supplemented and exalted by the anastrophe of 'Ausgeleert hab ich / Der Worte Köcher . . . '(ll. 439–40). Don Cesar's simple question,

> Denkst du von deinem Bruder nicht geringer?

and Manuel's response,

> Du bist zu stolz zur Demut, ich zur Lüge, (ll. 474–5)

form part of a passage of stichomythia from which the context of ordinary speech is utterly remote. The process of elimination of the colloquial, which had begun in *Maria Stuart*, is here completed.

The touchstone of the anastrophic genitive confirms the high degree of stylization. This trope occurs with a frequency far surpassing its incidence even in *Die Jungfrau von Orleans*.[1] Almost every other known rhetorical device finds its place in the play, but it is anastrophe (not only of the genitive) together with the variants of repetition which gives the play its special tension. These re-arrangements of word-order result especially in powerful, emphatic accents at the onset of sentences, as in Manuel's

Nicht Kleinmuts zieht Don Cesarn, wer ihn kennt, (l. 472)

or Isabella's

Nicht pflichtvergessen konnte meine Tochter... (l. 1616)

or Cesar's

Nein, Bruder! Nicht dein Opfer will ich dir
Entziehen — (ll. 2822–3)

The strong negative beat shown in these examples is one of the most notable rhetorical formulations in the play,[2] and is an important factor in producing the extraordinary emphasis and impressive attack of its style.

Less obtrusive, but commoner, is the reversal of subject and object, as in

Nur eure Pflicht zu leisten seid bedacht (l. 94)

or

Den begünstigten Sohn der Götter beneid ich. (l. 1230)

And the third powerful, though less frequent, use of anastrophe is the forward transfer of a participle, such as

Doch nachgezogen mit allmächtgen Zaubers Banden
Hast du mein Herz (ll. 1130–1)

or

Denn ausgesetzt ward ich ins fremde Leben. (l. 1022)

[1] The average incidence in *Die Braut von Messina* is 1 per 9.3 lines, in *Die Jungfrau von Orleans* 1 per 21.
[2] It occurs 61 times.

If the power of the speech in *Die Braut von Messina* derives largely from the prevalence of anastrophe, its eloquence is closely linked with the use of repetition. Up to this play the characteristic form in Schiller's work is the group of three. In *Die Braut von Messina* the pair comes into its own. It occurs repeatedly in simple forms, such as 'ihres Lebens Licht und Ruhm' (l. 7), or 'Von diesem Ort des Schreckens und des Todes' (l. 1924), or 'was hast du hier zu horchen und zu hüten' (l. 1720), where the dual expression is underlined by alliteration. It appears syntactically in the anaphora of 'Nicht dich, / Nicht deine Mutter will ich wiedersehen' (ll. 2552–3), or 'Ein Frevel führte mich herein, / Ein Frevel treibt mich aus' (ll. 2503–4). It takes the form of hyperbaton—'Dein Staunen lob ich und dein sittsam Schweigen' (l. 1162) and 'Schnell will ich Licht mir schaffen und Gewißheit' (l. 1670). Terse sentences appear in parallel—'Da ist das Fürchten! Da ist das Hoffen!' (l. 894) or 'In seine Arme! / An seine Brust!' (ll. 1107–8). Simple repetitions such as 'Mord! Mord!' (l. 1905) are underlined by an immediately following parallel pair of sentences—'Greift zu den Waffen alle! / Mit Blut gerächet sei die blutge Tat!' The exclamations of 'Wehe!', too, are usually in pairs or double pairs; and a stark duplicated repetition occurs with

> Rache! Rache! Der Mörder falle! falle!          (l. 1909)

The pattern of pairs is extended by the considerable element of stichomythia, so that the whole play may be said to be permeated by a dual linguistic design. One of the most dramatic strokes in the tragedy is executed by means of repetition. When Beatrice learns the identity of her lover the following dialogue takes place:

BEATRICE. Du wärst Don Manuel, Don Cesars Bruder?
DON MANUEL. Don Cesar ist mein Bruder.
BEATRICE.                                      Ist dein Bruder!

> (ll. 1824–5)

The numbing blow is poignantly expressed by this helpless echoing of the words, which anticipates an important feature in the dialogue of Heinrich von Kleist.

The recurrent double pattern is so important because it corresponds to the double character of the tragedy. The theme of unity expressed in duality is given by the presence of the two brothers as the protagonists. It is a mistake to see the death of Don Manuel as the elimination of one of these brothers from the play. Don Manuel, though dead, continues to play as powerful a part as in life. And it is his spiritual presence in the final scene, symbolized by the catafalque-borne coffin, that enforces upon Don Cesar his apparently free, but truly unfree, determination to die. Nothing could be clearer than Don Cesar's final speech addressed to the dead man, beginning as an answer to an injunction, unspoken and yet imperative:

> Nein, Bruder! Nicht dein Opfer will ich dir
> Entziehen — deine Stimme aus dem Sarg
> Ruft mächter dringend als der Mutter Tränen
> Und mächtger als der Liebe Flehn... (ll. 2822–5)

### 3. THE VOCABULARY

Schiller's alert geographical imagination was quick to seize upon and exploit certain conspicuous features of the Sicilian scene. So the sun symbolizes in its power intense life and in its setting death. The crux of this recurrent image, in which the measurement of time also represents the term of life, is contained in the assertion by the two brothers of their imminent happiness. Don Manuel leads with

> Eh dieses Tages Sonne sinkt, führ ich
> Die Gattin dir Don Manuels zu Füßen, (ll. 1402–3)

which Don Cesar caps a moment later with a virtual refrain:

> Eh dieses Tages Sonne sinkt, führt auch
> Don Cesar seine Gattin dir entgegen. (ll. 1415–16)

These solar allusions receive an important augmentation through two utterances made as the play draws to its end. With pathetic irony the Chorus alludes to these confident hopes, now dashed, in the words—

Diese Sonne, die jetzo nieder
Geht, sie leuchtete eurem Bunde                    (ll. 1965–6)

and Don Cesar expunges the whole world, which the sun of this day has symbolized, with the words

Die nächste Sonne finde von Verbrechen rein
Das Haus, und leuchte einem fröhlichern Geschlecht.
                                                  (ll. 2620–1)

The brooding presence of Etna contributes brief but vital images. All the sultriness of this intense and precarious family life is crystallized in the evocation, first by Isabella and then by the Chorus, of the quiescent, yet potentially explosive, volcano. Isabella stresses surface quiet and hidden fires in the lines:

— Wer möchte noch das alte Bette finden
Des Schwefelstroms, der glühend sich ergoß?
Des unterirdschen Feuers schreckliche
Geburt ist alles, eine Lavarinde
Liegt aufgeschichtet über dem Gesunden,
Und jeder Fußtritt wandelt auf Zerstörung.        (ll. 398–403)

And in similar terms the Chorus asserts the treacherous nature of the truce:

Auf der Lava, die der Berg geschieden,
Möcht ich nimmer meine Hütte bauen.               (ll. 946–7)

Schiller provides a climate subject to sudden and violent change. Storms furnish a series of prominent images, falling into two categories. The suddenly swollen, raging mountain stream (instanced in 'Jene gewaltigen Wetterbäche . . .', ll. 242–7, and 'Vom Berge stürzt der ungeheure Strom . . .', ll. 1553–6) supports the image of the lava stream. More prominent is the image of the lightning flash or its associated thunder. It reflects violent shifts of fortune, sudden onslaught or swift reversal. Even Isabella's first casual allusion is seen to be an unconscious stroke of irony:

Nicht Blitzen gleich, die schnell vorüberschießen,
Und plötzlich von der Nacht verschlungen sind,
Mein Glück wird sein, gleichwie des Baches fließen. (ll. 664–6)

A more potent irony operates when Isabella expresses her relief that the brothers have been spared the danger of loving the same woman:

Wenn in den aufgehäuften Feuerzunder
Des alten Hasses auch noch dieser Blitz
Der Eifersucht feindselge Flamme schlug —
Mir schaudert, es zu denken ...                    (ll. 2060-3)

Isabella goes on to speak of

... diese donnerschwere Wolke,
Die über mir schwarz drohend niederhing.           (ll. 2066-7)

But the lightning has already struck, all unknown to her, and the dead Manuel is its victim. The image, significantly enough, has been used by both the brothers with reference to their love. First Don Cesar speaks:

Und diesen festlich ernsten Augenblick
Erwählte sich der Lenker meines Lebens,
Mich zu berühren mit der Liebe Strahl.             (ll. 1520-2)

Almost immediately the words are echoed by Don Manuel:

Das ist der Liebe heilger Götterstrahl,
Der in die Seele schlägt und trifft und zündet.    (ll. 1542-3)

This destructive image applied to the power of love is, on the part of the brothers, a piece of unconscious self-characterization, and a prophecy.

Twice more the image appears in the closing stages. Don Cesar releases the truth of the murder upon the anxious Isabella with all the sudden impact of an utterly crushing blow—

Falle
Der Donner nieder, der dein Herz zerschmettert     (ll. 2473-4)

—so expressing all the flaming anger which, for the time being, saves him from remorse. The Chorus, too, develops the motif to its fullest extent in a famous passage in which Schiller once had the assistance of the elements themselves.[1] The 'message' of the lines is trite and threadbare, but the terms in which it is set fix the mood and the atmosphere of electric explosiveness which permeates the play:

Wenn die Wolken getürmt den Himmel schwärzen,
Wenn dumpftosend der Donner hallt,
Da, da fürchten sich alle Herzen
In des furchtbaren Schicksals Gewalt.
Aber auch aus entwölkter Höhe
Kann der zündende Donner schlagen...                    (ll. 2297–302)

These lines graphically sum up the sultrily oppressive temper of *Die Braut von Messina* and the sudden devastating blow which is its mode of action. And the references to *Feuer, glühen, Feuerzunder, Flamme*, and *zünden* revive in concentrated form a tract of vocabulary which had seemed to die out in the closing stages of *Don Carlos* and thereafter to be of irregular occurrence and minor importance.

These words of fire come fully into their own again in *Die Braut von Messina*, burning with a new and frightening intensity. They do not occur singly, but in reinforcing pairs. So the combination of *Flammen* and *schüren* is used both by Isabella ('Nur eures Hasses Flammen heftger schüre', l. 314) and by Don Manuel ('Die Flammen schürten, die sie löschen konnten', l. 494); and Don Cesar twice links a similar pair of words ('Der den erloschnen Funken unsers Streits / Aufbläst zu neuen Flammen' ll. 579–80, and 'Fragt man / Woher der Sonne Himmelsfeuer flamme', ll. 1463–4). When the feud breaks out again, Don Cesar's words are repeated by his brother Manuel ('Was für ein Dämon reizt euch an, / Des alten Zwistes Flammen aufzublasen', ll. 1753–4). From all this emerges an atmosphere of ardour, violence, and destructiveness. The maximal point of verbal incendiarism is attained in two passages, both spoken by Isabella,

[1] At the Lauchstädt performance on 3 July 1803 (see Schiller's letter to his wife dated 4 July 1803, Jonas, 7. 49). E. M. Butler (*The Tyranny of Greece over Germany*, 1935, p. 198) wrongly attributes the elemental intervention to the first performance (Weimar, 19 March 1803), a confusion which, when recognized, blunts the edge of her witty paragraph.

which are central to the tragedy. In her passionate anger at the frustration of all her efforts at reconciliation, she paints early in the play a picture of the brothers' end, and though her words are dictated, not by belief, but by uncontrolled temper, they truly anticipate in images of fire the outcome of the tragedy:

> Leib gegen Leib, wie das thebanische Paar,
> Rückt aufeinander an und wutvoll ringend
> Umfanget euch mit eherner Umarmung,
> Leben um Leben tauschend siege jeder
> Den Dolch einbohrend in des andern Brust,
> Daß selbst der Tod nicht eure Zwietracht heile,
> Die Flamme selbst, des Feuers rote Säule,
> Die sich von eurem Scheiterhaufen hebt,
> Sich zweigespalten voneinander teile,
> Ein schaudernd Bild, wie ihr gestorben und gelebt.      (ll. 450-9)

The speech receives an urgent underlining and an incisive finality by the unexpected trimeter at its close.

A second and more vivid prefiguration of the outcome is given in the father's dream with its vision of destruction by fire:

> Sie ward
> Zur Flamme, die der Bäume dicht Gezweig
> Und das Gebälk ergreifend prasselnd aufschlug,
> Und um sich wütend, schnell, das ganze Haus
> In ungeheurer Feuerflut verschlang.      (ll. 1311-15)

The imminent consummation of the tragedy is symbolically announced by the action of the aged anchorite, who repeats the motif of the dream by setting fire to his own hut—'und schnell in Brand steckt er die Hütte' (l. 2135)—, whilst Isabella greets the impact of the tragedy with an almost exact repetition of her earlier narration of the dream (ll. 2339-42). And finally Don Cesar embraces the depth of the tragedy and the ultimate conciliation of death with the image of extinguished flames:

> Ein mächtiger Vermittler ist der Tod.
> Da löschen alle Zornesflammen aus,
> Der Haß versöhnt sich, und das schöne Mitleid
> Neigt sich ein weinend Schwesterbild mit sanft
> Anschmiegender Umarmung auf die Urne.      (ll. 2702-06)

Beside this powerful deployment of the vocabulary of fire, four other groups of words stand out. They are, typically, *Macht*, *Haß*, *Blut*, and *Herz*. The most common of these is *Herz*, alone or in compounds. Next comes *Macht* with its associates *Gewalt*, *Stärke*, and *Kraft*, followed by the group composed of *Haß*, *Hader*, *Fehde*, and *Streit*. The least frequent of the four is *Blut*.

The words of power and violence could hardly fail to occur frequently in such a play, and they provide obvious epithets and adverbs for the dead father and the two rival brothers. Their reiteration establishes an atmosphere and their striking and original forms arrest attention. So Isabella refers to the father's autocratic rule with 'Der mächtigwaltend dieser Stadt gebot' (l. 16) or speaks of his 'Herrschermacht' (l. 2073). Similarly *Macht* and *Gewalt* appear in reinforcing conjunction:

> es herrschte noch im Lande
> Des Vaters Macht, und beugete gewaltsam
> Der Jugend starren Nacken in das Joch.          (ll. 681–3)

Most significant is the surprising association of *Macht* with words of emotion, especially *Herz* and *Blut*. So we hear of 'der Mutterliebe mächtge Stimme' (l. 1332). Isabella uses the phrase 'Wie mich des Herzens Stimme mächtig trieb' (l. 2037) and speaks of

> Den Trieb des Bluts, der mächtig wie des Feuers
> Verschloßner Gott aus seinen Banden strebte!          (ll. 2080–1)

The brothers, in their wooing, constantly insist on the idea of power. Thus Don Cesar addresses Beatrice,

> Nicht verborgen
> Blieb dir die Macht, mit der du mich bezwangst;          (ll. 1120–1)

and Don Manuel counters her apprehensive 'es gibt hier mächtge Menschen' with 'keinen mächtigern als mich' (ll. 1807–8). As the tragedy approaches the catastrophe, the note of *Macht* is emphatically reiterated. The echo of the fateful word recurs, whether Don Cesar contemplates his death—'Ein mächtiger

Vermittler ist der Tod' (l. 2702)—or inclines for a moment to
the thought of life—

> Da steht der holde Lebensengel mächtig
> Vor mir (ll. 2784–5)

or when Isabella bewails his resolution—

> Wenn der tote Bruder
> Ihn so gewaltig nachzieht in die Gruft. (ll. 2772–3)

To the last the word retains its dominance, occurring in a moving
and compelling parallelism in Don Cesar's final speech—'Ruft
mächtger dringend als der Mutter Tränen / Und mächtger als
der Liebe Flehn' (ll. 2824–5).

It was equally inevitable that the words of discord should be
prominent in *Die Braut von Messina*, but they, too, have a scope
extending far beyond the marking of moments of clash or gestures
of hostility. Their constant recurrence denotes the fundamental
character of the opposition between the brothers. And they do
not disappear when reconciliation is achieved; on the contrary,
both Don Manuel and Don Cesar continue to refer to their
harmony in terms of discord:

> Die unser Herz in bitterm Haß entfremdet (l. 490)

and

> Ist dieser freundlich sanftgesinnte Jüngling
> Der übelwollend mir gehäßge Bruder? (ll. 507–8)

and

> Du siehst die Liebe aus des Hasses Flammen
> Wie einen neu verjüngten Phönix steigen. (ll. 539–40)

So the reiterated words of discord reflect the persisting presence
of enmity beneath the surface, concealed yet potent.

The role of the words of blood in the play is notably ambiguous.
On the one hand it is linked with discord and its outcome,
murder. In the last third of the tragedy it is used to symbolize the

death of Don Manuel, both in the repeated allusions of the Chorus and in the utterances of Don Cesar, such as,

> Redlich wollten wir
> Den Frieden, aber Blut beschloß der Himmel (ll. 2440–1)

or

> mag dies Blut
> Anklagend gegen mich zum Himmel rufen. (ll. 2510–11)

It is besides generally associated with fraternal strife, which is 'der Söhne blutgen Hader' (l. 68) or 'der blutige Kampf' (l. 170) or the matter 'warum wir blutig stritten' (l. 611). Parallel with this, however, runs a second association of blood, the conception of blood relationship, seen in 'Brüder durch Blutes Bande' (l. 528), 'die Macht des Bluts' (l. 1662), or 'Erprobe *du* jetzt die Kraft des Bluts' (l. 2669). The motif of *Blut* links *Haß* and *Herz*.

The incidence of *Herz* is, at first sight, a surprising feature. Power and violence, hatred and discord, blood as a bond and blood as a price of strife, all these are evident elements in the pattern of the play. Yet the single word *Herz* is more frequent than either of the groups *Macht* and *Haß*, and if the cognate use of *Brust* is included it greatly exceeds them. It is seldom used by the Chorus and is concentrated upon the three characters Isabella, Don Manuel, and Don Cesar.[1] This striking emphasis suggests powerful subliminal currents of emotion, deep and lasting bonds of attachment holding together these irascible and violent characters. The constant reiteration of *Herz* turns the murder from crime to tragedy; it balances horror with compassion; and it affirms elements of personality which consciousness denies. It is the source of pity and the means of understanding. No interpretation can stand which does not take account of the truly vital role of the heart, which is so insistently yet discreetly presented in the ceaseless reiteration of the word *Herz*. It is no mere chance that it is the focus of Don Cesar's last words:

> Die Tränen sah ich, die auch mir geflossen,
> Befriedigt ist mein Herz, ich folge dir. (ll. 2833–4)

[1] In the speech of these three the word occurs on average once every 32 lines.

Schiller's deliberate adoption of classical conventions imposes upon his play a static quality, which must express itself on the stage through stylized gestures and calculated groupings. In all this there was a danger of degeneration into the statuesque. But there is nothing of the plaster-cast in Schiller's play. Even when his style is static it is full of tension. The verse conveys the tremendous sense of power contained and ready to break forth, especially in threatening form—

> Versöhnt, vereinigt, sind sie mächtig gnug,
> Euch zu beschützen gegen eine Welt,
> Und Recht sich zu verschaffen — gegen euch! (ll. 98–100)

—or, with more obvious dynamism—

> Den streck ich tot auf dieses Rasens Grund,
> Der mit gezuckter Augenwimper nur
> Die Fehde fortsetzt und dem Gegner droht! (ll. 1750–2)

Such utterances are themselves gestures and provide the vitality and decisive energy which the action, in virtue of its conception, necessarily lacks. And yet the verse is capable also of perfect tranquillity, a serene surface, which at the same time suggests depth:

> Wir zogen ein
> Mit Friedenshoffnungen in diese Tore,
> Und friedlich wollen wir zusammen ruhn,
> Versöhnt auf ewig in dem Haus des Todes. (ll. 2750–3)

Ambition was a spur to which Schiller always responded, and with *Die Braut von Messina* it took the form of emulation. Writing to Iffland on 22 April 1803 he avowed: 'Bei der Braut von Messina habe ich, ich will es Ihnen aufrichtig gestehen, einen kleinen Wettstreit mit den alten Tragikern versucht.'[1] And he has indeed produced a remarkable likeness of an antique tragedy. Yet the play is something more than a pastiche of Greek drama. Emulation implied ardent striving and stern wrestling with a task. And as with *Wallenstein* Schiller's creative powers

[1] Jonas, 7. 34.

warmed to the task imposed upon them. Out of this tension is wrought the special style which is the life of *Die Braut von Messina*. Since the peak of *Wallenstein* Schiller had sought to escape from the tyranny of the 'real', to shake off the hampering confinement of every day. His irrepressible impulse towards magnification and elevation prompted him to seek a new solution to the problem of form in an extension and intensification of rhetoric. And the lyrical elements which had always been present became entangled in the mesh of exalted oratory. The outcome of these aspirations, *Maria Stuart* and *Die Jungfrau von Orleans*, though widely applauded, provide only a dubious solution to the formal problem. In *Die Braut von Messina* Greek tragedy offered in ready-made form what was to turn out to be the formula for success. The separation of the lyrical from the dramatic permitted a new aptness of style, in which rhetoric became subservient, conforming to need, instead of taking over in generalized form. An imitative exercise thus brought forth an unexpected masterpiece. But it could not be repeated. The sense of imitation was in the long run unbearable and the high concentration, running against Schiller's instinct for complexity and ramification, was uncongenial. *Die Braut von Messina* solved Schiller's stylistic aspirations in the years 1800–3, but it did so in terms that he could not permanently adopt.

# IX · WILHELM TELL

## I. THE ELEMENT OF REALISM

SCHILLER seems scarcely to have been conscious of the peculiar rhythmic alternation in his work, by which a play of expansion is succeeded by one of tautness, to be followed in turn by a work of breadth. Or, if he was aware of it, he did not think it worthy of remark. Yet it is so regular and so pronounced that it must have corresponded to a deep-seated mental need. He recovered from constriction and enclosure by relaxation in a world of wide perspectives, and he paid for relaxation with a fresh indulgence in constriction. Nevertheless his work is not a pendulum alternation. The swing to and fro is complemented and complicated by a linear progression. Each swing achieves something new. *Die Braut von Messina* had seen a maximal stylistic concentration, achieved by the adoption of two distinct foci, one lyrical, the other rhetorico-dramatic. *Wilhelm Tell*, easing the concentration, turns from the lyrical to the epic, yet handles epic elements in a way that is new in Schiller's work. Schiller's sensitiveness in devising his plays so that the formal expression, though in his own tradition, is unique receives confirmation here from the history of the subject. Not only was the historical theme, derived from Tschudi and Johannes von Müller,[1] necessarily 'epic'; it was actually to have been the subject of an epic poem by Goethe, who according to Eckermann, recounted the plan to Schiller and eventually relinquished the subject to him.[2] Schiller went even further, not only giving his play epic breadth, action, and heroism, but

[1] Aegidius Tschudi: *Chronikon Helveticum*, 1734. Tschudi (1505–72) left this work in MS., and it was published a century and a half later by J. R. Iselin. Johannes von Müller, *Geschichte schweizerischer Eidgenossenschaft*, 1780–8.
[2] J. P. Eckermann, *Gespräche mit Goethe*, 6 May 1827.

creating in it a tangible solidity, a reality of nature, as well as truth of character.

The stage direction with which the play opens at once suggests a visual documentation which is new in Schiller's work. An actual view of a portion of the Lake of Lucerne is described with specific reference to familiar place and mountain names:

Hohes Felsenufer des Vierwaldstättersees, Schwyz gegenüber.... Über den See hinweg sieht man die grünen Matten, Dörfer und Höfe von Schwyz im hellen Sonnenschein liegen. Zur Linken des Zuschauers zeigen sich die Spitzen des Haken, mit Wolken umgeben.

Though Schiller is nowhere else in the play so topographically exact, his preoccupation with local colour is attested by his letters. On 16 March 1802 he asks Cotta for maps and books,[1] and a year later there comes a request for engravings and more books (9 August 1803),[2] quickly followed by a similar appeal to Körner (12 September 1803), which he justifies by the special need of the subject for local material: 'Ich bin genöthigt, viel darüber zu lesen, weil das Locale an diesem Stoffe so viel bedeutet, und ich möchte gern soviel möglich örtliche Motive nehmen.'[3] The same note is sounded again a month later[4] and in December Schiller makes the unprecedented announcement that he intends to visit the scene of his play: 'Ohnehin bin ich entschlossen, eh ich das Stück drucken lasse, nach der Schweiz zu gehen.'[5] Though Schiller had already written plays set in Italy, Spain, England, France, and Sicily, there had never been an expression of such a wish as this—not even a sigh over its impossibility. He had visited Eger, where Wallenstein was assassinated, but this had been a casual visit in 1791 while convalescing in Carlsbad and had nothing to do with his still unwritten tragedy. He could easily have visited Pilsen, where the greater part of *Wallenstein* is set, but he took no steps to do so. In *Maria Stuart* he had shown no interest in the map and had brought Fotheringhay southward to a point a few miles north of London. *Die Jungfrau*

---

[1] Jonas, 6. 365.          [2] Idem, 7. 61.          [3] Idem, 7. 74.
[4] Letter to Körner, 10 October 1803 (Jonas, 7. 83).
[5] Letter to Iffland, 5 December 1803 (Jonas, 7. 98).

*von Orleans* profited by the evocative names of Chinon, Orleans, and Rheims, but Schiller did not take the slightest trouble to adumbrate the localities. Etna, which had powerful symbolical potentialities, broods over *Die Braut von Messina*, but it is only an undefined presence, and the city itself and the Sicilian scene remain uncharacterized.

In the end Schiller did not visit Switzerland. All the same, the expressed intention suggests a regard for visual authentication which is elsewhere absent. Since he did not go, he had to rely on his astonishing faculty for absorbing visual facts through books. *Wilhelm Tell* exhibits a remarkable local vividness which it owes to guide books and engravings. And yet it is a curious fact that its tone abstains even from the modified degree of realism evident in *Wallenstein*.

In *Wilhelm Tell* the realism of common speech is a limited element, occurring only in short stretches and spoken by the common people. It is perceptibly stylized throughout. In the opening dialogue of three peasants the sentences are short and simple, dotted with Swiss words such as 'Naue', 'Talvogt', and 'Firn'. Yet the underlying structure is poetic. The two brief balanced sentences of the first line ('Mach hurtig, Jenni. Zieh die Naue ein', l. 37) are followed by a period composed of five co-ordinate clauses. Such a construction is well enough fitted to express the simple thoughts of countrymen, but its alternating pattern of normal and inverted order is clearly symptomatic of artful poetic arrangement:

> Der graue Talvogt kommt, dumpf brüllt der Firn,
> Der Mythenstein zieht seine Haube an,
> Und kalt her bläst es aus dem Wetterloch,
> Der Sturm, ich mein, wird da sein, eh wirs denken.     (ll. 38–41)

Kuoni rejoins with a brief sentence including a Swiss aphaeresis —' 's kommt Regen, Fährmann' —and completes his speech with a balanced pair of parallel clauses:

> Meine Schafe fressen
> Mit Begierde Gras, und Wächter scharrt die Erde.     (ll. 42–3)

To this Werni adds a syllogistic triad:

Die Fische springen, und das Wasserhuhn
Taucht unter. Ein Gewitter ist im Anzug.          (ll. 44–5)

The line unit, emphasizing the metrical pattern, is maintained until Baumgarten's entrance, which is the signal for a change of tone. The stylization clearly harmonizes with the introductory Swiss song, which establishes a poetic tone, not only by its simple lyrical quality, but also by its symmetrical distribution among the three typical figures of the Swiss rural scene, *Fischerknabe*, *Hirte*, and *Alpenjäger*, who are symbolically posed, the first by the lakeside, the other two on the mountains on opposite sides of the stage.

The use of Swiss words derived from Schiller's reading (in addition to the three already mentioned there are *Matte*, *Senne*, *Lug*, *Alp*, *Föhn*, *Runsen*, *kreucht*, *kommlich*, and *Gransen*) gives a Swiss mental climate without the need of detailed realism. They are reinforced by the aphaeresis *'s ist*, which Schiller employs sporadically as a localizing dialectal form. But these specific features are carefully limited. They are most prominent at the beginning of the play when the scene has to be set. They are spoken by minor rural characters among themselves. They mark the speech of the three countrymen of the opening scene, but disappear as soon as they address Baumgarten, a man of higher standing. Patches occur during the building of the fortress (I. iii), in the introduction to the Rütli scene (II. ii), in the dialogue between the two soldiers at the beginning of III. iii, and in the first words of the fisherman's son in IV. i. It is always introductory and, having served its indicative purpose, is abandoned when the real business of the scene begins. In relaxed moments it maintains the popular touch.

## 2. CHARACTERIZATION AND TYPIFICATION

The elements of symmetry and rhetorical arrangement, which even in the relaxed rural scenes are unobtrusively perceptible, run through the whole play; and the anastrophic genitive, sign of a conscious elevation, occurs as often as in *Maria Stuart* or *Die Jungfrau von Orleans*. The rhetorical tone of *Wilhelm Tell* tends to minimize differences between characters and to unify the texture. When Baumgarten enters (i. i) the first anastrophic genitive ('Des Landvogts Reiter kommen hinter mir', l. 72) immediately lifts the tone, which the countrymen support in more formal dialogue. Vulgar words are excluded and dualisms abound, such as '*Der* schadet nicht mehr, ich hab ihn erschlagen' (l. 79) or 'Am Schänder meiner Ehr und meines Weibes' (l. 83), both spoken by Baumgarten. But the peasants show themselves equally adept at this stylized speech, with such expressions as 'Ich kann nicht steuern gegen Wind und Wellen' (l. 110) or 'Und wärs mein Bruder und mein leiblich Kind' (l. 145). And they, as well as Baumgarten, make use of the anastrophic genitive, which was absent from the first part of the scene.

The style thus fixed is the basic tone of the play, used by all the characters at times, and almost exclusively by Stauffacher, Walter Fürst, and Attinghausen, the representative figures of Swiss independence. In heightened form it is used by the younger characters. Tell, however, of whom more must be said later, is sparing in its use.

This basic style is capable of subtle adaptation, as is immediately apparent in the second scene in the conversation between Stauffacher and his wife. The static nature of this domestic interchange allows a freer development of sonorous periods than the first scene, with its urgent action, could permit. It is the wife, a statuesque, almost Roman, matron who provides the first initiative for revolt, and her contribution to the dialogue is noticeably higher pitched than Stauffacher's. Her periods, with their parallelisms, accumulations, and anastrophic genitives, are fuller:

> Gesegnet ist dein Fleiß, dein Glücksstand blüht,
> Voll sind die Scheunen, und der Rinder Scharen,
> Der glatten Pferde wohlgenährte Zucht
> Ist von den Bergen glücklich heimgebracht
> Zur Winterung in den bequemen Ställen.      (ll. 202–6)

The visually characterizing effect of this 'rounded' period, together with the emphasis in the vocabulary on prosperity, good feeding, good 'condition', and comfort, all serve to delineate the speaker as well as to describe a successful farmer's state. And her self-possession and conscious self-importance emerge in the lengthy prelude to her analysis of the political situation:

> Mein lieber Herr und Ehewirt! Magst du
> Ein redlich Wort von deinem Weib vernehmen?
> Des edeln Ibergs Tochter rühm ich mich,
> Des vielerfahrnen Manns. Wir Schwestern saßen,
> Die Wolle spinnend, in den langen Nächten,
> Wenn bei dem Vater sich des Volkes Häupter
> Versammelten, die Pergamente lasen
> Der alten Kaiser, und des Landes Wohl
> Bedachten in vernünftigem Gespräch.          (ll. 238–46)

The dual address, the formal epithets (epic perhaps in origin, but characteristic in their effect), and the slowly and spaciously unfolding period make up an exercise in the fulsome, which Schiller has allowed himself only with this character.

Attinghausen's slow, weighty, deliberate speech provides another variation of the poetic style. His short sentences, used alone or in co-ordinate pairs, are so completely shorn of ornament that they appear almost starkly realistic:

> Ja leider bist dus. Leider ist die Heimat
> Zur Fremde dir geworden!          (ll. 776–7)

But the appearance is deceptive: the apparently colloquial is artfully arranged with anaphora (above), parallelism (Sie ergriff / Dein offnes Ohr, sie hat dein Herz vergiftet', ll. 820–1), or anastrophe ('Ich hab es fechten sehen bei Favenz', l. 910). The straightforwardness and simplicity of this poetic style correspond to the integrity and great age of the character. Attinghausen, despite his years, is still capable of being moved by a great cause, and twice in his interview with Rudenz (II. i) and once in the deathbed scene (IV. ii) his speech rises to a tirade; but simplicity and directness persist even in the flight of eloquence. In the address to Rudenz the rhetoric never soars; it speaks straight to its object, seeming to aim each phrase separately and to seek response at every pause:

> Die angebornen Bande knüpfe fest,
> Ans Vaterland, ans teure, schließ dich an,
> Das halte fest mit deinem ganzen Herzen.          (ll. 920–2)

This is the eloquence of sincerity, the persuasion of the old man who no longer cares about the image he creates.

In the deathbed scene Schiller interpolates a significant stage direction— *Er spricht das Folgende mit dem Ton eines Sehers — seine Rede steigt bis zu Begeisterung*. And this indication of tone is necessary because the verse outwardly remains the same, reflecting the sober and sincere character of the dying man. The peroration consists of three simple sentences and one compound sentence of the simplest kind, adorned with simple repetition, plain in vocabulary, and with barely noticeable anastrophe:

> Drum haltet fest zusammen — fest und ewig —
> Kein Ort der Freiheit sei dem andern fremd —
> Hochwachten stellet aus auf euren Bergen,
> Daß sich der Bund zum Bunde rasch versammle —
> Seid einig — einig — einig —.          (ll. 2447–51)

The final repetition in these lines serves as an emphasis, but from the point of view of the speaker it is a failure of syntax, and this in turn is a symbol of death. Altogether Attinghausen's speech is marked by retardation and a descending tone which conform with his great age and awareness of the approach of death. The structure of his compound sentences is usually such that the stress falls early, so that the latter part loses pace; or an ellipsis occurs in the second of two parallel sentences—'Mein Schatten bin ich nur, bald nur mein Name' (l. 763). And in one instance the retardation is achieved by a final dragging iambic trimeter with an extra prolonging syllable—'Wohl dem, der mit der *neuen* nicht mehr braucht zu leben' (l. 957).

Geßler and Tell also are characterized by stylistic means, but not by an adaptation of Schiller's poetic *continuum*. Schiller here carried further something he had begun in *Maria Stuart*, where in certain scenes the Queen's utterance has a simplicity and directness which contrasts with the speech of those around her. Schiller could have used his mastery of powerful rhetoric to give the tyrant a formidable eloquence. Yet Geßler speaks no tirade, and his speech is devoid of the tropes which even the peasants in *Wilhelm Tell* employ. Instead his words are tense, terse, and direct; and by this reticent presentation the man of violence is rendered more formidable than any tirade could have made him. Geßler marks his first entry by a series of brief, imperious commands and questions:

> Treibt sie auseinander!
> Was läuft das Volk zusammen? Wer ruft Hilfe?
> (*Allgemeine Stille*)
> Wer wars? Ich will es wissen. *Du* tritt vor!
> Was bist du und was hältst du diesen Mann? (ll. 1854–7)

It is important to note that the silence indicated includes Geßler himself, and his boding pause suggests the dangerous and threatening character of the man more plainly than a torrent of words. The brief intermission is followed by the formula *Ich will*, which is so significant a symptom of Geßler's harsh and forceful personality that it occurs in his speech eleven times. It is no coincidence that these two words of obstinate volition recur as Geßler's last utterance before he is transfixed by Tell's arrow.

Geßler's formulation is throughout strikingly laconic. The 133 lines he speaks contain no fewer than 122 sentences, and most of these are either of the simple type or co-ordinate groups of two or three. His tone has a deceptive familiarity, compounded of brevity, address by name, and the second person singular, with its note of intimacy:

> GEßLER. Ist das dein Knabe, Tell?
> TELL. Ja, lieber Herr.
> GEßLER. Hast du der Kinder mehr?
> TELL. Zwei Knaben, Herr.
> GEßLER. Und welcher ists, den du am meisten liebst?
>
> (ll. 1877–9)

The contrast between homely tone and threatening situation is felt by all those present. It corresponds to Geßler's intelligence, his psychological acumen, and his cold inhumanity. It is the means by which he plays on human beings as on an instrument. For a moment he prolongs the tone, then suddenly the mask is dropped; the sentences, as short as ever, become staccato, harsh, and imperious:

> Nimm die Armbrust —
> Du hast sie gleich zur Hand — und mach dich fertig,
> Einen Apfel von des Knaben Kopf zu schießen . . . . (ll. 1883–5)

There is nothing accidental in this performance. After Tell's miraculously successful shot Geßler repeats his move with a like success. The opening words are just as informally familiar as before:

> Du stecktest
> Noch einen zweiten Pfeil zu dir — Ja, ja,
> Ich sah es wohl — Was meintest du damit? (ll. 2048–50)

And once again the tone shifts in a flash from the intimate to the menacing.

Even when, in his thwarted rage, Geßler comes close to delivering a tirade (IV. v), he speaks in a succession of short direct sentences, which express fury without a touch of rant:

> Ein allzu milder Herrscher bin ich noch
> Gegen dies Volk — die Zungen sind noch frei,
> Es ist noch nicht ganz, wie es soll, gebändigt —
> Doch es soll anders werden, ich gelob es,
> Ich will ihn brechen, diesen starren Sinn,
> Den kecken Geist der Freiheit will ich beugen.
> Ein neu Gesetz will ich in diesen Landen
> Verkündigen — Ich will — (ll. 2778–85)

And, as the arrow transfixes him, his last words, 'Das ist Tells Geschoß — ', remain true, not only to his character, but to his style.

Tell's style is equally distinctive. He is one of Schiller's most laconic characters. Eponymous hero though he is, he speaks only

13 per cent of the total number of lines. And even when he is actually on the stage he speaks only one line in three. Yet, for all his reticence, Tell dominates the stage by the quality of what he speaks and the significance of his silences. His speech is brief and homely, and its expression is balanced and self-contained. The majority of his utterances take up two lines or less of verse.

Tell's first entry is characteristic. It is a blunt direct question in one line:

> Wer ist der Mann, der hier um Hülfe fleht?          (l. 127)

For all its simplicity, the line is not colloquial, as the verb *flehen* reveals. It belongs to a highly concentrated and intensely poetic style, by which Schiller implies Tell's robustness, balance, and independence. Frequently the terseness assumes the polished form of epigram, salted with ironic wit:

> Der See kann sich, der Landvogt nicht erbarmen,          (l. 143)

Or lines are constructed with forensic skill, as Tell vigorously outlines a situation and powerfully puts his plea:

> Mit eitler Rede wird hier nichts geschafft,
> Die Stunde dringt, dem Mann muß Hülfe werden.
> Sprich, Fährmann, willst du fahren?          (ll. 147–9)

At the same time Tell is a man of the people and so his epigrammatic leaning expresses itself most readily in the popular form of the proverb. Several of these are so convincing in their phrasing, so apt, and so homely that they have passed into common use, and are no doubt sometimes employed by people who are unaware that they are quoting Schiller. Such are 'Früh übt sich, was ein Meister werden will' (l. 1480) and 'Wer gar zuviel bedenkt, wird wenig leisten' (l. 1531). 'Die Axt im Haus erspart den Zimmermann' (l. 1513) is equally familiar, though its provenance is better known. All three have found their way as 'geflügelte Worte' into Büchmann.[1]

Though these, all drawn from a single scene (III. i), are the best known, such new-minted proverbs fall readily from Tell's

[1] G. Büchmann, *Geflügelte Worte*, 1864 and many later editions.

lips. And always they come fresh because of their vigour and economy. Examples of such crisp and homely formulations are 'Ein rechter Schütze hilft sich selbst' (l. 1478) and 'Ein jeder wird besteuert nach Vermögen' (l. 1523), both in the same scene; whilst the conversation with Stauffacher yields no fewer than eight proverb-like sayings, including 'Was Hände bauten, können Hände stürzen' (l. 387) and 'Der Starke ist am mächtigsten *allein*', (l. 437). Tell's speech, however, is not always studded with these homely epigrams. In the central scene of the play where he reluctantly displays his marksmanship, they disappear, except for a single *sententia* occurring before Geßler's entry. After Tell's deliverance they are renewed, though in modified form.

The proverbial style is thus confined to periods of relaxation and reflection, giving ground at once at the onset of tension. It represents the collected and balanced style of a collected and balanced personality in moments of easy equilibrium when poise is not threatened. But this proverbial style also corresponds to Tell's independence and self-reliance. The proverbs simulate a screen; they enable him to maintain contact without giving himself away. This becomes obvious in the conversation with Stauffacher (I. iii), in which certain proverb-like formulations are at variance with Tell's known or implied opinions, especially in the apparent 'appeasement' of 'Die Schlange sticht nicht ungereizt' (l. 429), a piece of brilliant irony since it suggests an ignoble quietism, yet unmistakably prefigures Tell's assassination of Geßler in the later action. Furthermore, Tell in the same scene, and by the use of a sententious generalization, reveals and yet conceals his true nature with the words 'Das schwere Herz wird nicht durch Worte leicht' (l. 418), in which the implied antithesis of *Taten* is apparent to the listener, but not to Tell's preoccupied and anxious interlocutor.

Even more conspicuous is the ironical use of proverbs by which Tell screens his preparations for the assassination of Geßler. When he is accosted by the garrulous Stüssi four of his seven laconic replies are self-coined proverbs, including 'Ein ernster

Gast stimmt nicht zum Hochzeithaus' (l. 2657) and 'Dem Schwachen ist sein Stachel auch gegeben' (l. 2675), which picks up the motif of *sticht* just mentioned. Both of these utterances are dramatically ironical, for they allude to Tell's situation in a way which Stüssi is unable to grasp. Even more revealing, yet equally impenetrable to Stüssi, is the *sententia*

> Es kann der Frömmste nicht im Frieden bleiben,
> Wenn es dem bösen Nachbar nicht gefällt. (ll. 2682–3)

The proverbs prove to be a defensive weapon by which Tell holds others at arm's length in accordance with his own aphorism that the strength of the strong man is most effective when he stands alone.[1]

Thus Schiller has used stylistic means to express the character of the self-contained man. With equal skill he fixes stylistically the essential Tell when a direct brutal assault from outside breaks through his outer defences and threatens to breach the sanctuary of his spirit. In Act Three the real Tell emerges, laid bare by Geßler's savagery. The proverbs evaporate. Tell, whose speech has hitherto followed a linear pattern, gasps out broken phrases in which the line rhythms are completely disrupted:

> Herr — Welches Ungeheure sinnet Ihr
> Mir an — Ich soll vom Haupte meines Kindes —
> — Nein, nein doch, lieber Herr, das kömmt Euch nicht
> Zu Sinn — Verhüts der gnädge Gott — das könnt Ihr
> Im Ernst von einem Vater nicht begehren! (ll. 1889–93)

From this disarray he quickly recovers and in two lines, in which the linear firmness is restored, he asserts his willingness to die:

> Ich soll
> Mit meiner Armbrust auf das liebe Haupt
> Des eignen Kindes zielen — Eher sterb ich! (ll. 1895–7)

But Geßler is not the man so easily to relinquish his advantage and with diabolical skill he forces Tell closer to the edge of the precipice. From this point on, the ultimate stylistic device—that of silence—is used to portray the self-contained character subjected to the extreme of stress. In the next 147 lines Tell speaks

---

[1] Quoted above, p. 271.

only twenty-seven words in four speeches. Yet this tract of verse includes Tell's terrible internal struggle, his first failure to bring himself to the point of shooting, his miraculously successful shot, and his reunion with his son. One of his four speeches occupies two lines, in which he makes one more desperate attempt to escape by inviting death (ll. 1983–4). For the rest, his silence is broken only by short exclamations which he cannot repress— 'Öffnet die Gasse! Platz!' (l. 1979), 'Mir schwimmt es vor den Augen!' (l. 1982), and 'Es muß!' (l. 1990).

The unspoken processes of Tell's inner struggle are demonstrated in unusually full stage directions at two critical points, before and after the shot. Once the crisis is past and the inner fortress of his heart secured, his guarded self-containment reasserts itself in evasive linear speech—'Herr, das ist also bräuchlich bei den Schützen' (l. 2051). But the recollection of the crisis breaks through and disrupts the rhythm of a three-line speech exposing to Geßler, in its barbed intensity, the peril in which he stands:

> Mit diesem zweiten Pfeil durchschoß ich — Euch,
> Wenn ich mein liebes Kind getroffen hätte,
> Und Eurer — wahrlich! hätt ich nicht gefehlt.          (ll. 2059–61)

Thereupon the second storm breaks over Tell and once again he seeks refuge in a silence, broken only by three brief involuntary outbursts in thirty-six lines.

Tell next appears in the scene of his self-rescue. He gives the necessary explanations in a vivid narrative of conventional type, but otherwise speaks with his earlier concision and control. The rhythms are again linear, but the searing experience he has passed through has brought in a new element, a menacing irony, especially evident in his last four lines:

> Sie sollen wacker sein und gutes Muts,
> Der Tell sei *frei* und seines Armes mächtig,
> Bald werden sie ein Weitres von mir hören,          (ll. 2296–8)

and

> Ist es *getan*, wirds auch zur Rede kommen.          (l. 2300)

Very different is the scene which culminates in the assassination of Geßler (IV. iii). The previously reticent Tell, who, except when telling a story (III. i and IV. i), has never put more than eight lines together in a single speech, and usually not more than two, now speaks a monologue of ninety-one lines. There is only one other soliloquy in the play, Attinghausen's speech of sixteen lines at the end of II. i, but this is a mere reverberation of the dispute between uncle and nephew which has just ended. Tell's monologue, in both extent and function, stands by itself. Up to this point he has solved his problems without reference to the outside world. The operation which he now undertakes is one which he can no longer carry out within his self-imposed limits. The assassination of Geßler oversteps the law and thereby becomes a public matter; and in this situation Schiller evidently felt obliged to shine into the workings of Tell's mind a light by which the unlawful act might be justified. By his reticent nature Tell was debarred from unburdening himself to a fellow man; his balanced detachment is one of the pillars on which the play rests. Schiller's solution is a monologue, a communing of Tell with himself, which the audience is privileged to overhear. That it is not addressed *to* the audience is underlined by the recurrent apostrophes, four invoking Geßler, one the arrow, one the bowstring, and one Tell's children.

The opening lines of the monologue remain consistent with Tell's normal speech. They consist of a number of short simple sentences dealing with matters of strategy:

> Durch diese hohle Gasse muß er kommen,
> Es führt kein andrer Weg nach Küßnacht — Hier
> Vollend ichs — Die Gelegenheit ist günstig.
> Dort der Holunderstrauch verbirgt mich ihm,
> Von dort herab kann ihn mein Pfeil erlangen,
> Des Weges Enge wehret den Verfolgern.       (ll. 2560–5)

It is the exposition of a plan in the form of a military appreciation. At the sixteenth line a compound sentence appears for the first time, and at once the style changes, shifting from the matter-of-fact to the rhetorical. But it is a rhetoric tempered by lyrical elements, as Tell reflects upon past innocence and contrasts the tranquil passage of the carefree world which passes him by with the darkness in his own heart. Only once does the intensity of hatred show clearly through—at the moment when he recalls the fearful inhumanity to which Geßler has subjected him. Schiller faces the situation of his hero squarely, the motif of *Mord* runs through the passage, but it is each time neutralized by the image of the children, for whose protection the murder is designed. The concluding lines, moreover, divert the mind from murder to sport. Tell is seen as the hunter—'Ich laure auf ein edles Wild' (l. 2635)—who is about to attain the climax of a career in the mastery of his weapon. The monologue reveals itself as a dialectical master-piece of extenuation, achieved by the interplay of two opposed emotional currents. It cannot at the same time, be gainsaid that it comes as something of a stylistic shock, contrasting sharply with the means which Schiller has so far used to delineate Tell. It is one of those sudden shifts to which Schiller's spasmodic mind was liable, recalling such abrupt changes as the emergence of Buttler as a chorus or the shift to trimeters in *Die Jungfrau von Orleans.*

The episodic character of the monologue is further emphasized by the immediate switch, at the close, to Tell's accustomed tone. The rejoinders he gives to Stüssi are as lapidary as any of his previous utterances.

Tell's last speaking appearance in the play is in the so-called Parricida scene, and here once more the reticent Tell becomes both fluent and rhetorical. He opposes to Johannes Parricida a barrage of 'rhetorical questions', supported by parallelisms of epithet and clause:

> Darfst du der Ehrsucht blutge Schuld vermengen
> Mit der gerechten Notwehr eines Vaters?
> Hast du der Kinder liebes Haupt verteidigt?
> Des Herdes Heiligtum beschützt? das Schrecklichste,
> Das Letzte von den Deinen abgewendet? (ll. 3175-9)

He employs sharp antithesis, compact synecdoche ('Laß rein die

Hütte, wo die Unschuld wohnt', l. 3188), and indulges in Schiller's characteristic, vivid, gruesome hyperbole:

> Von dem Blute triefend
> Des Vatermordes und des Kaisermords.          (ll. 3168–9)

Schiller's powerful rhetoric is here once again evoked by a scene of judgement. Two apparently similar cases are submitted to a court and a verdict demanded. The unease which this scene commonly causes in Schiller's listening or reading public is not a consequence of the rhetoric, which is properly applied to the purpose of advocacy. It arises from a moral objection to what is intended to be a highly moral scene. Tell is judge in his own cause, and even the compassion of the close (in which he reverts to his accustomed homely style) is judicial, an act of clemency to the condemned murderer.

The stylistic restraint which Schiller, for the most part, imposes upon himself in portraying Tell is abandoned in the treatment of an important group of characters. Exalted rhetoric in this play is primarily the speech of youth, and to that extent it serves to characterize. The principal speakers of this elevated language are Melchthal, Rudenz, and Bertha von Bruneck. All three display a powerful eloquence in political passages. Melchthal declaims with an *élan* which recalls *Don Carlos*, though on closer inspection it becomes apparent that he has not Carlos's swift yet easy flow. A sense of effort is felt; he seems to collect himself for each section and to hurl himself at it, advancing by a series of leaps rather than in continuous movement. An element of reflection is seen in the series of zoological parallels in the following passage:

> Jedem Wesen ward
> Ein Notgewehr in der Verzweiflungsangst,
> Es stellt sich der erschöpfte Hirsch und zeigt
> Der Meute sein gefürchtetes Geweih,
> Die Gemse reißt den Jäger in den Abgrund —
> Der Pflugstier selbst, der sanfte Hausgenoß
> Des Menschen, der die ungeheure Kraft

Des Halses duldsam unters Joch gebogen,
Springt auf, gereizt, wetzt sein gewaltig Horn
Und schleudert seinen Feind den Wolken zu.       (ll. 644–53)

Bertha speaks with a masculine vigour which is undifferentiated from the style of the two men:

Knechtschaft wollt Ihr ihm bereiten!
Die Freiheit wollt Ihr aus dem letzten Schloß,
Das ihr noch auf der Erde blieb, verjagen.       (ll. 1630–2)

And Rudenz pours out his new-won defiance in a torrent of words in which the groupings impetuously overrun the line endings:

Mein Volk verließ ich, meinen Blutsverwandten
Entsagt ich, alle Bande der Natur
Zerriß ich, um an euch mich anzuschließen.       (ll. 2010–12)

Yet, when this eloquence leaves the field of politics, it at once begins to sag. When Rudenz discovers that Bertha will esteem him more as a patriot than as a pro-Austrian, he celebrates his change of front in verse of linear structure, weak at the joints and slack of tension:

Fahr hin, du eitler Wahn, der mich betört!
Ich soll das Glück in meiner Heimat finden.
Hier wo der Knabe fröhlich aufgeblüht,
Wo tausend Freudespuren mich umgeben,
Wo alle Quellen mir und Bäume leben,
Im Vaterland willst du die Meine werden!       (ll. 1691–6)

Melchthal, too, expresses private emotion in the loftiest rhetorical terms. His anguish at the blinding of his father is conveyed in a passage adorned with anastrophe, repetition, anaphora, parallelism, and metaphor. Notwithstanding its brilliance (or perhaps because of it), a sense of unease arises in the reader at this extravagant public display of private grief.

Nevertheless Melchthal's vigorous oratory has its point for Schiller. It facilitates the shift from personal shock to political activism, which is the essence of Melchthal's function in the play. With the words 'Jetzt rede / Mir keiner mehr von Bleiben, von

Verbergen!' (ll. 610–11) he embarks on a series of passionate tirades which, in despite of the prudent reluctance of Stauffacher and Walter Fürst, prefigures the eventual action.

Melchthal's eloquence is, in one aspect, a typification of youth. Yet political rhetoric is not restricted to the young men of this play. Attinghausen, standing at the end of a long and rich life, delivers two important political tirades. In his interview with Rudenz (I. ii) he speaks a long passage in praise of the Swiss people, in which he seeks to arouse Rudenz's patriotism to an awareness of imminent peril. It is in the original sense rhetorical, for it seeks by the arts of speech to persuade and convince. In contrast to Melchthal's fiery personal revolutionism, Attinghausen's vision is broad and general, as the repeated use of the first person plural shows:

> — Nein, wenn wir unser Blut dransetzen sollen,
> So seis *für uns* — wohlfeiler kaufen wir
> Die Freiheit als die Knechtschaft ein!          (ll. 904–6)

By this assertion of community Attinghausen shifts the speech from the duologue demanded by the dramatic situation, and speaks to a greater audience, the Swiss people, present in spirit throughout the play—speaks, too, it may be thought, in those days of Napoleonic imperialism, to a wider public still. Attinghausen's function here is virtually that of a chorus. In his dying speech (IV. ii) he goes further, directing his words 'through' and across his stage listeners to an audience of all time, as the stage direction indicates (*Er spricht das Folgende mit dem Ton eines Sehers*). Both of these speeches are cut off from the tract of dialogue which encloses them by a sudden and sharp rise in the elevation of the style.

The double action of *Wilhelm Tell*, its constantly shifting pattern of characters and its language, by turns homely and rhetorical, set the play far away from its immediate predecessor, *Die Braut von Messina*. Yet the dawn oath on the Rütli unexpectedly revives choric procedure. The solemnity of the moment, in which nature underlines the significance of the undertaking, is expressed by the stage direction: *Alle haben unwillkürlich die Hüte abgenommen und betrachten mit stiller Sammlung die Morgenröte*. In this atmosphere of dedication the oath is sworn in a ceremony recalling that of the German oath to the colours (*Fahneneid*). The oath itself has a solemn threefold articulation, each phase is spoken by a single voice and then repeated in chorus by all, each man repeating the symbol of the triple oath in the elevation of three fingers of the right hand:

> RÖSSELMANN. Wir wollen sein ein einzig Volk von Brüdern,
> In keiner Not uns trennen und Gefahr.
> (*Alle sprechen es nach mit erhobenen drei Fingern*)
> — Wir wollen frei sein, wie die Väter waren,
> Eher den Tod, als in der Knechtschaft leben.
> (*Wie oben . . .*)
> Wir wollen trauen auf den höchsten Gott
> Und uns nicht fürchten vor der Macht der Menschen.
> (*Wie oben . . .*)                    (ll. 1447–52)

This use of a true group chorus, together with its military analogy, establishes the strength of firmly based popular feeling, the power of a healthy democracy, and represents the central point of the political action.

A further scene of chorus-like commentary occurs in Act IV. i, the scene of Tell's rescue. The persons present are Kunz and the Fischer. Their speech is functionally differentiated; Kunz narrates, the Fischer comments. Kunz speaks in a homely style with aphaeresis (' 's ist alles so geschehn') and elisions ('Ich sahs mit Augen an, Ihr könnt mirs glauben', l. 2098), though here and there a heightened touch, such as 'eilends' (l. 2107), shows that this is more than simple colloquialism. The Fischer's manner is noticeably more elevated, with parallelisms such as 'Der beste Mann im Land, der bravste Arm' (l. 2101), anastrophic genitives ('in des Vogts Gewalt', l. 2109; 'des Tages Licht', l. 2111), a formal vocative ('O glaubt', l. 2110), and a traditional literary image ('So bricht der letzte Anker unsrer Hoffnung!', l. 2116). The Fischer's selective and stylized speech is a preparation for what is to come. No sooner has Kunz left the scene than he breaks into a tirade in Schiller's loftiest manner:

> Erheb die freche Stirne, Tyrannei,
> Wirf alle Scham hinweg, der Mund der Wahrheit
> Ist stumm, das sehnde Auge ist geblendet,
> Der Arm, der retten sollte, ist gefesselt! (ll. 2123–6)

An ironical apostrophe, a parallel, a triad, and carefully chosen physical images given abstract meaning, all this is Schiller's full rhetorical style. Soon the apostrophes proliferate in a torrent of hyperbole in which the ravening beasts of Schiller's youthful poetic imagination are reinvoked as symbols of total desolation:

> Raset, ihr Winde, flammt herab, ihr Blitze,
> Ihr Wolken berstet, gießt herunter, Ströme
> Des Himmels und ersäuft das Land! Zerstört
> Im Keim die ungeborenen Geschlechter!
> Ihr wilden Elemente werdet Herr,
> Ihr Bären kommt, ihr alten Wölfe wieder
> Der großen Wüste, euch gehört das Land,
> Wer wird hier leben wollen ohne Freiheit! (ll. 2129–36)

The cataclysmic words mount in ever wilder hyperbole until the implied biblical allusion is crystallized in the explicit reference to the Deluge:

> O mich solls nicht wundern,
> Wenn sich die Felsen bücken in den See,
> Wenn jene Zacken, jene Eisestürme,
> Die nie auftauten seit dem Schöpfungstag,
> Von ihren hohen Kulmen niederschmelzen,
> Wenn die Berge brechen, wenn die alten Klüfte
> Einstürzen, eine zweite Sündflut alle
> Wohnstätten der Lebendigen verschlingt! (ll. 2142–9)

The avalanche of rhetoric seems to take charge and carry Schiller willy-nilly along with it. Yet there are unexpected signs of deliberation. The Fischer's thunder is punctuated by his son's homespun interjections, such as

> Es hagelt schwer, kommt in die Hütte, Vater,
> Es ist nicht kömmlich hier im Freien hausen. (ll. 2127–8)

Thus the scale of reality is set beside the scale of hyperbole, which is recognized for what it is.

The Fischer acts as a chorus, passionately delivering a moral commentary on the world which has (apparently) crushed the representative of goodness, courage, and freedom (ll. 2100–2). But his metaphors are not drawn from a vacuum. They are derived from a real storm taking place before his (and our) eyes. His son's naïve comments serve to stress reality and so to link hyperbole and fact. Without the boy the rhetoric would have to be damped down, so as not to push exaggeration to the point of disbelief. His presence and interventions allow Schiller to pull out all the stops and yet maintain a relevance to the physical situation. By this development of technique he can take a scene similar to that of the charcoal-burner in *Die Jungfrau von Orleans* and dovetail it closely into the action.

The Fischer's oblique portrayal of the storm, which in its later stages, with the boy's assistance, takes the classical form of running commentary from a point of vantage (teichoscopy), is only one of a number of passages of narration in this play, some of which, such as Melchthal's account of his journey (ii. ii), are written in the rhetorical mode, whilst others show sobriety of style. There are in all nine such narratives, a higher proportion than in Schiller's other plays.

The use of narrative in drama brings with it retardation. This the dramatist can accept and exploit. Retardation in its various forms, especially when applied in suspense, is one of his most powerful weapons. But retardation through narrative involves a danger; it substitutes history for action, past for present. The spectator, keyed to actuality, responds all too readily with disappointment and boredom. Each narrative is an implied challenge to the writer, so to frame its form and knit its style that the evidence of the eyewitness can hold its own with the evidence of the senses. Schiller has for the most part successfully solved this problem. Only the account of remote and legendary Swiss history inserted into the Rütli scene in the mouth of Stauffacher arouses doubts. This must, we feel, be the passage to which

Kirms, the manager of the Weimar theatre, referred in a letter to Böttiger,[1] as 'das Langweilige der Versammlung auf dem Rütli'. The remoteness posed the problem which baffled Schiller. He had to emphasize the Swiss tradition and to demonstrate the deep roots from which Swiss conservative libertarianism grew. And it proved difficult to relate the remote past with the present. It was perhaps a mistake to deal with this theme in one single and very long narration. Schiller uses all the art of a skilled rhetorical poet, but the long passage refuses to blend into the texture of the play.

The other narrations concern the experience of characters or act directly on their prospects and are conceived dramatically. Each mounts to a climax and represents a dramatic action in miniature; and each supplies a facet of character or gives an impulse to action. But Stauffacher's narration does neither of these things. The return to the present is made in a separate concluding section, a frankly political speech, delivered with impassioned rhetoric to an audience *on the stage*. It adds to the long arguments of reason the quick appeal to emotion. Schiller deploys all his rhetorical expertise, but the special tone of the passage is produced by emotively loaded words and phrases, including 'Tyrannenmacht', 'der Gedrückte', 'Rechte', 'unerträglich' . . . 'Last', 'seine ewgen Rechte', 'unveräußerlich und unzerbrechlich', 'Mensch', 'Schwert', and 'Gewalt'. This gives it a demagogic character which is emphasized by the final irresistible appeal to the protective instincts—'Wir stehn vor unsre Weiber, unsre Kinder!' (l. 1287). So powerful was the dynamism of this speech that it aroused the misgivings of Iffland, who felt it to be politically impossible at any rate on the Berlin stage.[2] Schiller conceded the point and shortened the speech, without, however, sacrificing his fundamental intention. Indeed, he even inserted a new and potent line—'Wenn rohe Willkür alles Recht zertritt' —and the abridged version is a remarkable demonstration of Schiller's ability to make drastic cuts without any loss in power.

---

[1] 24 November 1804.
[2] Schiller's reply is dated 14 April 1804 (Jonas, 7. 138 f.).

One of Schiller's principal sources was a sixteenth-century account, Ägidius Tschudi's *Chronikon Helveticum*. Its homely direct style appealed to Schiller just as Abraham a Santa Clara's idiosyncrasies had captivated him while he was at work on *Wallenstein*. And, just as he had done with Abraham, he lifted whole sentences and wove them into his work. The sections which owe most to Tschudi are the story of Baumgarten's homicide (i. i), the account of Melchthal's brush with the bailiff and the blinding of his father (i. iv), Stauffacher's conversation with his wife (i. ii), the apple scene (iii. iii), and Tell's escape (iv. i). They include most of the scenes in which appear Tell, Stauffacher, and Geßler, the principal exponents of a modified realism of speech.

Baumgarten's savage irony 'Und mit der Axt hab ich ihm 's Bad gsegnet' (l. 97) is already in Tschudi in the form 'ich will ihm das Bad gesegnen, daß Ers keiner Frowen mer tut'. Stauffacher's story of his encounter with Geßler gives in direct speech ('Wessen ist dies Haus?', l. 225) what Tschudi gives in indirect ('fragt In der Landvogt, weß das Huß wäre?' The chronicle gives in dialogue much of the material for the apple scene. Tell speaks as follows: 'Lieber Herr, es ist ungewärd und nit uß Verachtung geschehen; verzichend mirs, wär ich witzig, so hieß ich nit der Tell; bitt umb Gnad, es soll nit mer geschechen'. This Schiller renders almost literally:

Verzeiht mir, lieber Herr! Aus Unbedacht,
Nicht aus Verachtung Eurer ists geschehen,
Wär ich besonnen, hieß ich nicht der Tell,
Ich bitt um Gnad, es soll nicht mehr begegnen.    (ll. 1869–72)

Schiller's Tell, evading the question about the second arrow, says, 'Herr, das ist also bräuchlich bei den Schützen' (l. 2051), where Tschudi's Tell answers in indirect speech: 'es wäre also der Schützen Gewohnheit'. And Geßler's rejoinder runs in Tschudi, 'die gegebene Antwurt nimm ich nit an, es wird etwas anders bedut haben', which Schiller gives as

Nein, Tell, die Antwort laß ich dir nicht gelten,
Es wird was anders wohl bedeutet haben.    (ll. 2052–3)

In all this it is clear that, indebted though Schiller is to Tschudi, he does more than convert the chosen phrases into verse. Thus in the last example he gives to Geßler a more ingratiating tone where Tschudi is brusque, and he underlines in this way a feline and stealthy element in Geßler's predatory nature. Moreover, in amplifying phrases from Tschudi and transposing them into verse, Schiller has been able to integrate them so that the passages from the sixteenth-century source are indistinguishable from those which are independent. A particularly good example of this is provided by the speech beginning 'Du bist ein Meister auf der Armbrust, Tell' (l. 1873), which is approximately half Tschudi and half original and yet makes up a consistent whole, preserving unity of tone.

### 3. THE VOCABULARY

The choice of words in Schiller's plays seems sometimes to be determined by undisclosed preoccupations, but the vocabulary of *Wilhelm Tell* is predominantly functional. The words are tied to the theme, and the language gives an impression of straightforwardness. So the abundant words of freedom outweigh their opposites, the words of tyranny, and so emphasize the optimistic political climate of the work. Similarly the vocabulary of tradition is exceptionally strong, with such expressions as 'Die alten Zeiten und die alte Schweiz', 'nach den alten Bräuchen', or 'die alte Treue'. And epithets indicating robust integrity and a sense of right (*wacker, bieder, fromm*) also play an important part. These two groups together fit the conservative revolt which is a major part of the action. The symbolism of the Alps powerfully reinforces this feeling of stability and power, which is amplified by the signs of mountain dynamism, avalanche and flood and the storms of Alpine lakes. And the background of unflinching integrity and stable political consciousness is further supported by the word *Herz*, which, though not so frequent as in *Die Braut von Messina* and *Die Jungfrau von Orleans*,[1] is still the most

---

[1] It occurs more than sixty times.

abundant emotive word. *Herz* is used by all the Swiss. It is applied to the mobile emotions of Rudenz, to the womanly fears and suffering of Tell's wife; but most of all it is used to denote the fortitude and sincerity of the Swiss patriots, as in 'Unbilliges erträgt kein edles Herz' (l. 317), 'Das Herz muß jedem Bieder-manne bluten' (l. 558), 'Das halte fest mit deinem ganzen Herzen' (l. 922), or 'Die Herzen alle dieses biedern Volks' (l. 1050). Geß-ler's only and resentful use of the word ('um die Herzen / Des Volks zu prüfen', ll. 2717–18) is an unconscious tribute to the integrity of the Swiss, whom he oppresses.

It is remarkable that Tell makes much more sparing use of *Herz* than any of his compatriots. Twice he uses it untypically as the focus of his hostility to Geßler ('Der kann auch treffen in das Herz des Feinds', l. 2576, and 'Daß meines *nächsten* Schusses *erstes* Ziel / Dein Herz sein sollte', ll. 2586–7), once it refers to the failing courage of Geßler's oarsmen, and once it occurs in one of Tell's defensive aphorisms ('Das schwere Herz wird nicht durch Worte leicht', l. 418). Only twice does he use the word with the aura and weight which it has elsewhere in the play, once in his confrontation with Parricida and again when in the apple scene he speaks of the father's heart (l. 1901). Tell's neglect of this keyword emphasizes his distinct and separate identity. He is not heartless, he is heart-whole, free from self-questionings and has no need ever and again to invoke the heart. And so Tell's abstention from the emotive word provides a negative means of characterization.

When all is said and done, it remains true that the vocabulary of *Wilhelm Tell* is almost devoid of distinctive features which could not be foreseen by anyone reading the title of the play. No doubt this is a sign of an estimable sobriety and a trenchant adaptation to purpose. But it also suggests a faltering imagination. And, when the style is looked at as a whole, it is seen to have only two new features. In its local elements, derived from maps, topographical works, and Tschudi's chronicle, it takes a step towards later documentary drama. And the inclusion of an epic perspective with corresponding epic elements of style seems also to be an innovation with far-reaching possibilities. Schiller has up to a point integrated the local factor, though the epic aspect remained largely recalcitrant. But he was not prepared to go far enough. These new features subsist beside modes of style which have become traditional with him, and the rhetoric, to which he inclined temperamentally as well as by habit, accords ill with his new techniques. At the central points of the play Schiller's mastery of theatrical effect is as assured as ever, and the close of the Rütli meeting and the two great scenes of Acts Three and Four never fail to grip the spectator; nevertheless at other points *longueurs* are felt, and on dispassionate examination it seems likely that Schiller's creative imagination was not sufficiently roused to achieve successfully a harmonization of disparate materials.

Though Schiller, at the time of writing *Tell*, was a sick man and had less than two years to live, it would be unsafe to guess that his health was impeding his vision, so astonishing was his power of subduing physical infirmity. And, indeed, in his last and unfinished play, *Demetrius*, the imagination, despite declining health, is as vivid and creative as it had ever been. It seems that *Wilhelm Tell*, the last play of the Schiller canon, stimulated him to experiment and yet failed to rouse him to the point of solving the problems inherent in his experiments. Its deserved reputation rests on a number of individual strokes and performances rather than on the achievement of a fully coherent whole.

# CONCLUSION

SCHILLER'S *Demetrius* fragments, dealing with the pretender who opposed Tsar Boris Godounov, have a special interest, for they reach out into the uncharted sea of the future, offering the only clue to his intended course. They consist of two versions of a first act, an unfinished second act, and numerous other fragments, ranging from scenes in verse, through scraps of dialogue in prose or verse, to the initial prose scenario, which Schiller was accustomed to draft at an early stage of his writing. In the second (and quite different) version of Act One Schiller sensationally breaks entirely new ground. The mode of address is already familiar in various plays of Schiller, and notably in *Maria Stuart*. Though the convention of dialogue is retained, the speech is designed to convince and persuade the audience. In the first act of *Demetrius* the dramatic frame is enlarged, drawing the audience into the play. The scene is the Polish Diet, and the initial stage directions give no hint of innovation. The entry of Demetrius, however, is accompanied by the following indication: *Alsdann stellt er sich so, daß er einen großen Teil der Versammlung und des Publikums, von welchem angenommen wird, daß es im Reichstag mitsitze, im Auge behält* ... This implied extension of the stage is something unprecedented in Schiller's work, and, indeed, in the drama of his day. His bold step in abolishing the demarcation between stage and auditorium represents the avowal of a hitherto concealed aim—the direct address to the public. Parallel with this development there appears a reversion to the function of exalted speech as Schiller had practised it in *Wallenstein*, though in *Demetrius* it is applied with an intensity and pungency surpassing its treatment in the earlier play. The language of this first act is almost exclusively lofty rhetoric. It is spoken at close quarters, and is used as a screen for the concealment of motives and as a weapon to achieve selfish ends. Suspicion of integrity is everywhere and becomes the more obvious for the proximity of the audience. The impassioned speeches ring hollow. All too readily the archbishop eloquently accepts Demetrius's pretensions. Even the vehement opposition of Sapieha, the champion of law, is suspect (ll. 675–6). And Demetrius unwittingly reveals his own egotism in the motifs of gold and silver by which he appeals to the self-interest of his hearers:

> Euch öffnen sich des Glückes goldne Tore;
> Mit euch will ich den Raub des Feindes teilen.
> Moskau ist reich an Gütern, unermeßlich
> An Gold und Edelsteinen ist der Schatz
> Des Zars; ich kann die Freunde königlich
> Belohnen, und ich wills. Wenn ich als Zar
> Einziehe auf dem Kremel, dann, ich schwörs,
> Soll sich der Ärmste unter euch, der mir
> Dahin gefolgt, in Samt und Zobel kleiden,
> Mit reichen Perlen sein Geschirr bedecken,
> Und Silber sei das schlechteste Metall,
> Um seiner Pferde Hufe zu beschlagen.          (ll. 366–77)

Thus the exalted tone is adapted without difficulty or hesitation to a base motive. There is an affinity here with the screening use of rhetorical speech in Wallenstein. New is the direct address to the implicated spectator.

This sophisticated treatment of elevated style is a form of irony. Schiller turns the rhetoric of his politicians inside out and shows its shabby lining. In the other great scene, the attempt to persuade Marfa, the Tsar's widow, that Demetrius is in fact her son, Schiller writes some of his most dynamic and powerful rhetoric and yet imbues it with a subtle and finespun irony. Marfa's language in the second act passes through three stages. At first it is laconic, compressed, a reserved and reticent rhetoric, constantly ridden on the curb. A symptom of the restraint is the occurrence of only one anastrophic genitive in forty lines. When she finds herself in the presence of Hiob, the style rises to display dignity and resolution. The anastrophic genitives begin to multiply and the nouns to acquire epithets:

> Durch welcher Zeichen und Beweise Kraft
> Beglaubigt sich der kecke Abenteurer
> Als Iwans Sohn, den wir als tot beweinen?                    (ll. 1047–9)

When at last the full conviction of her new position of strength joins forces with her long-repressed yearning for revenge, she bursts into a rhetoric of a power new in Schiller's verse. The speech of *Maria Stuart* and *Die Jungfrau von Orleans* had been noble and eloquent persuasion; and the rhetoric of *Don Carlos* or of Max in *Wallenstein* had made music to which the speaker had indulgently listened. Marfa's speech is a tense, steely, finely wrought outburst, exactly expressing the passion she experiences. She looks into no mirror, she cares not who hears her words. She speaks with absolute directness, yet responds to a discipline derived from long-acquired restraint.

The onset of this passage coincides with Marfa's recognition of the transformation which her situation has undergone. Her reserve suddenly recedes, giving way to an invocation of God with repetition and alliteration, with an air of spontaneity induced by the omission of *und*:

> O höchste Allmacht, habe Dank, Dank, Dank,
> Daß du mir endlich Rettung, Rache sendest!                   (ll. 1096–7)

Her speech uses short, stabbing, simple sentences, then flares up into more complex movements. So her second passionate outburst begins staccato and then rises to a ringing climax:

> Er ist mein Sohn. An diesen Zeichen allen
> Erkenn ich ihn. An deines Zaren Furcht
> Erkenn ich ihn. Er ists. Er lebt. Er naht.
> Herab von deinem Thron, Tyrann! Erzittre!
> Es lebt ein Sprößling noch von Ruriks Stamm,
> Der wahre Zar, der rechte Erbe kommt,
> Er kommt und fordert Rechnung von dem Seinen!               (ll. 1102–8)

And her final passage glows, flashes, and blazes in a coda, in
which cosmic, incendiary, and military images are fused—

> Du ewge Sonne, die den Erdenball
> Umkreist, sei du die Botin meiner Wünsche!
> Du allverbreitet ungehemmte Luft,
> Die schnell die weitste Wanderung vollendet,
> O trag ihm meine glühnde Sehnsucht zu!
> Ich habe nichts als mein Gebet und Flehn,
> Das schöpf ich flammend aus der tiefsten Seele,
> Beflügelt send ichs in des Himmels Höhn,
> Wie eine Heerschar send ich dirs entgegen!
>
> (ll. 1219–27)

Yet the overtly sincere rhetoric, which Marfa here uses so
passionately, involves an element of deceit. All the weight of her
resolute and powerful personality is thrown into a cause which,
in the deepest recesses of her heart, she knows to be false. The
clue to her inner uncertainty is provided by her repeated insistence on her *will* to believe, as she exclaims, 'Es ist mein Sohn,
ich will nicht daran zweifeln' (l. 1196) and 'Er ist mein Sohn, ich
glaub an ihn, ich wills' (l. 1205). She wills the silence of the voice
within, and in this disclosure shows that the most powerful as
well as the shallowest rhetoric is in the service of deceit. Yet the
scale of the rhetoric corresponds to the nature of the pretence.
The contrast is sharply brought out in the confrontation of
Marfa's dynamic self-deception and Hiob's calculated imposture.
The difference in inner tension is immediately apparent if Hiob's
words are set beside Marfa's speech. To her power, derived from
deep commitment, he can only rejoin with lines such as these:

> Ein frecher Trugner in der Polen Land,
> Ein Renegat und Rostriga, der, sein
> Gelübd abschwörend, seinen Gott verleugnet,
> Mißbraucht den edeln Namen deines Sohns,
> Den dir der Tod geraubt im Kindesalter.          (ll. 1021–5)

The epithets are commonplace, the rhythm lacks compulsion,
and a revealing weakness of phrase occurs at the end of the second

line, with its close-set double pause, and another at the beginning of the fifth ('Den dir der' . . . ).

Schiller offsets his pervasive rhetoric with the crude and aggressive speech of coarse-grained and brutal characters. Thus in the Diet Odowalsky, after a few clumsy attempts to live up to the style of what is going on around him, slips, as soon as his plan begins to go awry, into his natural bludgeoning tone:

> Was kümmert Eur Vertrag uns! Damals haben
> Wir so gewollt, und heute wollen wir anders!          (ll. 413–14)

And he reveals in our hearing that the whole procedure is a put-up job—'Das schlug uns fehl' (l. 485). Such forthright interjections remind us that the surrounding rhetoric is not mere ornament, but has a serious interpretative purpose.

Finally, it is necessary to draw attention to the prevalence of the word *wollen* in *Demetrius*. Short though the extant text is, it occurs abundantly, and the following are some of its forms: 'Wir wollen ihn hören', 'Eher will ichs tropfenweis verspritzen', 'ich kann die Freunde königlich belohnen / Und ich wills', 'ich fodr es, ich begehrs und wills', 'Zerreißen will ich dies Geweb von Arglist, / Aufdecken will ich alles', 'Will ich die Freiheit meines Worts behaupten', 'Ich will aus Sklaven freie Menschen machen', 'Verdienen will ich deine Gunst', 'Nicht deinen Arm bloß will ich', 'Nur du willst ewig, deinem Gram zum Raub . . .', 'Ich will mich nicht beruhigen, will nicht / Vergessen'. The word extends to every important character and its omnipresence suggests that *Demetrius* would have been a tragedy of the convergence of inflexible wills. The importance of the will in Schiller's poetic character, and, indeed, in his whole mature outlook, has often been stressed, and none has expressed it with such terseness and force as Schiller himself in *Über das Erhabene*: 'Alle andere Dinge müssen, der Mensch ist das Wesen, welches will.' The power and the integration of the language in *Demetrius* suggest that Schiller had found a theme nearer to his heart than anything that had gone before. The tension of *Wilhelm Tell* at its best is here present in every fragment.

Schiller was a poet and language was his business; and like many other poets he rarely wrote about his tools. Now and then he made some passing reference in his letters, say to his newly acquired mastery of blank verse in *Carlos*,[1] or to his inability to understand how he could ever have thought of writing *Wallenstein* in prose.[2] But in general he contented himself with writing dramatic speech, and left writing about it to others. On one occasion, however, he departed from his usual reticence and set down in a letter to Körner[3] his views on language at some length.

Schiller's opinions are at first sight surprising; for he writes of language with barely concealed hostility. He conceives words as general signs, unapt to express the individual and unique experience which is the stuff of art. The poet does battle with them, seeking to impose his will upon them:

Soll also eine poetische Darstellung frey seyn, so muß der Dichter *die Tendenz der Sprache zum Allgemeinen durch die Größe seiner Kunst überwinden, und den Stoff* (Worte und ihre Flexions- und Constructions-Gesetze) *durch die Form* (nehmlich die Anwendung derselben) besiegen.

And the restrictive, impeding tendency of language is emphasized by repeated stress on the metaphor *fetter* (*Fessel*), which makes a decisive appearance in the final summary: 'Die Schönheit der poetischen Darstellung ist *freie Selbhandlung der Natur in den Fesseln der Sprache.*'[3]

These strictures on the poet's medium bear some relation to the time at which they were written. Schiller's poetic writing had been at a standstill for six years and seemed then unlikely ever to be set in motion again. In that time his output consisted merely of two poems, and the more recent of these already lay five years back. For four years he had been driving a reluctant pen through the Thirty Years War, compelling words to do his bidding in a task which he himself valued only as a source of income. By their number and weight words had temporarily got the better of him,

[1] Letter to H. v. Dalberg, 24 August 1784 (Jonas, 1. 208).
[2] See above, p. 149.
[3] 28 February 1793 (Jonas, 3. 299).

and the sour tone of his remarks is at least partly conditioned by his situation at that time.

But even if his comments were unduly severe they cannot be lightly dismissed. The underlying attitude must long have been present. Doubtless all poets are engaged in a struggle with intractable material. Yet in some the quest, the wrangle, and the fashioning take place beneath the level of consciousness. Eichendorff and Mörike seem to produce their poems as effortlessly as a conjuror draws his rabbit from a hat. Their revisions, however, testify that they, too, must skirmish with words. And the task of the dramatic poet, who must direct his words to expression, argument, emotion, motives overt and concealed, inherent character, and past and future action, is not fully susceptible to the inward creative processes of the lyric poet.

Schiller, moreover, was not a patient writer, prepared to sit and wait until the voice within was ready in the fullness of time to speak its word. The powerful, relentless will, by which he subdued ill-health which would have paralysed the creative impulse in most men, exerted itself in his poetry, so that he sought to compel the seemingly intractable medium in which he worked. Indeed, the recalcitrance of words was in part self-created. It corresponded to Schiller's own need to assert his formidable will. And something of the shaping of his style is related to the changing function of that will.

The shift which takes place in the temper of Schiller's mind is something more than a general development from angry young man to mellow senior. What took place was a redirection of the will. Its rock-like constancy and steely resistance remained undiminished. But, whereas in youth it had been harnessed to his impulses, in maturity it opposed them. Uncontrolled dynamism was exchanged for dynamic discipline. The processes take place at levels beyond our vision, but the end-product is clearly expressed in *Über die ästhetische Erziehung des Menschen in einer Reihe von Briefen*, in the concept of balance. It is not a balance of forces converging from without, but a balance of potencies within the personality. The newly acquired positive discipline, the seeds of which reach far back beyond Schiller's period of philosophical study into the years in which *Don Carlos* was reluctantly taking shape, is the factor governing the change in Schiller's style.

Schiller's newly developed power to select and control was an urgent necessity for him. He was by temperament an extravagant writer, as the multiplication of plots in the early plays, the plethora of incident and situation, clearly show. What would have served many dramatists for three plays Schiller squandered on the single work *Don Carlos*. The same excessive generosity is apparent in his style. In the first four plays the images, the clauses, the words themselves, luxuriate and proliferate so that the sense of direction is often obscured. It says much for Schiller's dynamism that the retarding effect of such rich growth is minimized. The urge towards repetition, parallelism, and triadic structure remains a permanent symptom of this early prodigality in the use of words. Though Schiller retained the impulse he learned to curb it.

The growth of command was in part the consequence of increasing skill. The first signs of a mastery of language, as distinct from a prodigious gift for it, are to be found in *Kabale und Liebe*, especially in the realistic scenes involving Miller and, most notably, in the attempted arrest of Luise in Act Two. In *Don Carlos* Schiller moved a further step forward, writing with fluency and power in a medium that was new to him. But the new skill had its own dangers, and the verse betrays, through a perceptible self-indulgence, the author's pleasure in writing it. The long gap of nine years between the publication of *Don Carlos* and the commencement of work on *Wallenstein* is the period of maturation, the evidence of which is apparent in the poems, in the historical and aesthetic writings, and especially in the letters. By the time he committed himself to *Wallenstein* his forces were redeployed. The basic elements were still the same, but they no longer jostled each other. They took their place in a controlled and disciplined whole.

Among Schiller's completed plays *Wallenstein* marks the

highest pitch of discipline, with only here and there a point where the control slips. The standard of disciplined consistency in the *Demetrius* fragments is even higher, and it is tempting to think that this might have been Schiller's greatest achievement if he had lived to finish it. The plays between these peaks show some relaxation with touches of self-indulgence in *Maria Stuart* and, to a lesser extent in *Wilhelm Tell*. In *Die Jungfrau von Orleans* there is a distinct recession, and a self-indulgence, less crass than in the early plays, nevertheless pervades the whole work. This temporary slackening in the effort to maintain stylistic discipline may well have been therapeutic, a necessary phase of ease between two stages of exertion. It was a relaxation in every sense, and it is understandable that Schiller *enjoyed* writing *Die Jungfrau* more than any other of his later works, for it provided him with a stylistic spree.

In the earlier plays free expression was the rule. Strong feelings were given their head, and the resultant language did more, and less, than serve the interest of the play. An intrusive personal element manifested itself in explosive or tempestuous rhetoric, accompanied by a vocabulary with undertones relating to Schiller's personal life, his prejudices, and his private passions. He learned to control such irrelevances, and if in some of the later plays words and phrases still have such private points of reference it is no longer apparent. This self-discipline was not, for Schiller, something which, once acquired, could be taken for granted. It was maintained by a persistent effort of will and by constant vigilance; and it was subject to lapses, as *Die Jungfrau von Orleans* and rare passages in other plays reveal. Where, however, Schiller's control operates, vocabulary and tone are fully explicable in terms of the work itself and require no private gloss.

That the basic dynamic vehemence survives, though under duress, is demonstrated by the prevalence of emphasis in the plays. The typographical equivalents of underlining occur with a truly remarkable profusion—a hundred or more times in most of the plays and more than three hundred in *Kabale und Liebe*. The desire to emphasize is a symptom of the battle with words, a sign of the urge to impose the will upon them and to *force* them into conformity with thought and feeling. It is noteworthy that emphasis is least frequent in *Die Jungfrau von Orleans*, the play in which Schiller was most ready to go *with* words, relaxing the usual pressure of the will.

The materials of Schiller's style remain constant throughout his life. It is their proportion and manner of employment that change. These elements are realism and rhetoric, and the use of these seeming incompatibles is in conformity with one of the basic aspects of Schiller's psychological structure. The realistic element, with its sobriety and idiomatic fluency, has roots in his ordinary life. It is the manner of his letters, especially of those written after the maturation period in Leipzig and Dresden. As a correspondent he is direct, unaffected, unadorned. Even the access of joy in the letter sent to Körner on receipt of the news of the Danish benefaction is bare of rhetoric.[1] Exultation there is, but it does not turn into exaltation. Addressing himself directly to a friend, Schiller does not raise his voice. The style corresponds to its function of intimate, personal communication.

Schiller's rhetoric is functional, too, though it is only in the mature plays that he learned to apply it without irrelevance or extravagance. The plays are necessarily unintimate. Even in the most realistic moments of *Kabale und Liebe* the fourth dimension of the drama, reaching out into the audience, is preserved. The spectator is never an eavesdropper, his presence is acknowledged, and when in *Demetrius* Schiller elected his audience to membership of the Polish Diet he was only giving unusually graphic expression to a tendency which had always been present in his work. Rhetoric is the mode of persuasion, and in his plays he sought to persuade.

Though Schiller's dramatic speech is persuasive, it is not ingratiating. It does not woo his hearers, it seeks to convince. Its affinities outside the theatre are with courts of law. It is no coincidence that so much of the vocabulary of the tragedies relates to

[1] 13 December 1791 (Jonas, 3. 174).

law and crime, to judges and judgment, to punishment and execution. This range of words is indicative of the forensic character of Schiller's eloquence. His persons speak to convict or to exculpate themselves or others. Every one of Schiller's plays is a tribunal, in which both human and divine justice are at issue. The ultimate arbiter is God, and the frequent references to the final divine instance bring many apparently non-judicial passages into the framework of judgment. So the Gräfin Terzky pleads for mercy from the highest judge because it is denied on earth:

> Ich vertraue mich
> Der Gnade eines größern Herrn.[1]

And Octavio Piccolomini, who has left God out of his political reckoning, makes his admission of guilt in a gesture which acknowledges the true seat of judgement: '*erschrickt und blickt schmerzvoll zum Himmel*'.[2] It can hardly be chance that Schiller's last words, spoken as consciousness faded, invoked the judge above:

Auch am letzten Morgen seines Lebens riß er sich einigemal auf, sah edel in die Höhe, als habe er alle Kraft gesammlet, und sagte einigemal „Judex".[3]

Schiller, especially in his later plays, makes plentiful use of rhetoric to suggest subterfuge, concealment, and deceit, matters which seem to have little to do with justice. Yet deception is a matter which courts are accustomed to unravel. By the oblique use of delusive rhetoric Schiller sets his characters at work to persuade each other, and simultaneously succeeds in persuading us, in reverse, of the injustice of their aims. His style is aimed at engaging our conscience in the processes of law, human and divine, in which his figures are enmeshed.

The brilliant display of Schiller's rhetoric has tended to obscure both the quality and the extent of his colloquial speech. The rhetoric cannot be overlooked; indeed, it forces itself upon

---

[1] *Wallensteins Tod*, ll. 3842–3.

[2] Ibid., final stage direction.

[3] Karoline von Wolzogen, *Aus Schillers letzten Tagen*, 1805, quoted in J. Petersen, p. 423, *Schillers Gespräche*, 1911.

the attention even of those whose response to it is disapproving. The realism, except perhaps in *Kabale und Liebe*, makes no parade. It is a relative realism, not an absolute naturalism. It is never sustained. Either it is intermittent or, as in the extreme example *Kabale und Liebe*, it turns into over-emphasis and caricature, by which it approaches rhetoric. For the most part it makes up a subtle pattern of inconspicuous reminders. From *Don Carlos* onwards a thread of colloquial phrasing runs through all but the most exalted passages. A verse style evolves which is rhythmically persuasive and yet maintains touch with the speech of real life. This solid basis of recognizable reality provides a substratum of fact, a body of evidence, without which the eloquence of advocacy would ring hollow. The appeal which Schiller's works continue to exert, in the face of periodic efforts at detraction, rests upon the simultaneous presentation of reality and of the will which stretches to the utmost the human endeavour to subdue reality.

Though we may speak (and not without justification) of Schiller's style, yet each play has its own stylistic individuality, which one may term its tonality, compounded of subtle variations in the quality and the proportions of rhetorical and colloquial speech. And each variation is derived from the special requirements of the particular play, not imposed arbitrarily upon it. What Schiller wrote to Goethe about the shaping of *Die Jungfrau von Orleans* is applicable to all aspects of his work, and not least to his style: 'Man muß, wie ich bei diesem Stücke sehe, sich durch keinen allgemeinen Begriff fesseln, sondern es wagen, bei einem neuen Stoff die neue Form zu erfinden . . .'.[1] The style reflects a fresh and vital approach to the successive problems which the plays pose for Schiller. Schiller is not, as has often been supposed, a stylistically rigid author; on the contrary, his language responds sensitively and flexibly to each new demand which is put upon it.

It has often been said that Schiller created his works consciously and deliberately, that he calculated his effects and allowed his reason to shape his style. Certainly he applied thought to his

[1] 26 July 1800 (Jonas, 6. 177).

work, sketched prose scenarios, wrote prose dialogue for subsequent conversion into verse, and argued the pros and cons of his structure and text with his friends. Yet what was so discussed came from the depths. Not only does his restless behaviour when writing, his Beethoven-like grunting, his dependence on pungent smells and strong coffee, bear witness to difficult parturition; even the apparently rational processes prove to be an aspect of creation, a patient and persistent striving for the only right expression.[1] Only when that was found could the artist within him be satisfied. Language did not come easily to Schiller, and in moments of doubt he could despair of communication by its means:

> Warum kan der lebendige Geist dem Geist nicht erscheinen?
> Spricht die Seele, so spricht, ach! schon die Seele nicht mehr.[2]

But for all its intractability and incalcitrance, language was also inseparably dear to him:

> Laß die Sprache dir sein, was der Körper dem Liebenden; er nur
> Ists, der die Wesen trennt und der die Wesen vereint,[3]

If his dramatic poetry fell short of imagined perfection, he achieved his own prescribed condition: 'Jeder Stoff will seine eigene Form, und die Kunst besteht darin, die ihm anpassende zu finden.'[4]

---

[1] See H. B. Garland, 'Schiller the Revisionist—the poet's second thoughts', in *Reality and Creative Vision in German Lyric Poetry*, ed. A. Closs, 1963.
[2] Votivtafeln, 84.　　　　　　　　　　　　　　　　　　　　　[3] Ibid. 85.
[4] Letter to Körner, 28 July 1800 (Jonas, 6. 182).

# BIBLIOGRAPHY

## I. WORKS, LETTERS, ETC.

*Schillers Werke.* Nationalausgabe, ed. J. Petersen, L. Blumenthal, B. von Wiese, 1943– . Of 43 projected volumes 16 have so far (1969) been published: 1, 3, 5, 8, 9, 13, 14, 16, 20–3, 27, 30, 35, and 42. Vols. 23–32 embrace Schiller's letters, vols. 33–40 letters to Schiller.

*F. Schiller. Sämtliche Werke.* Säkular-Ausgabe, ed. E. von der Hellen, 16 vols., 1904–5.

*Schiller. Sämtliche Werke,* ed. G. Fricke and H. G. Göpfert, 5 vols., 1958–9.

*Schillers Briefe,* ed. F. Jonas, 7 vols., 1892–6.

*Schillers Briefwechsel mit Körner,* ed. K. Goedeke, 2nd edn., 2 vols., 1874.

*Briefwechsel zwischen Schiller und Goethe,* ed. H. G. Gräf and A. Leitzmann, 3 vols., 1912.

*Briefwechsel zwischen Schiller und Wilhelm von Humboldt,* ed. A. Leitzmann, 1900.

*Schillers Persönlichkeit,* ed. M. Hecker and J. Petersen, 3 vols., 1904.

*Schillers Gespräche,* ed. J. Petersen, 1911.

## 2. CRITICAL AND THEORETICAL WORKS

I. Appelbaum-Graham, 'Reflection as a function of form in Schiller's tragic poetry', *Publications of the English Goethe Society,* New Series, 24, 1955.

—— 'Passions and possessions in Schiller's *Kabale und Liebe*', *German Life and letters,* New Series, 6, 1952.

—— 'The structure of the personality in Schiller's tragedies', in *Schiller bicentenary lectures,* London, 1960.

E. Auerbach, *Mimesis, dargestellte Wirklichkeit in der abendländischen Literatur,* 3. Aufl., 1964.

W. Babilas, *Tradition und Interpretation,* 1961.

L. Bellermann, *Schillers Dramen. Beiträge zu ihrem Verständnis,* 2 vols., 1888–91.

K. Berger, *Schiller,* 6. Aufl., 1924.

W. Binder, 'Schiller, *Kabale und Liebe*', in *Das deutsche Drama,* ed. B. von Wiese, Bd. II, 2. Aufl., 1960.

R. Buchwald, *Schiller. Leben und Werk*, 4. Aufl., 1959.

E. M. Butler, *The tyranny of Greece over Germany*, 1935.

H. Cysarz, *Schiller*, 1934.

—— *Die dichterische Phantasie Friedrich Schillers*, 1959.

M. L. Gansberg, 'Zur Sprache in Hebbels Dramen', in *Hebbel in neuer Sicht*, ed. H. Kreuzer, 1963.

H. B. Garland, *Schiller*, 1949.

—— *Schiller revisited*, 1959.

—— 'Some observations on Schiller's stage directions', in *German studies for Walter Horace Bruford*, 1962.

—— 'Schiller the revisionist—the poet's second thoughts', in *Reality and creative vision in German lyrical poetry*, ed. A. Closs, 1963.

M. Gerhard, *Schiller*, 1950.

W. Kayser, *Das sprachliche Kunstwerk*, 10. Aufl., 1964.

H. Knudsen, *Goethes Welt des Theaters*, 1949.

E. Kühnemann, *Schiller*, 7. Aufl., 1927.

H. Lausberg, *Elemente der literarischen Rhetorik*, 2. Aufl., 1963.

W. F. Mainland, *Schiller and the changing past*, 1957.

Th. Mann, *Versuch über Schiller*, 1955.

K. May, *Friedrich Schiller: Idee und Wirklichkeit im Drama*, 1948.

M. Parzeller, 'Die Sprache bei Schiller', in *Goethe*, Neue Folge des *Jahrb. der Goethe-Gesellschaft*, 25, 1963.

E. L. Stahl, *Friedrich Schiller's drama: theory and practice*, 1954.

E. Staiger, *Friedrich Schiller*, 1967.

G. Storz, *Der Dichter Friedrich Schiller*, 1959.

A. Streicher, *Schillers Flucht von Stuttgart*, ed. P. Raabe, 1959.

F. Strich, 'Der junge Schiller', in *Der Dichter und die Zeit*, 1947.

W. Vulpius, *Schiller-Bibliographie, 1893–1958*, 1959.

B. von Wiese, *Schiller*, 1959.

W. Witte, *Schiller*, 1949.

K. von Wolzogen, *Schillers Leben*, 1830.

J. Wychgram, *Schiller*, 5. Aufl., 1906.

PRINTED IN GREAT BRITAIN
AT THE UNIVERSITY PRESS, OXFORD
BY VIVIAN RIDLER
PRINTER TO THE UNIVERSITY